1984

The China Quandary: Domestic Determinants of U.S. China Policy, 1972–1982

Also of Interest

†Available in hardcover and paperback.

Westview Special Studies in International Relations

The China Quandary: Domestic Determinants of U.S. China Policy, 1972–1982
Robert G. Sutter

Although the United States has established formal diplomatic relations with the People's Republic of China (PRC), achieving major advances in economic and cultural relations, it continues to be bedeviled by serious dilemmas regarding such issues as future relations with Taiwan, U.S.-PRC military ties, the extent and type of U.S. aid to China, and the need for secrecy in U.S. China policy versus traditional American demands for "open" diplomacy. U.S. scholars have been clear about the international factors influencing current U.S.-PRC relations; however, the domestic political factors that have contributed in a major way to the creation of the dilemmas we face in formulating China policy today remain poorly understood.

This book concentrates on these domestic determinants of recent U.S. China policy. Pointing to the compromises and contradictions in policy choices made by leaders who have sharply differing conceptions of the goals of policy and their appropriate implementation, Dr. Sutter draws on a wide array of recent U.S. government publications and more than one hundred interviews with officials of the Carter and Reagan administrations and Congress to examine differences in views, divergencies in policy approaches, and the confusion that results. He specifically treats key issues such as the Taiwan Relations Act and possible U.S. arms sales to China, as well as summarizing and assessing domestic and foreign policy interests of the United States in relation to China and offering policy options for the problems that lie ahead.

Dr. Robert G. Sutter is a specialist in Asian affairs at the Congressional Research Service of the Library of Congress. He served as an analyst for the CIA in East Asian affairs from 1968 to 1977, specializing in Chinese foreign policy.

To my mother, Marie B. Sutter,
and to the memory of my father, Leonard L. Sutter

The China Quandary:
Domestic Determinants of
U.S. China Policy, 1972–1982

Robert G. Sutter

Westview Press / Boulder, Colorado

Westview Special Studies in International Relations

Copyright © 1983 by Westview Press, Inc.

Published in 1983 in the United States of America by
  Westview Press, Inc.
  5500 Central Avenue
  Boulder, Colorado 80301
  Frederick A. Praeger, President and Publisher

Library of Congress Cataloging in Publication Data
Sutter, Robert G.
  The China quandary.
  (Westview special studies in international relations)
  Includes bibliographical references and index.
  1. United States—Foreign relations—China. 2. China—Foreign relations—United States. I. Title. II. Series.
E183.8.C5S878 1983   327.73051   82-23736
ISBN 0-86531-579-5

Printed and bound in the United States of America

Contents

Preface

The American reconciliation with the People's Republic of China (PRC) begun by President Richard Nixon and developed by succeeding U.S. presidents has enjoyed wide support in the United States as one of the most important breakthroughs in U.S. foreign policy since the cold war. In broad terms, each American administration, from Richard Nixon's to Ronald Reagan's, has sought to use better relations with China as a means to position the United States favorably in the U.S.-Soviet-PRC triangular relationship; to stabilize Asian affairs, secure a balance of forces in the region favorable to the United States and its allies and friends, and foster a peaceful and prosperous future for Taiwan; to build beneficial economic, cultural, and other bilateral ties; and to work more closely with the PRC on issues of global importance such as world food supply, population control, and arms limitations. China has supported the opening of relations with the United States as a means to strengthen China's national security against the Soviet threat and to oppose the expansion of Soviet power in Asian and world affairs; to obtain U.S. and other Western economic commodities, investment, and technology; and to benefit from cultural, educational, and tourist exchanges.

Despite this broad community of interests, however, Sino-American relations are often delicate and uncertain and need seemingly constant nurturing more than ten years after President Nixon and Chinese Communist Party Chairman Mao Zedong started the process of reconciliation during Nixon's landmark visit to China in 1972. In part, this has been caused by developments in the PRC and in international affairs beyond the control of the United States. But it has also been caused by contradictions and controversy in the United States that have adversely affected Sino-American relations.

This book is an examination of domestic determinants of American policy that have complicated U.S. efforts to develop close relations with

China. It shows that divisions of opinion in the United States over Taiwan policy, U.S.-Soviet-PRC relations, U.S.-PRC economic relations, and the management of U.S. China policy have threatened at times to upset the ongoing Sino-American reconciliation.

Of course, these American domestic considerations have generally played a secondary role to the overriding U.S. interest in seeking advantage, especially strategic advantage, from the new relationship with China. During the period of U.S.-Soviet détente in the first half of the 1970s, the United States sought to use improved relations with China to elicit positive Soviet foreign policy regarding U.S. interests and to use improved relations with Moscow to elicit positive Chinese foreign policy. U.S. planners tried to develop good relations with *both* communist countries, striving to have better relations with each of them than they have had with each other.

In the face of expanding Soviet military power and political influence in such Third World areas as Angola, the Horn of Africa, Afghanistan, and Indochina, U.S. willingness to pursue détente with the Soviet Union declined in the late 1970s. U.S. policy was also affected by a rising concern over American military preparedness to meet Soviet and other foreign challenges that were seen after the collapse of U.S.-supported governments in Indochina, the fall of the Shah, the capture and detention of the American hostages in Iran, and the acrimonious debate over U.S. strategic preparedness during Senate consideration of the SALT II treaty.

As a result, the administration of President Jimmy Carter, especially in its last two years, shifted away from the policy of "evenhandedness" that had characterized the American approach to the Sino-Soviet powers in the past. Improved relations with China increasingly came to be seen as an important factor in the matrix of U.S. regional and global power and influence, useful to the United States and its allies in the developed world as a means of countering the major strategic problem of the next decade—the containment of expanding Soviet military power and influence in world affairs. At the start of the Reagan administration, U.S. officials seemed to agree with that basic position. In an effort to consolidate ties with China, Secretary of State Alexander Haig traveled to Peking in June 1981 and announced that for the first time the United States was willing to consider selling weapons to the PRC.

Dealing with Soviet power is likely to preoccupy U.S. leaders for some years to come. Because of the perceived cost to the United States of tackling the USSR on its own, Americans will probably try to elicit increased support from their allies, which are also influenced by ideological, economic, and political trends that undercut a firm defense posture against the Soviet Union. Thus, Washington will have to cast its net wider in the search for anti-Soviet leverage, assuring China a continuing important role in future U.S. strategic calculations (provided that the PRC remains cool to the USSR). In this context, the United States can be expected to accommodate secondary considerations—including the domestic determinants that have complicated its China policy—to maintain and develop improved relations with the PRC. Of course, U.S. domestic tensions over China policy may sometimes pose a threat to reconciliation with the PRC. Accordingly, it would be wise if Americans paid closer attention to the potentially troublesome domestic determinants of China policy in order to manage that policy more effectively and to build a more solid consensus behind an improved U.S. relationship with the PRC.

In the course of preparing this book, I benefited greatly from over one hundred interviews with U.S. government officials and other leaders concerned with U.S. China policy. Since those interviews were intended to elicit, as frankly as possible, differing perspectives on issues in U.S. China policy, and since many of the questions touched on matters of institutional and personal sensitivity, all were assured that their comments would not be for attribution. Nevertheless, it goes without saying that if they had not given of their time and effort, this study would not have been possible.

The author is also indebted to Henry Tom, Bradley Rymph, Kathleen Jones, Michele McTighe, Alice Levine, and Lynn Arts for their editorial support and guidance. Finally, it should be noted that the views expressed in this book are solely my own and not those of the Congressional Research Service or any other U.S. government organization.

Robert G. Sutter

The China Quandary:
Domestic Determinants of
U.S. China Policy, 1972–1982

Dilemmas in Contemporary U.S. China Policy

The U.S. reconciliation with the People's Republic of China (PRC) begun by President Richard Nixon and continued by his successors has won wide bipartisan support in the United States as one of the most important breakthroughs in U.S. foreign policy since the cold war. Although President Nixon made the initial overture to China, President Jimmy Carter played a special role in pushing the relationship forward. His historic decision to normalize diplomatic relations with the PRC opened the way to extensive Sino-American cooperation in economic, strategic, and cultural relations. Under his guidance, relations with the PRC advanced rapidly to a point where the president referred to the Chinese—the former implacable foes of the United States—as "our new and great friends,"[1] and newspaper headlines welcomed the visit of the U.S. defense secretary to Peking in 1980 with reports of an emerging Sino-American strategic "alliance" against the Soviet Union.

Underneath such rhetoric, the two powers appeared to enjoy a relationship based on a firm foundation of enduring mutual interests. Both countries opposed the expansion of Soviet power in Asian and world affairs; both benefited from improved bilateral economic ties; and growing cultural, educational, and tourist exchanges were binding the two peoples more closely together.[2]

But the progress in Sino-American relations failed to obscure persistent serious disputes among American leaders over China policy. Presidents Nixon and Gerald Ford were generally sensitive to the strong domestic disagreements over China and took care that their policies did not substantially exacerbate those tensions. President Carter adopted a different approach. He repeatedly pushed the U.S. relationship with the PRC forward despite sharp resistance from American leaders in the Congress, the administration, and elsewhere. Ronald Reagan also triggered a major public debate over U.S. policy concerning Taiwan during the presidential campaign of 1980. Peking responded with strong public pressure and new demands for further U.S. compromise over the Taiwan issue—a stance that led to a slowdown in U.S.-PRC relations.[3]

Historical Roots of U.S.-PRC Relations

Debate and controversy are deeply rooted in the history of U.S. China policy. Quarrels in the United States during the late 1940s and early 1950s effectively blocked U.S. ability to communicate with the PRC for almost two decades. It became an article of faith that the United States would check potential communist Chinese expansion—with military force if necessary—would isolate the PRC diplomatically and economically, and would maintain support for the Nationalist Chinese government in Taiwan. To advocate change in this policy was thought to be suicidal in American politics, particularly in the face of the so-called China lobby—a group of lobbyists, legislators, and other officials who were able to use the anti-communist atmosphere in the United States during the cold war to foster policies of strong opposition to the PRC and firm support for Taiwan.[4]

During the Vietnam War in the mid-1960s, American disillusionment with military involvement in Asia helped to prompt change in the U.S. opinion of the PRC. Prominent officials began to call publicly for a reassessment of U.S. policy in East Asia—particularly in relation to China. They advocated an end to U.S. isolation of the PRC, though they frequently added that the United States should remain militarily vigilant against possible PRC expansion in the region.

Although President Nixon's announcement in July 1971 that he would travel to the PRC in February 1972 caught the United States by surprise, his initiative subsequently received broad U.S. support. For the first time in over two decades, a consensus among U.S. leaders supporting improved relations with the PRC emerged. Nixon's opening promised some important short-term advantages for the United States. Over the longer term, it seemed to represent a suitable compromise between two historically opposing approaches in U.S. foreign policy—to fulfill American moral yearnings and commitments and to follow the American sense of practicality and toughness.

Nixon's visit represented an adroit maneuver to begin negotiations with North Vietnam's major Asian ally to help extricate the United States from the Vietnam quagmire. The visit also allowed U.S. officials to assess, firsthand, Chinese intentions throughout East Asia, thereby helping to smooth the way for the major U.S. military withdrawal from the region envisioned in the Nixon Doctrine. Indeed, the more cooperative Sino-American relationship became a useful substitute for previous U.S. military deployments that had maintained a balance of power in East Asia favorable to U.S. interests since the Korean War. At the same time, by placing the United States in an advantageous position in the U.S.-Soviet-PRC triangular relationship, Nixon's opening complemented U.S. efforts to reach arms control and other agreements with the USSR. In particular, it prompted the Soviet Union to be more forthcoming in negotiations with the United States, for fear that to do otherwise would be to risk the establishment of a Sino-American partnership against the USSR.[5]

Nixon's handling of the Taiwan issue avoided offending most Americans, who judged that it was improper for the United States to show itself as "changeable" or "unreliable" in international affairs by cutting off ties with an ally of thirty years for the sake of practical gains to be made in cooperation with the PRC. Nixon managed to put aside the issue for the time being, although press reports suggested that he planned to follow up his initial opening with a deal with the PRC over Taiwan during his second term. However, he soon became absorbed by the Watergate scandal and resigned in 1974. President Ford, concerned about political attacks from the Republican right wing, endorsed the inherited Nixon policy but avoided new initiatives. The sudden collapse of pro-U.S. governments in Indochina in 1975 seemed to harden the administration against further withdrawals and other signs of "weakness" in East Asia. It caused President Ford to be especially wary of any new approach on the Taiwan issue that might be seen as another affront to U.S. honor or as a decline of U.S. commitment to Asian allies.

Nixon and Ford both attempted to use improved relations with China as leverage in the U.S.-Soviet-PRC relationship, but their policies also reassured Americans who opposed the development of the U.S. relationship with China at the expense of U.S.-Soviet relations. Both presidents took numerous steps to advance U.S.-Soviet relations, and the United States never did appear to be aligning with China in direct confrontation with the USSR.

Nixon and Ford also sidestepped controversy by neither involving the United States too closely in Chinese domestic politics nor committing the United States to the massive task of supporting China's economic development. The new relationship developed smoothly, based on practical U.S. and Chinese interests that were generally understood by American leaders. Sino-American trade grew, but no U.S. aid was offered, and there was little cost to be borne by the American taxpayers.

President Carter at first followed the cautious policy he inherited from President Ford. Secretary of State Cyrus Vance tried to reach a compromise agreement with Peking over the Taiwan issue during a visit to China in August 1977, but no substantial results were achieved.

High-level diplomatic and defense officials in the Carter administration later confirmed that the administration, at its outset, was committed to the normalization of U.S.-PRC relations but was uncertain of the conditions and the timing of the move.[6] The officials added that in mid-1977 other policy issues acted to limit Secretary Vance's flexibility in negotiations with the mainland Chinese over Taiwan. (According to some press reports, Vance offered a compromise formula proposing that the United States retain some sort of liaison office in Taipei following the normalization of U.S.-PRC relations. The proposal was thought to have only a relatively small chance for success, as the PRC leaders had turned down similar proposals in the past.)

For one thing, the administration anticipated submitting the controversial Panama Canal treaties to Congress and was reluctant to create a controversy over Taiwan that might complicate the delicate treaty-ratification process. Of more strategic importance, a consensus among upper-level officials in the administration at this time held that relations with China should not have priority over relations with the USSR. In particular, they decided, the United States should avoid undue compromise over Taiwan and other gestures toward the PRC that might upset concurrent efforts to renew talks with the Soviet Union on arms control.

By spring 1978, the administration had won congressional approval for the Panama treaties. And its view of the USSR had changed. Soviet interference in the Horn of Africa at that time was seen by many as the latest in a series of Soviet expansive moves in the Third World that had to be countered by the United States. Some leaders, like Secretary Vance, favored improved relations with China but were wary of moves toward Peking that might upset the important Strategic Arms Limitation Talks (SALT) negotiations with the USSR. The consensus of the U.S. leadership, however, swung in favor of those who, like Presidential Advisor on National Security Zbigniew Brzezinski, were calling for a move ahead in relations with China, regardless of its possible negative effect on U.S.-Soviet relations.

In May 1978, Brzezinski traveled to China, where his warm meetings with Chinese leaders were marked by repeated Sino-American statements of opposition to the USSR and the start of secret negotiations on normalizing diplomatic relations. The talks culminated in the communiqué announced by President Carter and Chinese Premier Hua Guofeng in December 1978. The administration quickly followed with further steps during 1979 and 1980 that were designed to establish closer political, economic, and security ties with the PRC.

The Carter administration's initiatives were successful in pushing U.S.-PRC relations forward and in establishing a remarkably friendly atmosphere for relations between administration representatives and Chinese officials. But they had the serious side effect of promoting repeated quarrels and controversy among American leaders, which undermined the administration's efforts to build support in the United States for its new relationship with China. They alienated four important groups in Congress, the administration, and elsewhere:

1. Those who emphasized the need to preserve American honor and reliability in Asian and world affairs by maintaining commitments to long-standing allies. These leaders were particularly upset by the Carter administration's treatment of Taiwan throughout 1978–1980. Senator John Glenn, chairman of the Subcommittee on East Asian and Pacific Affairs of the Senate Foreign Relations Committee, was a persistent critic of the administration on this issue.

2. Those who judged that American collaboration with China—especially closer U.S.-PRC military ties—would lead to serious adverse consequences for what they judged were far more important American interests vis-à-vis the Soviet Union. They were strongly opposed to the Carter administration's increasingly transparent efforts to develop ties with China in an effort to punish and pressure the USSR. Secretary Vance and his special advisor on Soviet affairs, Marshall Shulman, were leading examples of those in the administration who opposed closer military ties with China on these grounds.[7]

3. Those who were traditionally suspicious of China's communist system and its intentions in East Asian and world affairs. These leaders were especially upset by the Carter administration's unusually deferential treatment of China at a time when several long-standing noncommunist American allies and friends in Asia were being subjected to criticism or neglect. Many conservative U.S. senators and congressmen, led by such prominent Republicans as Senators Barry Goldwater, S. I. Hayakawa, and Jesse Helms, identified themselves with this view.

4. Those who favored an open approach in U.S. foreign policy designed to inform the American people and their representatives of the full implications of major departures in U.S. foreign policy, like the administration's initiatives to China. They were greatly irritated by the administration's secretive approach to the conduct of U.S.-PRC relations, especially U.S.-PRC security ties. Most outspoken in this regard was Congressman Lester Wolff, chairman of the Subcommittee on Asian and Pacific Affairs of the House Foreign Affairs Committee.

After the announcement of U.S.-PRC normalization, the Carter administration made strenuous efforts to build congressional and public support for its new approach toward China—efforts that were far greater than those made by the Nixon and Ford administrations to build support for their China policies. Given enough time and effective leadership, Carter administration officials might have been able to put together a well-coordinated information and lobbying campaign that would have won over enough skeptics to establish a new consensus on China policy. Unfortunately, their efforts to build a consensus were hampered by serious problems. For one thing, unlike President Nixon at the time of the Vietnam War, the Carter administration was unable to point to a major international crisis that could easily justify the compromises and commitments it made to China.

Furthermore, consensus-building was extremely difficult because of constant advances in the administration's policy during 1979 and 1980. These initiatives were brought about by new Sino-American agreements and other U.S. moves toward China announced during high-level U.S. leadership meetings with PRC officials during 1979 and 1980. In particular, U.S.-PRC relations advanced greatly as a result of Vice President Walter Mondale's visit to China in August 1979 and Secretary of Defense Harold Brown's visit there in January 1980. During Mondale's visit, the United States signaled, with a series of economic initiatives to the PRC that were denied to the USSR, the end of its previous policy of evenhandedness in dealing with the PRC and the Soviet Union. During Brown's visit, the United States went further in this regard by scrapping its previous embargo on U.S. military sales to China.

Some administration officials subsequently said that the American overtures were prompted in large part by a perceived need for visiting U.S. leaders to announce major accomplishments (i.e., advances in policy) at the end of their visits. They called this phenomenon "visit diplomacy." Other administration officials said that the administration had planned at the outset to use the visits of high-level U.S. leaders as an important way to move the process of normalization forward. In any event, the result in the United States was that administration officials in their private talks and briefings for congressional officials and other U.S. leaders offered shifting rationales for U.S. China policy—justifications that were likely to change with the next visit of a high-level American official. Not surprisingly, the credibility of such rationales declined over time.

Efforts by the Carter administration to build support for its China policy also suffered because of persisting strong differences within the administration about the ultimate objectives of U.S. policy. Indeed, many officials in the administration judged that there were no clearly agreed-upon objectives for their China policy. Rather, they saw relations advancing largely on an ad hoc basis, notably as specific decisions were required by scheduled visits of American leaders to China or by visits from their Chinese counterparts to the United States. At these times, decisions would be made to push the relationship ahead by coalitions of officials who generally favored forward movement with China but who differed markedly on why they favored such movement.

National Security Advisor Brzezinski clearly identified himself with officials who wished to use improved relations with China as part of a broad plan to gain greater U.S. international leverage in competition with the Soviet Union.[8] Secretary Vance supported forward movement with China, but he was strongly opposed to Brzezinski's efforts to align with China against the USSR. He identified with those officials who judged that relations with China should not be developed at the expense of concurrent U.S. efforts to reach understandings with the USSR over strategic arms limitations and other issues.

China specialists in the administration were anxious to develop relations rapidly after thirty years of estrangement, and they frequently identified themselves closely with Chinese interests. They generally favored forward movement in the relationship, even though many of them had serious reservations about the increasingly obvious efforts by Brzezinski and others to manipulate relations with China against the USSR and, in particular, to develop closer U.S. military ties with China as a source of leverage against the USSR. Some other administration officials were concerned primarily with the American domestic political consequences of the opening to China, supporting progress in U.S.-PRC relations because it represented one of the most important accomplishments in the administration's foreign affairs record prior to the 1980 presidential elections.

President Carter's motivations in building the new relationship with China remained unclear. As a candidate for reelection in 1980, the president wished to avoid upsetting this major foreign policy accomplishment. His frequent well-publicized meetings with Chinese leaders and his appearances in campaign commercials dealing with China testified to his sensitivity regarding the potentially favorable domestic repercussions of his new China policy. The decline in U.S.-Soviet relations and persisting anti-Soviet arguments of officials like Brzezinski also influenced the president as he moved away from the evenhanded U.S. policy supported by Secretary Vance and other advisors toward an American tilt to China and against the USSR.

Meanwhile, the administration's efforts to build support for its China policy were also hampered by the veil of secrecy that surrounded U.S.

China policy. As a result, few officials were confident that they really knew what was going on at any particular time. Faced with conflicting signals regarding the administration's motives and lacking a full appreciation of the current policy, many administration representatives were, not surprisingly, less than effective in their efforts to persuade skeptics of the wisdom of the new approach toward the PRC.

Subsequently, Ronald Reagan seriously exacerbated U.S. tensions over China policy with statements of firm support for Taiwan during the 1980 presidential campaign. Peking's strong reaction had a major impact on U.S.-PRC relations. Thus, even though the Reagan administration announced in June 1981 that it was willing to consider the sale of weapons to China, PRC leaders made it known that China would not consider purchases of U.S. military equipment until the United States clarified its position on Taiwan. More important, Chinese officials began to demand that the United States agree to cut off all U.S. arms sales to Taiwan over a period of several years. China threatened to downgrade relations with the United States if Washington went ahead with new sales to Taiwan before such an American agreement.

Faced with strong PRC pressure and the danger of a substantial setback in Sino-American relations, the Reagan administration adopted an increasingly cautious policy upon taking office. It avoided any substantial upgrading of relations with Taiwan, decided against the sale of more advanced fighter aircraft to Taiwan, and began discussions with the PRC on the question of future U.S. arms sales to Taiwan. At the same time, it tried to restore some momentum in U.S.-PRC relations through such gestures as an announced U.S. willingness to sell weapons and consider granting aid to China.

Current Dilemmas

As we have seen, Carter administration initiatives toward the PRC were repeatedly assailed and countered by opponents, especially in the Congress; they were also resisted more quietly by opponents inside the administration. Ronald Reagan's remarks on Taiwan sparked the most serious public controversy on China policy since the normalization of U.S.-PRC diplomatic relations. The result has been a series of compromises and contradictions in U.S. policy that provide the basis for current dilemmas, which can be seen in four major areas.

Policy Toward Taiwan

The normalization of U.S. diplomatic relations with the PRC announced by President Carter and Premier Hua Guofeng on December 15, 1978, settled some major outstanding issues in the prolonged debate over the "Taiwan question" in U.S. foreign policy. The United States finally decided to recognize the PRC, to break its official ties with the Chinese Nationalist administration in Taiwan, and to terminate the U.S. defense treaty with Taiwan. The administration also strongly reaffirmed U.S. adherence to the principle of one China, seen originally in the Shanghai Communiqué signed by President Nixon during his visit to the PRC in February 1972. Thus, it acknowledged the Chinese position that Taiwan is part of China and recognized the PRC as the sole legal government of China. To the Chinese and many international observers, the normalization communiqué signaled that the United States expected Taiwan eventually to be reunited with the mainland.

However, no sooner had the normalization agreement been announced than U.S. leaders demonstrated strong differences over policy toward Taiwan. Their disagreements were seen especially during congressional consideration of the Taiwan Relations Act in February and March 1979. Congress added a series of amendments—dealing with U.S. protection for Taiwan, arms sales to the island, and other matters—to the bill proposed by the Carter administration. The resulting legislation contradicted the thrust of the normalization communiqué by clearly implying that the United States expected Taiwan to remain separate from the mainland and under U.S. protection for the foreseeable future.

Peking protested the contradiction in U.S. policy even before the act was passed.[9] But Americans remained largely unaware of its importance until the presidential campaign of 1980, when Ronald Reagan complained that the Carter administration had treated Taiwan badly. Reagan claimed that the administration had violated the Taiwan Relations Act by placing restrictions on U.S. official interchange with representatives from Taiwan, on U.S. arms transfers to the island, and on the activities of Taiwan's representatives in the United States. Despite repeated complaints from Peking, candidate Reagan went on to formulate a comprehensive statement on policy toward Taiwan that sidestepped the implications of past U.S. statements supporting the principle of one China and based his policy firmly on implementation of the Taiwan Relations Act.[10] The resulting controversy during summer and fall 1980 saw PRC and Carter administration spokesmen warn of dire consequences for Sino-American relations if Reagan were elected and proceeded to upgrade U.S.–Taiwan relations according to his announced policy.

After taking office, President Reagan adopted a more ambiguous policy toward Taiwan. Although he continued to voice support for the Taiwan Relations Act, his administration stopped short of restoring official contacts with Taiwan and set aside—at least for a time—Taiwan's calls for upgrading the relationship and for providing the island with sophisticated U.S. fighter aircraft and naval missiles. Perhaps more important, Reagan administration spokesmen began to reaffirm the U.S. commitments made in the normalization communiqué and pledged repeatedly to strive to improve relations with the PRC.

This approach did little to solve the continuing debate over U.S. policy toward Taiwan. Most notably, the Taiwan Relations Act still called for the United States to continue selling arms to Taiwan, and supporters of Taiwan in the United States favored the sale of sophisticated weapons to the island. Peking warned that China's tolerance of such sales was limited. In early 1981, Peking downgraded diplomatic relations with the Netherlands after the Dutch government agreed to sell two submarines to Taiwan and warned that similar actions would be taken against other countries that sold weapons to the island.[11] Later that year, Peking hardened its policy and claimed that any U.S. weapons sale to Taiwan would be grounds for downgrading U.S.-PRC relations, unless the United States first agreed to cut off all weapons sales to Taiwan over a period of several years.

The Reagan administration attempted to meet the new PRC demands while avoiding a basic compromise in U.S. interests regarding Taiwan or the islands' future. On January 11, 1982, it announced that the United States would not sell Taiwan fighter aircraft more advanced than those then being provided. After several months of intensive negotiations, the United States and the PRC on August 17, 1982, issued a joint communiqué that established at least a temporary compromise over the arms sales question. As a result, two days later the administration was able to announce, without prompting a major, hostile PRC response, the proposed sale of 60 F-5E/F aircraft to be coproduced in Taiwan from 1983 to 1985. Reaction to the communiqué was mixed, particularly among President Reagan's constituency in the Republican Party.

The PRC remained very sensitive over the Taiwan issue, demanding strict U.S. adherence to the communiqué and criticizing U.S. interpretations of the accord. An August 17 *People's Daily* editorial commenting on the accord warned that Sino-American relations would "face another crisis" like the recent impasse over arms sales if U.S. leaders continued to adhere to the Taiwan Relations Act, which Peking called "the fundamental obstacle to the development of Sino-U.S. relations."

U.S.-PRC Security Ties

After the establishment of normal diplomatic relations between the PRC and the United States, as well as the passage of the Taiwan Relations Act in early 1979, American leaders began to turn their attention to the implications of improved Sino-American relations for broader U.S. foreign policy interests, especially vis-à-vis the Soviet Union. The result has been a strong debate based on profound disagreements among American leaders over how U.S. relations with China have affected broader American interests in the triangular relationship. The debate has focused most recently on whether the United States should increase the transfer of military equipment, including arms, to the PRC.

Some have called on the United States to adopt a manipulative policy designed to exploit differences between China and the Soviet Union—to use improved relations with China to gain greater leverage in America's continuing competition with the USSR. They have urged the United States to "play the Chinese card"—a loosely defined concept referring to building closer U.S. political, economic, technical, or military ties with the PRC to gain greater U.S. advantage over the Soviet Union. Emphasizing that Chinese preoccupation with the Sino-Soviet rivalry in international affairs has clearly resulted in substantial benefits for the United States, they add that Washington should take initiatives, including the sale of weapons and the transfer of advanced technology to China, that will enhance Peking's strength vis-à-vis the USSR.

Other officials have been less sanguine about Chinese intentions or have remained skeptical that closer ties with China represent the most effective way to deal with the USSR. Some have pointed out that China has remained one of the most unpredictable major powers in world affairs and have warned that a major shift in the policies of either the Soviet Union or the United States could result in substantial changes in Chinese policies. Others have seen negotiations with Moscow or increased U.S. and allied defense efforts as better ways to deal with Soviet power than closer strategic ties with China.

Still others have advocated a "balanced" approach to the Chinese and the Soviets. They have judged that the United States in the past has gained considerable international benefit within the triangular great-power relationship by trying simultaneously to improve relations with the USSR and the PRC. Thus, for example, these spokesmen supported U.S. efforts to follow up the normalization of relations and high-level U.S. contacts with China during early 1979 with a SALT agreement and high-level U.S.-Soviet talks.

A steady decline in U.S.-Soviet relations during 1979, capped by the Soviet invasion of Afghanistan, prompted an increasingly strong perception in the United States of a growing menace posed by Soviet military power. In response, American interest in closer ties with China, including security ties, grew rapidly. Chinese leaders for their part stressed repeatedly their desire to develop a "long-term strategic" relationship with the United States, adding on occasion their strong interest in obtaining weapons and other U.S. military equipment.

After Defense Secretary Brown's visit to China in January 1980, the United States announced that it was willing to consider sales to China of selected military items and technology with military-support applications. In March 1980, the administration listed categories of military support equipment the United States would consider, on a case-by-case basis, for export to China. Included on the list were trucks, transportation aircraft, unarmed helicopters, and radar, communications, and training equipment. The State Department announced that it would consider each export license application individually, bearing in mind the level of technology involved and the item's intended use.[12]

Secretary Brown announced in mid-1980 that the U.S. government had approved requests from several American firms to make sales presentations to the Chinese for certain articles of military support equipment and dual-use technology (items primarily of civilian use but with possible military applications). By late 1980, it was reported that several hundred such requests had been approved. Carter administration spokesmen tried to define the limits of such U.S. military cooperation with China by noting that "the United States and China seek neither a military alliance nor any joint defense planning" and that "the United States does not sell weapons to China." But they repeatedly implied that this policy could be subject to further change, especially if either country faced a "frontal assault" on U.S.-PRC common interests, presumably from the USSR or its proxies.

During the latter half of 1980, contending groups within and outside the U.S. government brought the debate to a new height. Although Peking was slow to purchase much of the U.S. equipment available for sale, the Chinese were pressing the United States to take what was widely seen as the next logical step forward in developing Sino-American friendship: the sale of weapons and weapons-related technology to China. American proponents of such sales were opposed by those who judged that the United States had already gone too far in developing military ties with China and should stop promptly.

Debate over the question continued after the inauguration of the Republican administration (which received divided counsel on the issue of military transfers to China) and following heightened Soviet military pressure on Poland, which prompted official speculation that the United States would strengthen military ties with China if Soviet forces took action against the Polish regime or its labor unions. Secretary of State Alexander Haig announced during a visit to Peking in June 1981 that the United States was now willing to consider the sale of weapons to China on a case-by-case basis. (Coincidentally, it was disclosed in Washington that the United States and China had been operating an intelligence monitoring station in China for a year. The station was designed to replace U.S. stations targeted against the USSR that were closed in Iran in 1979.) However, Haig did not formally commit the United States to sell any particular weapons to China.

Although Haig's announcement gave rise to renewed debate within the administration and Congress over how far the United States should go in developing a military relationship with the PRC, the issue was overtaken—at least temporarily—by the U.S.-PRC disagreement over Taiwan. Peking made clear that it would not purchase U.S. military equipment until the administration first clarified its policy toward Taiwan.

U.S.-PRC Economic Relations

Although economic relations generally have had few of the drawbacks that have made Sino-American security ties so controversial, U.S.-PRC economic relations have been linked from time to time with the debate over playing the China card. A case in point was the dispute that accompanied Vice President Mondale's visit to China in August 1979. The vice president pledged to provide China with U.S. Export-Import Bank (Ex-Im Bank) financing of up to two billion dollars on a case-by-case basis over the next five years; promised to submit to Congress before the end of the year the previously negotiated Sino-American trade agreement, which offered most-favored-nation (MFN) tariff treatment for Chinese goods entering the United States; and told Chinese leaders that the Carter administration would seek congressional action to provide investment guarantees of the Overseas Private Investment Corporation (OPIC) for U.S. investors in China. Since none of these benefits was planned for the USSR, critics argued that Mondale's remarks clearly altered—in favor of China and against the USSR—past evenhanded U.S. policy in the triangular relationship.

Administration and congressional supporters of closer U.S.-PRC cooperation used several different arguments in private efforts to win support for the vice president's initiatives. They noted, for example, that the United States would be prepared to grant similar trade and credit benefits to the Soviet Union, if only the Soviet government would provide the assurances on emigration and other questions that were needed to overcome the legal hurdles in the way of granting MFN treatment and Ex-Im Bank credits to communist countries. They added that the United States had a good opportunity to move ahead in economic relations with the PRC and that it should not allow such an occasion to pass or to be held "hostage" because of "stubbornness" on the part of the Soviet government regarding the needed assurances. Some officials claimed that by moving ahead in economic cooperation with China, the United States would prompt the Soviet Union to rethink its past position on the emigration issue and other controversies blocking U.S.-Soviet economic cooperation and to adopt more forthcoming policies. Finally, officials argued that even though the U.S. initiatives toward China would cause an imbalance of the administration's previously avowed policy of evenhandedness toward the Sino-Soviet powers, they noted that it would do so only in the area of economic cooperation and would avoid significant change in the more sensitive area of strategic cooperation with China.

The Soviet invasion of Afghanistan caused Congress—in a strong anti-Soviet gesture—to pass by wide margins on January 24, 1980, the U.S.-PRC trade agreement, opening the way for MFN and Ex-Im Bank loans for China. But concern over closer economic ties with China revived as the year wore on. Some leaders began to question the economic benefits and possible liabilities for the United States in developing closer economic ties to China. Erratic Chinese economic behavior, cutbacks in Chinese economic contracts with Western firms, and budget constraints in the United States combined to undermine the arguments of those who wished to push for closer economic ties— such as the granting of U.S. economic aid or technical assistance—to China. The Carter administration was compelled to put aside (at least until after the presidential elections) proposals by some U.S. officials that U.S. laws be changed to allow the United States to grant assistance to the PRC. Faced with similarly conflicting pressures, the Reagan administration was slow to take a position on granting U.S. aid to China.[13]

Secrecy Versus Openness in U.S. China Policy

The secrecy that has surrounded U.S.-PRC relations has exacerbated disagreements among U.S. leaders over policy toward Taiwan and U.S.-PRC security and economic relations. Presumably because the slow movement in China policy following President Nixon's initial breakthrough avoided provoking controversy in the United States, secrecy was not a major issue during the Nixon and Ford administrations, even though China policy was highly covert at that time. Secrecy became a significant problem only after President Carter's surprise announcement of the establishment of normal Sino-American diplomatic relations in December 1978.

Congressional officials were particularly upset and suspicious over the administration's handling of China policy matters. They were not sure, for example, how the administration's normalization agreement would fit in with U.S. interests in Taiwan and with broader American interests concerning Asia and the Soviet Union. They were also uncertain about the new policy's possible repercussions in the United States, judging that the president's actions represented a serious affront to their position and prerogatives in the formation of U.S. foreign policy.

Carter administration officials knew that keeping China policy secret hurt their ability to deal well with Congress. But they saw several important reasons for keeping Sino-American relations under wraps. They argued that secrecy protected the sensitivities of Chinese leaders, who reportedly preferred to deal with the United States behind closed doors; avoided signaling U.S.-PRC intentions to the Soviet Union; allowed for freer U.S. interchange with Taiwan than otherwise would have been possible; and avoided possible "interference" from those in Congress who might be inclined to use sensitive information about China policy for "demagoguery" or narrow personal political purposes. Administration officials repeatedly stressed that U.S. China policy was based largely on carefully calibrated ambiguity that allowed the United States a high degree of flexibility as it tried to "fine tune" its relationship with its new Chinese associate. Without such ambiguity, China policy would likely fail, they concluded.

Many congressional officials and some in the administration judged that, although there was some merit in a high degree of secrecy in making China policy, congressional leaders and other important American opinion leaders did not need to be kept in the dark on sensitive issues. These issues need not be subject to full public review, they maintained, but some advice should be sought, and congressional officials, at least those with responsibilities for Asian affairs, should be informed—in private, if necessary—about major new developments. Several in Congress suspected that the administration had "something to hide" in its China policy and had avoided consultations in order to avoid publicly baring its "pro-Peking bias." Others thought that the administration was using secrecy to cover up the alleged confusion and "wrong-headed assumptions" that had prompted the Carter government to "lurch ahead" in its China policy in the first place.

Congressional-executive tensions were high throughout the remainder of the Carter administration. Several congressional officials closely involved in East Asian affairs were especially suspicious of and resistant to further administration initiatives toward China. The election of Reagan and new committee leaders in the Senate and the House eased these tensions to some degree at the start of 1981. At first the Reagan administration's secret planning on U.S.-PRC military ties, culminating in Secretary Haig's unexpected announcement in Peking of a new U.S. policy on arms sales to China, provoked renewed congressional irritation and revived debate over secrecy in U.S. China policy. But the administration's subsequent cautious policy regarding ties with both the PRC and Taiwan, as well as its repeated efforts to consult with Congress over that policy, gave Congress little to complain about up to mid-1982.

China Policy During the
Nixon and Ford Administrations

Policy toward China became a bone of contention in American foreign policy after World War II. On one side were those in Congress and the postwar administrations who supported the views of what came to be known as the "China lobby" in American politics. The lobby was made up of loosely organized groups of pro–Chinese Nationalist legislators, lobbyists, publicists, and others. Taking advantage of the anticommunist atmosphere that prevailed in the United States during the later 1940s and early 1950s and of the harshly anti-American policies of the PRC, they persuaded government leaders to establish a strong American policy of containment and isolation of mainland China. They successfully discredited officials on the other side of the debate who favored moderation in U.S. policy toward Peking or reductions in U.S. support for Taiwan. Indeed, the lobby's strength seemed so formidable that U.S. officials were reluctant to incur its members' disfavor with initiatives in China policy that could be seen as moderating America's hard line.[1]

By the late 1960s, however, the relative decline in U.S. power in world affairs and more discriminating American attitudes toward communist countries after almost two decades of cold war caused U.S. policy makers to begin showing more openness toward possible improved relations with the PRC. The frustration of American military involvement in Vietnam, the emergence of a wide Sino-Soviet rift, and the perceived need for American communication with the world's most populous nation—a major nuclear power—were all cited as reasons compelling the United States to begin the process of seeking more normal interchange with Peking. Surveys of public opinion supported this trend, with 51 percent of the respondents in one major study on American attitudes toward the PRC, undertaken by the University of Michigan's Survey Research Center in the mid-1960s, favoring "exchanging ambassadors with communist China the way we do with other countries." Only 34 percent opposed this step.[2]

The Senate Foreign Relations Committee took one of the most important initial steps in 1966 with a series of hearings devoted to U.S. policy toward China. In an unmistakable sign of the China lobby's declining influence in American politics, the majority of witnesses proposed three basic changes in U.S. policy: official recognition of communist China by the United States, the development of trade relations with the PRC, and an end to the United States's prevention of its admission to the United Nations. In May 1966 the House Foreign Affairs Subcommittee on Far Eastern and Pacific Affairs released a report on its own hearings held earlier in the year, which recommended that the United States seek peaceful contacts with China while also blocking aggressive Chinese expansion.[3]

President Nixon's early initiatives toward China and congressional actions during the first two years of the Nixon administration demonstrated a further erosion of anti-PRC feelings among U.S. leaders. The administration's calls for improved trade and other interchange with China were complemented by similar appeals by many prominent legislators. In the fall of 1970, the House Foreign Affairs Subcommittee on Asian and Pacific Affairs held its first hearings on China policy since 1966. Most of the experts on China and the Soviet Union urged a normalization of relations with mainland China. Many of the same witnesses later testified in June 1971 before the Senate Foreign Relations Committee, again recommending improved relations with Peking.[4]

President Nixon's announcement in July 1971 that he would travel to Peking was greeted with general support in Congress, even by such conservatives as Senator Strom Thurmond. The administration had earlier announced on June 10 that the United States would end its trade embargo against the PRC. On August 2 it also disclosed that the United States would no longer oppose the admission of the PRC into the United Nations but would continue to fight efforts to expel Taiwan from the world body. The UN issue was a sensitive one for Congress since its members had voted in each of the past twenty years to oppose communist China's admission to the United Nations. They were particularly concerned that the PRC would exact undue influence as one of the five members of the UN Security Council. Nonetheless, 1971 marked the first year since the Korean War that such a resolution was not passed by Congress. In pressuring the United Nations during its vote on Chinese representation, members of Congress supported the Nixon administration's efforts to preserve Taiwan's seat; they reacted angrily to the October 25 vote expelling the Chinese Nationalists, but no formal congressional action was taken.[5]

President Nixon returned from Peking to bipartisan praise. Although some congressional leaders criticized parts of the communiqué governing U.S.-PRC relations that was released in Shanghai at the end of Nixon's visit, most echoed the favorable comments voiced by such disparate spokesmen as Senators George McGovern, Edward Kennedy, and Barry Goldwater.

The signing of the Shanghai Communiqué marked the end of twenty years of U.S. efforts to block the spread of Chinese communist influence in Asia and signaled the formal beginning of U.S.-PRC normalization. The communiqué had two major features: On the one hand, it noted that the two countries had reached general agreement about the international order in East Asia. In particular, they pledged to cooperate to insure that the region would not become subject to international "hegemony"—a code word used by the PRC to denote Soviet expansion. On the other hand, the communiqué affirmed that the Taiwan issue represented a major stumbling block in the normalization of Sino-American relations. The PRC claimed that Taiwan was a province of China, that its "liberation" was China's internal affair, and that all U.S. military forces had to be withdrawn from Taiwan. For its part, the United States acknowledged "that all Chinese on either side of the Taiwan Strait maintain there is but one China and Taiwan is part of China." The United States did not challenge that position and reaffirmed its interest in a "peaceful settlement of the Taiwan question by the Chinese themselves." With this in mind, the United States declared that its ultimate objective was to withdraw all U.S. forces and military installations from Taiwan. Both sides pledged to continue negotiations on the normalization of relations.

The Shanghai Communiqué showed that the United States and the PRC were willing at that time to defer problems of diplomatic relations to work together on the basis of their common strategic interests in East Asia. Prospects for such cooperation were enhanced during the Nixon administration by the reduction of the U.S. military role in Vietnam and along the PRC's periphery in East Asia. Facing heavy Soviet military pressure in the wake of the Sino-Soviet border clashes of 1969, the Chinese viewed the Soviet Union as their major adversary and now saw the United States as a source of useful leverage against the Soviet "threat."

The Developing U.S.-PRC Reconciliation

Over the next five years, the Nixon and Ford administrations emphasized common U.S.-PRC strategic interests in opposing international "hegemony" and encouraged closer U.S. contacts with the PRC, but they did not significantly alter formal U.S. diplomatic and defense ties with Taiwan. As promised in the Shanghai Communiqué, the United States gradually reduced its military forces in Taiwan to fewer than one thousand by the end of the Ford administration, down from around ten thousand at the height of the Vietnam War.

This policy seemed acceptable to the PRC, and relations gradually improved. In particular, Peking saw the withdrawal of U.S. forces from East Asia, under the Nixon Doctrine, as conducive to a slow expansion of Chinese influence in the region. Peking probably expected the United States to avoid a precipitous pullback, maintaining sufficient forces in the area—especially naval and air forces—to help the PRC offset possible Soviet expansion in Asia. At the same time, Peking assumed that the United States would continue vigilantly to check Soviet moves in Europe and the Middle East, thereby compelling the USSR to focus its strategic attention westward, away from China.[6]

The PRC and the United States veered from their collision course, toned down their ideological rhetoric, and began to explore cooperation rather than conflict. Sino-American understanding rested on several parallel strategic interests: (1) opposing Soviet expansionism, especially in Asia and the Pacific; (2) withdrawing American military personnel from Vietnam and some other parts of Asia; (3) maintaining a strong American naval and air presence in the Pacific to counteract possible Soviet expansion; (4) encouraging stability on the Korean peninsula to avoid the possibility of a war involving the United States, the PRC, and the USSR; and (5) dealing with the Taiwan issue in a way that would not provoke Taiwan to pursue independence, develop a strong nuclear arms capability, or seek alliance with the Soviet Union.[7]

Discovery and pursuit of these parallel goals helped bring greater stability to Asian affairs in the early 1970s, with considerable progress being made in several areas. However, many of the goals hinged on common PRC and U.S. tensions with the Soviet Union and thus were subject to the uncertainties of triangular politics. Although concern about Soviet expansion remained a key element in the foreign policy calculations of both Washington and Peking, it did not provide an enduring foundation for cordial, cooperative Sino-American relations. President Nixon and Secretary of State Henry Kissinger opened the door to reconciliation, but they failed to leave behind a clearly defined, long-term agenda for bilateral and multilateral relations in Asian and global affairs.

Sino-American relations in the areas of diplomacy, trade, and cultural and scientific exchange showed a pattern similar to that of strategic relations between the two nations—a peak of action from 1972 to 1974, followed by a plateau and some uncertainty from 1975 to 1977. In the early 1970s, Sino-American détente was a powerful new ingredient in world affairs, its chief engineers were still in power in Washington and Peking, and both sides assumed that diplomatic recognition would be forthcoming relatively soon. Then in the mid-1970s both nations became absorbed with the politics of domestic leadership succession, and Sino-American rapprochement lost some of its momentum.

Washington and Peking moved quickly from 1972 to 1974 to fulfill the content and spirit of the Shanghai Communiqué. In 1973 liaison offices, headed by senior diplomats, were established in Peking and Washington to perform most of the functions of full-scale embassies. Some U.S. observers saw Peking's approval of liaison offices as a major PRC concession, made in the expectation that normalized relations soon would follow. Secretary Kissinger started including Peking as a frequent stop in his various global missions. Bipartisan congressional delegations began to travel to the PRC, publishing lengthy reports of their impressions of the "New China."

Sino-American trade grew from $5 million in 1971 to $930 million by 1974. Exports from the United States to the PRC constituted over four-fifths of the trade, with agricultural goods composing half of the U.S. exports. Other exports included such high-technology items as Boeing 707 aircraft, Pratt and Whitney jet engines, and RCA satellite systems. Exchanges also grew apace. By 1975 several hundred Chinese had visited the United States and roughly ten thousand Americans had traveled to the PRC. Some exchanges made a spectacular public relations splash, as did the Chinese archaeological exhibit sent to the United States in 1975 and the tour of the Philadelphia Orchestra in the PRC in 1973. In terms of popular interest, the United States seemed particularly enamoured with the PRC in the early 1970s.

Beginning in 1975, however, the Sino-American relationship started to level off, and uncertainties and anxieties cropped up to complicate bilateral relations. Although the number of travelers continued to increase (in total, about one thousand mainland Chinese came to the United States and fifteen thousand Americans went to the PRC between 1971 and 1977), problems arose in cultural exchanges. In 1975 a visit of performing artists from the PRC was cancelled because of the last-minute inclusion of a song about "liberating Taiwan." Similarly, a visit of American mayors to China was cancelled because the Chinese objected to the inclusion of the mayor of San Juan, a gesture in keeping with their view of Puerto Rico as a U.S. colony chafing for independence. In 1976 Sino-American trade fell sharply, to $336 million. Some of the drop was due to improved harvests in the PRC and a resulting decline in Chinese need for U.S. agricultural products. The PRC leaders' desire for a balance in trade with the United States also contributed to the reduction, and China ran a small surplus in trade with the United States in 1976.

Behind the surface tensions in the mid-1970s were problems centering on Taiwan and on leadership issues in both Peking and Washington. The Taiwan problem remained the litmus test in relations between the two powers. The Shanghai Communiqué vividly demonstrated the gap between U.S. and PRC views on the issue, but it also seemed to imply that there was room for maneuver and negotiation in the interest of normalizing relations. The United States duly reduced its troop strength in Taiwan, though U.S. diplomatic recognition and security ties with Taipei remained intact. U.S. trade with Taiwan increased considerably, reaching $4.8 billion in 1976, over ten times the level of U.S.-PRC trade, and several new Taiwan consulates were opened in the United States.

Leadership problems in the United States exacerbated difficulties over Taiwan and other bilateral issues. President Nixon had appeared ready to establish diplomatic relations with the PRC during his second term. But, because of frequently strong opposition from the right wing of his own party, Gerald Ford was unable to exert strong leadership on China policy and had to be content with endorsing Nixon's policy while avoiding new initiatives toward Peking.

Congressional Visits to China, 1972–1977

Despite the loss of momentum in U.S.-PRC normalization from the Nixon to the Ford administrations and occasional flare-ups of U.S.-PRC differences over sensitive issues like Taiwan, the opinions of U.S. leaders appeared to support the initially rapid and subsequently cautious pace of American reconciliation with the PRC in the 1970s. These opinions were seen most vividly in reports issued by the approximately eighty members of Congress who traveled to China in the period between President Nixon's visit in 1972 and the Carter administration's start in 1977. The visits of the congressional delegations—made up of members of both parties and representing conservative as well as liberal political philosophies—were by far the most active channel of high-level communication between the United States and the PRC during this time.

The Shanghai Communiqué had specifically called for increased bilateral interchange and exchanges between the two countries to strengthen Sino-American understanding and to enhance progress toward the normalization of U.S.-PRC relations. With this in mind, most of the congressional members who went to China wrote reports on their visits that were published as official documents of the U.S. Congress. At the time, these reports were the most important vehicle American leaders had to voice their opinions on issues that concerned Sino-American relations and on the development of PRC foreign and domestic policies that had direct implications for American interests.

The American visitors were generally pleased about the new U.S.-PRC relations, seeing them as likely to remain both a source of strategic leverage for the PRC and the United States against the Soviet Union and a stabilizing influence in Asian affairs for some time to come. The government in Peking was seen as preoccupied with domestic affairs, no longer opposed to the presence of American forces in East Asia, and anxious to work with the United States and other noncommunist countries to offset Soviet pressure against the PRC. The Americans saw the Taiwan question as the main impediment to improved bilateral relations with China. They differed on how the United States should tackle this problem, although most delegates seemed to agree with the Ford administration's cautious and slow approach. The members of Congress also disagreed strongly in their lengthy commentaries about the pros and cons of the PRC's political and economic system.

U.S.-PRC Relations

As I noted above, the visitors were in general agreement regarding the status of U.S.-PRC relations. Most of them portrayed the relationship as beneficial to both Peking and Washington, providing a particularly useful source of strategic leverage against the Soviet Union. The congressional visitors frequently claimed that Peking appeared unlikely—at least for the near term—to allow bilateral problems like Taiwan to lead to a serious reversal in U.S.-PRC relations. They also said that there appeared to be little likelihood of a major breakthrough in Sino-American diplomatic relations that would result in a rapid increase in bilateral trade and exchanges.

Concern over Vietnam and U.S.-Soviet Détente. The congressional reports mentioned that Chinese leaders sometimes viewed certain international issues as major complications in Sino-American relations. Delegates visiting the PRC in 1972 noted U.S. military involvement in Vietnam as a major source of difficulty in U.S.-PRC relations. Senator Mike Mansfield said that "certainly no problem loomed as large as the war in our discussions in Peking." Adding that Peking's opposition to U.S. involvement in Vietnam had been clearly linked by Chinese leaders to the development of Sino-American relations, Senator Mansfield warned that the Chinese had told him that "unless this [Vietnam conflict] can be settled, there can be no progress on other issues [between the United States and the PRC]."[8]

Following the signing of the U.S.-Vietnamese peace agreement signed in Paris in January 1973 that ended the U.S. ground combat role in the Vietnam War and the subsequent withdrawal of U.S. military forces from Indochina, congressional visitors noted a marked decline in PRC attention to the Vietnam issue. Over the next few years, PRC leaders began to show far greater concern over the development of U.S. détente with the Soviet Union. The signing of the European Security Conference agreement during the major East-West summit meeting in Helsinki in August 1975 and the earlier agreement on strategic arms limitation reached by President Ford and Soviet leader Leonid Brezhnev during their summit meeting in Vladivostok in November 1974 prompted pointed expressions of concern from the PRC about U.S. strategic resolve vis-à-vis the USSR. PRC leaders warned Washington repeatedly that it should not "appease" the USSR or be "taken in" by Soviet blandishments of détente. Not surprisingly, a group of congresswomen led by Margaret Heckler said in regard to their visit to Peking in January 1976 that "without question the dominant theme of our discussions was a series of warnings about the Soviet Union and its intentions in contemporary international affairs."[9]

Taiwan. The congressional reports showed that Peking remained uncompromising on its three main conditions for U.S.-PRC normalization: an end to U.S. diplomatic ties with the Republic of China (ROC) on Taiwan, a withdrawal of U.S. military forces from the island, and the termination of the U.S.-ROC mutual defense treaty. At the same time, Peking leaders were generally moderate in their demands about Taiwan during talks with congressional visitors; several reports depicted the Chinese as "patient" over the issue. Thus, for example, the delegation led by Congresswoman Heckler said:

> At no time did the Chinese choose to initiate direct discussion of Taiwan. The sole reference occurred in their response to a question about how our two countries might move more closely together. In answering they mentioned the Shanghai Communiqué of 1972 and the need for its implementation. . . . They added, however, that they understood that the American government felt it was difficult to implement [Peking's conditions on Taiwan] and they, the Chinese, could wait.[10]

Similarly, congressional members led by Congressman John Anderson noted that during their visit to the PRC in 1975, "the Chinese gave no hint of willingness to compromise regarding the complicated Taiwan issue. At the same time, they are not insistent that the issue be rapidly resolved."[11]

U.S. visitors occasionally reported that PRC leaders were impatient over Taiwan. Most notably, Senator Hugh Scott reported that during his talks with Chinese leaders in July 1976 "they talked about Taiwan at length upon their own initiative. . . . [Their views were] stated with a vehemence which suggested they were surprised and resentful that any American would not know that this was their view." Senator Scott judged from his encounter that even though Peking was prepared to acquiesce in some delay of U.S. withdrawal from Taiwan, the PRC was "not willing to acquiesce in such postponement for an indefinite period."[12]

Congressional visitors had different views on the question of what steps the United States should take to help resolve the Taiwan issue. Some stressed that the United States should end its ties with Taipei and accept Peking's conditions for normal diplomatic relations, warning that to do otherwise would lead to dangerous friction in Sino-American relations and instability in Asia. Senator Mansfield, for example, warned that unless the United States pushed ahead and accepted Peking's conditions, "stagnation . . . the enemy of a sound constructive foreign policy would overtake U.S.-PRC relations and would lead to an exacerbation of U.S. international differences over China policy."[13]

Most others, however, felt no sense of urgency, judging that the status quo in Sino-American relations would suffice until the balance of costs and benefits for the United States in normalizing with the PRC became more favorable. Thus, Senator Robert Byrd said in regard to his visit to the PRC in 1975:

> In my opinion, the effort to normalize relations with the PRC, first initiated by President Nixon's visit in February 1972, should be continued. This normalization process can only be slow and gradual, but it ought to go forward. I think we ought not be overly eager to speed up the process, nor do I think we should press too hard; but a gradual evolution toward normalization will be in the best interests of the United States and the PRC in the long run—especially given the present obvious efforts and intent of the Soviet Union to expand her sphere of influence and authority and the continuing buildup of Soviet naval and nuclear strength.[14]

A few others opposed any further forward movement in U.S.-PRC relations, especially if it might have a negative impact on Taiwan. Congressman Edward Derwinski said in a report on his visit to the PRC in 1975 that "personally I see no reason for the United States to grant formal diplomatic relations to the PRC; while we should continue communications with them, to formally recognize their regime would be in conflict with our moral responsibility and inconsistent with our traditional policy."[15]

Trade and Exchanges. Congressional visitors were more uniform in their comments on Sino-American trade. Most saw only limited prospects in this area, inasmuch as PRC leaders continued to stress the importance of "self-reliance" in China's program for economic development and continued to show only limited interest in trade with developed Western countries like the United States. Thus, there was no reported PRC interest in importing U.S. consumer goods, in purchasing U.S. military equipment, or in securing long-term economic loans from the United States. U.S. grain and technology were seen as having some appeal for China, inasmuch as they could provide Peking with the means to fill gaps in its food supply system and in its technological base.[16] Congressional delegates were frequently outspoken in favor of larger and more active exchange programs, but they were also quick to note some of the problems involved in developing these programs. Senator Hugh Scott reported in 1972 that "one got the impression that the Chinese were very desirous of increasing exchanges between the two countries, but did not at this time have the facilities to handle a great influx of visitors."[17]

PRC Foreign Policy

Congressional visitors voiced general agreement regarding recent developments and trends in PRC foreign policy. The Chinese communist leaders, the Americans said, were concerned primarily with pressure from the Soviet Union and viewed the United States not as a threat to the PRC but rather as a source of international leverage against the USSR. Many congressional visitors advised that the PRC was not a superpower and had far to go before its strategic influence would come close to rivaling that of the United States and the Soviet Union. They frequently added, however, that Chinese leaders appeared determined to employ their nation's resources effectively to develop sufficient economic and military capability to reach great-power status by the end of the century.

During conversations with congressional leaders, PRC spokesmen repeatedly condemned the Soviet Union in harsh terms for its allegedly "expansionist" foreign policy ambitions and its desire to establish "hegemony" over other countries, including the PRC. By contrast, the Chinese spokesmen were relatively relaxed regarding U.S. military actions abroad and in many cases frankly encouraged the United States to maintain forces in other nations to offset suspected Soviet expansion.[18]

Congressional officials saw little immediate threat to U.S. interests posed by the PRC. Some judged that Peking's preoccupation with the Soviet Union and with Chinese internal economic and political developments would require the PRC to maintain a cordial relationship with the United States for the foreseeable future. Thus, Senator Robert Byrd reported:

The PRC does not seek to become a superpower. . . . The PRC seeks mainly to build up its own economic and industrial base, improve the living conditions of its own people, further develop the Dictatorship of the Proletariat, and protect its own territorial integrity against outside attack. It claims no designs on other countries in Southeast Asia, and is firmly opposed to attempts by any country to establish bases on foreign territory or to exercise hegemony over other countries. Homeland defense is now the determinant strategic military posture in the minds of the Chinese leadership, despite its rhetoric from time to time. . . .

The PRC no longer believes the United States poses any threat to its own territorial integrity or to its existence as a socialist state, but it is thoroughly distrustful of the intentions, words, and actions of the Soviet Union. . . .

In my judgment, the United States need have no fear of Red China as a viable threat to our own country in the foreseeable future or as long as the Sino-Soviet rupture continues. Nor do I foresee any rapprochement between the PRC and the USSR until such time as the USSR drastically revises its policies of hegemonism over other people—an event not easily anticipated.[19]

A few, like Senator Mansfield, adopted an even more positive view of PRC intentions, seeing China as a power with fundamentally peaceful motives in international affairs. These spokesmen placed blame on the United States for past Sino-American conflicts in Asia, which they claimed were caused—at least in part—by misguided American policies.[20]

Some other congressional spokesmen were somewhat more suspicious of PRC foreign policy objectives, noting that even though Peking was currently cooperating with the United States on certain foreign policy issues, there remained considerable potential for Sino-American conflict in foreign affairs. Following his visit to the PRC in 1975, Congressman Carl Albert warned of several "inconsistencies" in PRC foreign policy that he judged could lead to difficulties in Sino-American relations. He said:

It seems to me, however, that the Chinese are inconsistent in their foreign policy. While they reiterate their opposition to hegemony, which is defined as the exertion of authority or influence of one nation over others, and believe that no country has the right to interfere in the affairs of another, they freely admitted that they contributed assistance and support to their comrades in North Vietnam. They espouse the cause of the North Koreans and the Cambodians and lend support for their causes, while insisting that their interests lie only at home.[21]

PRC Internal Affairs

In contrast to the general agreement seen in the congressional reports regarding trends in U.S.-PRC relations and PRC foreign policy, the visitors differed markedly in their assessments of conditions inside the PRC. On the one hand, some judged that the PRC's political-economic-social system was uniquely well suited for the Chinese people and stood as a model that could be copied in many respects by the United States. On the other hand, some thought that the PRC system represented a veritable prison in which the Chinese Communist Party (CCP) controlled all major aspects of life and pursued domestic policies that were not in the best interests of the Chinese people. Between the two poles were the views of others who attempted to balance what they saw as the major accomplishments and major shortcomings of the PRC leadership.

Although these assessments were not of direct importance in determining how a member of Congress would judge U.S. policy toward China, they did tend to either reduce or increase a given member's enthusiasm for closer U.S.-PRC relations. It could be difficult, after hearing a congressional delegate's description of an economically poor and politically repressive China, to then argue that the United States should cut long-standing ties with its loyal ally and prosperous trading partner, Taiwan, for the sake of rapid consolidation of political relations with the PRC.

Reasons for Varying Assessments. Several congressional visitors tried to explain why they and other American travelers formulated sharply different assessments of the situation inside the PRC. A few suggested that visitors' general political orientations might have some effect on their observations of Chinese conditions. Thus, Congressman Derwinski noted that "a substantial number of prominent Americans who like to be identified as 'liberals' have returned with glowing reports of the progress made by the Peking regime. They tell us that the 'new China is a great experiment for all mankind' and a nation where hundreds of millions work happily and enthusiastically to build a 'new order.' "[22] At the same time, delegates led by Senator Charles Percy said a visitor's "background" and "interests" significantly affected his or her views of China.[23]

Differing assessments were also said to result from reported problems in obtaining accurate information on what was going on inside the PRC. Some congressional visitors were quick to note that their inexperience in Chinese affairs impeded their assessments of conditions there. Others noted that the relatively short time involved in the congressional visits to the PRC and the methods the Chinese used to handle foreign visitors impeded accurate reporting on conditions in the

PRC. In comments typical of reports given by members of Congress, Hale Boggs and Gerald Ford said in 1972:

> We do not pose as experts on China, or on Sino-American relations. All that we report must be evaluated in light of the views of others in and out of government who have devoted themselves to a study of China. We recognize as well as anyone that in a mere ten days in the vastness of China, we could do little more than become aware of the enormous amount of information and understanding we lack about the land.
>
> We are reminded of the blind men who sought to learn about an elephant, each coming away with a very different impression, and none with a complete account.[24]

There was also no agreement among congressional visitors on what kind of standards—those of the United States, the PRC, the United Nations, or some other body—should be used to measure conditions in the PRC. Indeed, there was some disagreement among congressional visitors over whether U.S. travelers should be trying to judge the situation in China by any standards.[25]

Many felt that, on the basis of the Shanghai Communiqué, U.S. observers should go to the PRC, not with an eye toward passing judgment on conditions there, but rather to gather information on China for Congress and for the American people, in the expectation that this exchange would help strengthen Sino-American relations.[26]

Senator Mansfield was particularly outspoken in his emphasis on the need for U.S. visitors not to dwell on what they may have seen as the shortcomings in China, but to accentuate the points of common ground between the United States and the PRC. He said:

> Nor should Chinese society be judged by American standards. It is a disciplined society with its people subjected to unremitting propaganda from an all-pervasive party-government apparatus. Westerners note the absence of individual freedoms in China and the subservience to an all-powerful state. On the other hand, the Chinese see our society as wasteful and disorganized. In fact, present conditions in the two nations are so different that to compare the two is to compare apples and oranges.
>
> To weigh the U.S.-China relationship in a reasonable context, Americans must look at common interests, not at our differences. That is what has brought our two countries together, almost in spite of themselves, in an official but unorthodox relationship.[27]

A different point of view was expressed by members of the delegation led by Congressman Anderson. They argued that American standards *should* be used in assessing conditions inside the PRC and in viewing prospects for Sino-American relations:

> It may be misleading for us to apply our system of values to a country whose history and culture have been so different from our own and which is still faced with problems so unlike ours in kind or magnitude. Nevertheless, we were struck by the fact that the basic individual liberties which we value, particularly freedoms of choice and expression, are considered not only irrelevant but antisocial and even counter-revolutionary. What work one does, where one lives, where one can travel, how much education a youngster can obtain, how much a person can earn, what views he can safely express—all these decisions are made for, not by, the individual.[28]

The delegation members added that neither the PRC nor the United States should try to hide its differences. Instead, each country should strive to deal with the other forthrightly in order to avoid illusions and misjudgments in future Sino-American relations.[29]

Material Standards. Congressional visitors differed markedly in their assessments of the material standards of living of people in the PRC. Most agreed that the people they saw appeared to be well fed and adequately clothed and housed and that the government of the PRC appeared to have made great strides in bettering the material standards of living of the average Chinese person since it gained power in 1949. However, some chose to emphasize the reported accomplishments of the PRC administration, while others accentuated continued shortcomings.

Senator Mansfield commented in 1972 that:

> It is difficult to look at China today, free of the distortions of national disparities, especially after two decades of separation. But the distinctions can be tempered by perspective. It is possible, for example, to judge a bottle as half full or as half empty. If China is measured by some of our common yardsticks, whether they be highway mileage, the number of cars, television sets, kitchen gadgets, political parties, or newspaper editors—the bottle will be seen as half empty. If China is viewed in the light of its own past, the bottle is half full and rapidly filling.[30]

Offering his own positive assessment of the standard of material welfare in the PRC, Senator Mansfield went on to point out:

> There has not been a major flood, pestilence, or famine for many years. The cities are clean, orderly, and safe; the shops well stocked with food, clothing, and other consumer items. . . . The housing is of a subsistence type, but is now sufficient to end the spectacle of millions of

the homeless and dispossessed who, in the past, walked the tracks and roads or anchored their sampans in the rivers of China and lived out their lives in a space little larger than a rowboat.[31]

In a report on his second visit in 1975, the senator echoed these themes in more emphatic language and added: "The livelihood of the people seems to be improved from what it was at the time of my first visit to the People's Republic almost three years ago. In Peking, for example, a great deal of new housing was evident. The people appeared to be better clothed. More trucks and other commercial vehicles and more sophisticated bicycles were on the streets. Shops offered a greater variety of consumer goods."[32]

Many other congressional observers reported on what they saw as the major accomplishments of the PRC administration, but they also noted several shortcomings. For example, the delegates led by Congressman Anderson in 1975 emphasized that China gave them the impression of a land of great contrasts. While acknowledging that significant material progress had been achieved in the PRC, they added that much remained to be done. They emphasized that the PRC was still a poor country and had achieved some of its material progress because of heavy ideological indoctrination and tight organizational control of the individual.[33]

Even some PRC leaders pointed up their country's shortcomings and advised congressional visitors against portraying what they saw in an overly positive light. Delegates led by Congressman Melvin Price, visiting Shanghai in 1976, heard a PRC official there admit that Shanghai still had a crime problem. According to the report, the official added: "When U.S. friends go back . . . they often make too good a report about conditions in China. They say that you don't have to lock your doors in China in the evening, for example. While this is basically correct . . . it is not entirely true. There are still class enemies. There are still thieves and theft. When you go into the street to shop, you must watch your handbag."[34]

Some congressional visitors thought that what they saw and heard in China did not provide a credible basis for judging the situation there. Congressman Derwinski was in the forefront of this group, believing that his PRC hosts had carefully orchestrated the reception of his delegation to create a positive impression. The congressman acknowledged that material progress had been made in China under the PRC administration over the previous thirty years, but he questioned whether or not the mainland Chinese would have achieved a better material life today had they been ruled by a democratic form of government during that period.[35]

Indoctrination and Control. Congressional observers generally agreed that the PRC placed great stress on the indoctrination of the Chinese people and on effective mobilization of the masses through party and government organizations responsive to the PRC leadership. Some observers saw this indoctrination and control as both consistent with traditional Chinese practices and accepted by the people. Many others, however, viewed the indoctrination and control as a basic affront to individual human rights and dignity in China.

Senator Mansfield, for one, adopted a positive view of these Chinese methods. He pointed out that the communists had managed to create "a well motivated and cooperative" populace that was striving toward national progress. He judged that Mao's theories "are now imbedded in the fabric of Chinese life. They have produced a system which is here to stay."[36]

Although they frequently expressed admiration for Chinese efficiency and organization in the PRC, many congressional visitors voiced serious reservations over what they saw as strong curbs on individual rights in China. Senator Robert Byrd, for example, said, "Much of what has been accomplished by the communist regime in China has been as I have stated heretofore at the expense of human liberty, freedom of choice and most of all at the expense of spiritual life."[37]

Leadership Stability and Economic and Military Development. The dramatic changes in PRC leadership in the 1970s had a considerable impact on some congressional visitors to China. Several expressed concern over the future political stability of the PRC, noting that the passing of such major leaders as Mao Zedong and Zhou Enlai might lead to domestic disorder and political competition, which might in turn serve to complicate the emerging U.S. relationship with the PRC. In a typical report, Congressmen Lester Wolff and J. Herbert Burke voiced several questions after their visit in April 1976:

> While there was no visible turmoil observed by the delegation and the impression gained during our week's visit is of a highly disciplined society, the present anti-revisionist campaign (against [Deng Xiaoping]) might well be an indication of an internal struggle. It is highly probable that the death of Mao has already been discounted in plans for the succession. It is by no means certain, however, that the means chosen for the post-Mao transition period will necessarily be as harmonious as the Chinese would have us believe.
>
> Since there is no apparent successor to Mao waiting in the wings, one speculates about the possibility of a consortium consisting of both the "moderates" and the "radicals." In this respect, three major questions arise:

(a) Could a consortium manage, as had the Mao-[Zhou] leadership, to keep the opposing factions in relatively peaceful tension?;

(b) What are the implications for the world scene should the post-Mao era be marked by visible upheavals? (A limited rapprochement with the Soviet Union? A turning inward?); and

(c) Should a relatively stable leadership emerge, does continuity in foreign policy necessarily follow?[38]

Following his visit three months later Senator Hugh Scott said:

When the President was in Peking last December, Premier [Zhou Enlai], though known to be ailing, still was alive. His death in early January, produced, I think, an impact on China's succession of power arrangements far more profound than anyone seemed to be anticipating. Shortly after Chairman Mao received Prime Minister Lee Kuan Yew and Prime Minister Bhutto in Peking last May the Central Committee of the Chinese Communist Party announced that Chairman Mao would no longer be receiving foreign visitors. The extraordinary procedure for admitting Chairman Mao's declining activity and involvement in Chinese affairs obscures, even more, who is likely to be taking charge. On the eve of our departure from Washington for Peking, Marshall Chu Teh died unexpectedly, and during our first two days in Peking national mourning exercises reached their climax. With two giants gone from the scene and the actual role of Chairman Mao unknown, it is obvious that the Chinese people are wondering who will be shaping China's future domestic and foreign policies.[39]

Senator Mansfield discounted such warnings of potential difficulties for China—and possibly for the United States—posed by leadershp struggles in Peking. He criticized those in the United States who focused on the PRC leadership struggle and implied that PRC policies and programs would continue basically unchanged, inasmuch as what he called the Maoist system had been effectively inculcated among the Chinese people. He explained:

The constant speculation over what will happen in China after Chairman Mao [Zedong] retires from the scene, in my opinion, is largely an exercise in irrelevance. It ignores the depth and the reality of the revolutionary changes which have taken place in China during the last quarter century. Mao is esteemed almost to the point of reverence because he has pointed the way and his leadership has restored China's self-confidence. Mao's precepts can be expected to guide China's destiny for a long time to come. "Serve the people" and "self-reliance" are more than slogans, they are the guideposts of Chinese society for the present and the future. . . .

> This is not to say that there will not be political turmoil. Indeed,
> periodic political shake-ups are an essential feature of Mao's thesis. They
> are regarded as a necessity in order to cleanse the system of ever recurring
> elitist tendencies. That was the significance of the Cultural Revolution.
> It is a principal factor in the current movement to criticize "Lin [Biao]
> and Confucius." The prospect of struggles for personal political power is
> also inherent in any political system. In China, however, the likelihood
> is that even these struggles will take place within the framework of
> Maoism.[40]

Congressional leaders voiced greater agreement regarding PRC economic and military policies. Spokesmen who sharply disagreed on other
issues generally saw Peking's policies in these areas as governed by the
principle of "self-reliance." The Chinese had advanced their economic
prosperity and improved their military power largely through their own
efforts and were thought likely to continue this trend in the future. The
PRC's leaders were seen as refusing most types of foreign aid because
such grants were against PRC ideology and they did not wish to become
dependent on foreign sources of revenue for matériel. The Chinese were
said to be open to trade with foreign countries, but such trade was
seen as ancillary in Peking's economic and military development programs.[41]

China's Approach to the United States, 1972–1977

Official support in the PRC for closer relations with the United
States was generally strong, although it was sometimes disrupted by
domestic political campaigns, leadership disputes, and changes in Peking's assessment of U.S. foreign policy.[42] Peking had welcomed opening
relations with the United States for several reasons: It marked the end
of U.S. containment of the PRC and all but eliminated Chinese concern
over U.S. forces stationed in Asia. It reflected a reduction in U.S.
support for the Taiwan government, providing greater leverage and new
opportunities for Peking in its continuing effort to gain control of
Taiwan. And it enhanced Peking's rising international stature by establishing a set of Sino-American principles to govern future developments in East Asia, especially cooperative U.S.-PRC efforts to coun-
terbalance Peking's main enemy, the USSR.

Over the next two years, Peking hailed improved U.S.-PRC relations
as the United States pulled back in East Asia, notably in Indochina.
It highlighted increased Sino-American contacts and welcomed the
February 1973 agreement to establish U.S.-PRC liaison offices. Peking
media also treated the United States more favorably than they had in

the past. The media had previously attacked the United States shrilly and repeatedly concerning American domestic problems, but PRC comment on such issues sharply declined after Nixon's 1972 visit. Their treatment of the U.S. domestic scene became generally confined to one or two reports a week on U.S. economic and social problems such as inflation, unemployment, and the plight of minorities. For the most part, these reports were brief, contained little or no critical comment, and almost never referred to U.S. internal political developments.[43]

A resurgence of critical media reports on U.S. domestic problems came in 1974, with an upsurge in PRC revolutionary fervor during the massive domestic political campaign to criticize the ancient Chinese sage Confucius and former PRC Defense Minister Lin Biao, who died in 1971. Reportage began explicitly to condemn the "rotten capitalist system" in the United States and the West. Peking media entered into a new area by criticizing aspects of popular U.S. culture for the first time since 1972. A July 27, 1974, New China News Agency (NCNA) report—widely broadcast by Peking radio and published in the CCP's daily newspaper, *People's Daily*—hailed the American people's resistance to the "decadent culture" fostered by the U.S. "ruling class," which NCNA said aimed to "poison the peoples' souls" with displays of sex and violence on television and in movies and magazines. The impact of the PRC campaign on coverage of U.S. events was graphically illustrated by another NCNA report that day praising popular resistance in San Jose, California, to the display there of a statue of Confucius that had been brought over from Taiwan.[44]

The anti-Confucius campaign in the PRC served to complicate the smooth development of Sino-American relations in a number of ways. The campaign featured harsh attacks against Western music, films, and other cultural works, which served to dampen PRC interest in cultural exchange with the United States. It prompted harsh criticism of foreign trade with capitalist countries, reducing the PRC's heretofore active interest in developing commerce with the United States. The campaign also prompted a PRC protest against the presence of U.S. military guards at the U.S. liaison office in Peking, resulting in the quick recall of the guards to the United States. And during the campaign, Peking took an unusually hard line on the Taiwan issue, giving atypical stress to Peking's determination to move across the Taiwan Straits to liberate Taiwan by force.

As the anti-Confucius campaign subsided in late 1974, the PRC approach toward the United States became especially influenced by U.S. strategic power in world politics. In particular, three major events coincided to cause serious concern over U.S. strength:

1. Although PRC media did not comment on the Watergate scandal, Peking representatives made clear in private talks with Westerners (reported in the Western press) that Chinese leaders were concerned that the United States might be entering a period of "isolation" in foreign affairs as a result of its preoccupation with internal problems.

2. The 1974–75 economic recession had a seriously weakening effect on the United States, according to PRC estimates. An outpouring of Chinese media reports repeatedly depicted the recession as the worst U.S. economic crisis since the 1930s and a vivid reflection of the "weaknesses" of the Western economic system.

3. The 1975 collapse of U.S.-backed regimes in Indochina caused PRC officials to question U.S. ability and determination to defend its interests in world affairs.

The PRC leaders did not feel that the Ford administration was following policies that would adequately restore U.S. credibility as a great world power. In fact, they expressed serious reservations over the Ford administration's willingness to compromise with the Soviet Union during the president's summit meeting with Soviet Party chief Leonid Brezhnev at Vladivostok in November 1974 and during the European Security Conference at Helsinki, Finland, in August 1975. PRC concern over the Ford administration's pursuit of U.S.-Soviet détente was heightened as a result of the president's firing of Defense Secretary James Schlesinger in late 1975.[45]

A November 7, 1975, NCNA dispatch reported critical U.S. and foreign comment on the firing. NCNA carefully refrained from comment in its own name, but the dispatch departed from Peking's past circumspect treatment of the U.S. administration by replaying comments that focused on the firing of Schlesinger as a clear sign of the Ford administration's determination to speed up détente with the Soviet Union and that criticized the decision as detrimental to U.S. national security.

Significantly, when the NCNA dispatch focused on the Schlesinger firing as an indication of the determination of the president and the secretary of state to "ease tensions" with Moscow, it did not follow the previously standard PRC media practice of noting U.S. leaders' countervailing determination resolutely to maintain their country's security interests against alleged Soviet encroachments. NCNA reported British press comment calling Kissinger the "arch-architect" of détente with Moscow. Again citing the British press, NCNA quoted the observation that President Ford's decision to release Schlesinger while retaining Kissinger "shows clearly which side he takes in the argument about détente."

NCNA reported comments by Senator Henry Jackson and others praising Schlesinger and criticizing his dismissal as "a loss to the nation . . . in the pursuit of a prudent defense and foreign policy." It cited statements that the firing had upset Western European leaders and could weaken the strength of the North Atlantic Treaty Organization (NATO) against the Warsaw Pact. The dispatch replayed Soviet and U.S. comment highlighting Moscow's pleasure over Schlesinger's departure and speculating that "the shuffle in Washington will certainly be regarded by the Kremlin as a step in the right direction." It concluded by citing *Washington Post* reports that Schlesinger's dismissal would broaden the "already widening debate in the United States over the pros and cons of détente with the Soviet Union."

The report was a clear departure from a then-standard practice of the PRC media: Peking in recent years had rarely reported U.S. cabinet changes, and it had invariably avoided replaying comments critical of such shifts. Indeed, Peking was not known to have reported Schlesinger's July 2, 1973, appointment as defense secretary. The media did note Secretary Kissinger's takeover in the State Department and William Rogers's departure, but only in a terse, four-sentence September 1973 NCNA report. The resignation of President Nixon and the inauguration of President Ford were also handled circumspectly in a brief August 9, 1974, NCNA dispatch.

On the same day that NCNA reported Schlesinger's dismissal, it carried two "international reference material" articles explaining to the Chinese people the significance of the 1938 Munich agreement on German territorial ambitions concerning Czechoslovakia and the 1940 Dunkirk evacuation. The articles, which were also published in *People's Daily* and broadcast by Peking radio, focused on the disastrous results of the Munich "policy of appeasement" followed by the British and French leaders in "conniving with the aggressive acts" of the fascists "to divert" the "spearhead of aggression toward the east." One report concluded by noting that "since then, people have often described similar schemes by several major powers in conniving at aggression and betraying other countries as a 'Munich' or a 'Munich plot.' " Recent NCNA replays of foreign comment highlighted articles labeling the East-West agreement signed at the Helsinki European Security Conference in August 1975 as a new "Munich," as well as characterizing Brezhnev as playing the "Hitler role" at that conference. This juxtaposition of reports on Schlesinger's dismissal with those on the 1938 Munich agreement reflected Peking's view of the Ford administration's dismissal of Schlesinger to ease U.S.-Soviet tensions as similar to Neville Chamberlain's efforts to appease Hitler at the Munich Conference in 1938.

Peking spokesmen also voiced their concern on this issue during the late 1975 visits of Secretary Kissinger and President Ford. Peking's treatment of Secretary Kissinger during his trip to China in the fall of 1975 was highlighted by a "friendly" meeting with Mao Zedong on October 21. Prior to the meeting, Kissinger received correct Chinese protocol treatment, but the PRC foreign minister's remarks at the usual welcoming banquet contained some indirect criticism of U.S. détente policy. In particular the minister issued a warning—not previously heard during a Kissinger visit—that détente was an "illusion" that should not blind the world to Soviet expansionism.[46]

PRC media treatment of President Ford and his party during their December 1975 visit generally adhered to the strict protocol pattern followed during Nixon's 1972 visit. The U.S. delegation's "friendly" meeting with Mao on December 2, as well as initial PRC comments welcoming the visitors, underlined the state of Sino-American relations during the previous three years. The need for formal normalization of bilateral relations was soft-pedaled; instead, the Chinese stressed that Peking was concerned about U.S. détente with the USSR. Vice Premier Deng Xiaoping on December 1 indicated, in the most explicit terms to date, that the PRC saw a stronger U.S. strategic resolve against the Soviet Union as the most important contribution the Ford administration could make toward enhancing Sino-American rapprochement.

Deng's remarks at the December 1 banquet echoed stock PRC assessments of Sino-American bilateral relations. He asserted that "on the whole" relations had improved, and he praised Nixon's 1972 visit and the resulting Shanghai Communiqué, calling the latter a "unique international document" underlining both the "fundamental differences" and the "many points in common" held by the two sides. Deng expressed Peking's "welcome" to President Ford's past affirmations that the United States would abide by the communiqué and seek to improve Sino-American relations, and he voiced routine confidence that relations would be normalized "eventually" through both sides' "joint efforts."

By contrast, Deng placed unusual stress on "a more important question"—the need for U.S. vigilance against Soviet international expansion. Though not explicitly mentioning the USSR, he harshly attacked "the country which most zealously preaches peace" as "the most dangerous source of war," and he added that "the crucial point is what line or policy" the United States and China would pursue in the face of this mutual threat. Deng exhorted the United States to follow China's example—not to fear such "hegemonism," but to form a broad international front against it and to wage a "tit-for-tat struggle." He added that the USSR was "weak by nature" and "bullies the soft" but "fears the tough." Deng underlined the joint U.S.-PRC cause against

Moscow by highlighting as "an outstanding common point" the Shanghai Communiqué's call for opposition to international hegemony.[47]

While PRC leaders continued to harp against U.S. "appeasement" of the Soviet Union, their emphasis shifted by early 1976 toward efforts to reassure the United States of their continued interest in improving Sino-American relations. This stemmed in part from Peking's desire to show that the PRC's December 27, 1975, démarche toward the Soviet Union—the unexpected return of a Soviet helicopter and crew that had been held in the PRC since it had strayed over China's frontier in March 1974—had not affected its efforts to foster better ties with the United States. Peking also endeavored to reassure Washington that Zhou Enlai's death on January 8, 1976, and the resulting succession crisis in the PRC would not result in a change in the nation's foreign policy.

In the wake of that unexpected release of the Soviet helicopter crew, Peking media treated U.S. visitors to the PRC with rare warmth and again softened criticism of U.S. policies. Julie and David Eisenhower were accorded an extraordinarily warm welcome during a December 29, 1975–January 2, 1976, stay (they even were allowed a visit with Mao), and media reports on a U.S. congressional delegation touring Peking from December 30 to January 4 were warmer than those describing previous visits by U.S. congressional delegations. At the same time, extensive Chinese year-end comment reviewing international developments in 1975 dropped the previous year's more evenhanded criticism of both superpowers to focus attacks on the USSR while markedly easing criticism of the United States.

After Zhou's death, Peking used Nixon's second visit to the PRC (in February 1976) to stress the continued importance of Sino-American rapprochement. The key tenets of Peking's moderate foreign policy were reaffirmed by China's new acting premier, Hua Guofeng, who was making his major diplomatic debut as Nixon's host. The Chinese leadership's commitment to improve Sino-American relations was underlined both by the cordial reception given the former president and by Hua's remarks at the welcoming banquet. Hua's banquet statements also included a call for greater vigilance against Soviet "expansionism."[48]

The PRC's protocol treatment and media coverage of Nixon's 1976 visit generally followed the pattern of earlier official visits. This visit's less official character was reflected, however, in the Chinese omission of references to some of the ceremonial trappings that had surrounded previous visits by U.S. chiefs of state. There were no descriptions of U.S. and PRC flags being displayed, no references to the playing of the national anthems of the two countries, and no honor guard to welcome the former president at the airport.

Hua Guofeng led the Chinese officials welcoming Nixon at the airport on February 21, 1976. On the following day, the former president held talks with Hua and paid a condolence visit to Zhou Enlai's widow. Hua hosted him at the welcoming banquet on the evening of February 22, and the two exchanged "toasts." Nixon, accompanied by Hua and other Chinese officials, met with Mao the next day for a "friendly conversation . . . on a wide range of subjects." NCNA's report on that meeting included a gesture to the Ford administration, noting that Mao had asked Nixon to convey his regards to President Ford. Nixon also held talks with Hua on February 23 and 24, and on the evening of February 23 he attended a soirée in the company of Hua and Jiang Qing, Mao's wife.

Hua's strong affirmation at the February 22 banquet of the importance of U.S.-PRC rapprochement may have been calculated to allay concern that the emerging leadership crisis in China, seen in the purge and political campaign against Vice Premier Deng Xiaoping during 1976, might jeopardize the Sino-American relationship. Hua echoed remarks made by Deng during a banquet for President Ford the previous December when he restated Chinese support for the Shanghai Communiqué, maintained that there was common ground between the two countries, and recalled Nixon's role in opening relations with China—adding that Nixon took this "courageous action" in his "far-sightedness." Hua went on implicitly to link Mao personally with this policy toward the United States, stating: "The Chinese Government has always pursued and will consistently pursue the line, principles, and policies laid down by Chairman Mao in the field of foreign affairs. We remain convinced that so long as both sides earnestly implement the principles of the Shanghai Communiqué, Sino-U.S. relations will further improve."

Following the death of Mao Zedong in September and the arrests of four leftist Chinese politburo members (later known pejoratively as the "Gang of Four") the following month, newly installed CCP Chairman Hua Guofeng took the lead in reaffirming Chinese interest in good relations with the United States. PRC media coverage also reflected a rejection of the policies of the Gang of Four earlier in the year, which had prompted a harder PRC line on Taiwan and the United States. PRC propaganda was now consistently moderate and restrained in treating the United States.[49]

Reflecting this trend, the *People's Daily* as well as the NCNA highlighted Peking's cordial welcome for an unusually large number of U.S. visitors to China in late 1976. In October Peking media reported that PRC officials led by Vice Premier Li Xiannian held "friendly" talks with a U.S. congressional delegation led by Senator Mike Mansfield, noted Foreign Trade Minister Li Qiang's "friendly" meeting with a

U.S. trade delegation, and recounted the enthusiastic welcome given a U.S. volleyball team touring the PRC. In November Peking media noted the activities of a U.S. congressional delegation led by Senator Carl Curtis and reported the warm welcome by the People's Liberation Army (PLA) high command for visiting *New York Times* correspondent Drew Middleton. On November 17 NCNA also commented warmly on the October tour of the United States by a Chinese volleyball team, observing that the team had seen first-hand that "the American people are very friendly to China."

PRC propaganda on the Taiwan issue remained low-key. Peking media took pains to emphasize increased interest in trade with the United States and other capitalist countries—a policy that the leftists had opposed. Peking was also restrained in its treatment of U.S. government policies. Chinese media sharply reduced attacks on alleged U.S. efforts to "appease" the Soviet Union under the cover of East-West détente. Their main criticism was aimed at the Soviet Union. Thus, for example, a November 11 speech by a PRC delegate at a UN committee meeting on the Middle East briefly criticized U.S. support for Israel but went on scathingly to denounce the Soviet Union as "more insidious and cunning." Peking did criticize the U.S. veto of Vietnam's application for UN membership, but the criticism was couched in mild terms that went no further than expressions of Chinese "regret" over the U.S. action.

Consistent with its reluctance in recent years to comment on changes in the U.S. administration, Peking made only passing references to President-elect Jimmy Carter in 1976. A terse November 3 NCNA report noted his election and an equally brief NCNA report on December 23 recounted his cabinet appointments. Peking's only other mentions of Carter that year came in NCNA items on November 12 and December 10. The November item noted that a U.S. "Committee on the Present Danger"—created by former U.S. government officials and others who were suspicious of Soviet intentions—had urged Carter to increase U.S. defense spending. The December 10 item reported on the NATO foreign ministers meeting in Brussels and noted, with obvious approval, that Carter had sent a message to the session affirming his commitment to the Atlantic alliance.

Peking and the Taiwan Issue

The PRC's approach to the sensitive issue of Taiwan was closely intertwined with the evolution of Peking's policy toward the United States. Thus, the first indication of PRC moderation and flexibility on the issue of Taiwan in over a decade came in the wake of the Sino-

American reconciliation in 1972, when Peking media abandoned their long-standing hard line against the Nationalist government in Taipei and its foreign supporters. Following Nixon's February 1972 visit and other Chinese diplomatic successes at that time, Peking began to encourage publicly "people-to-people" contacts with Taiwan, sharply reduced criticism of Chiang Kai-shek and other Nationalist leaders, and—for the first time since the mid-1950s—called for peace talks with the Nationalists and the "peaceful" liberation of Taiwan. There was also a sharp reduction in Chinese media criticism of alleged foreign "schemes" to promote "two Chinas" and keep Taiwan free of Peking's control.[50]

The PRC's approach hardened in 1974 following Taipei's rejection of its repeated overtures and a general stiffening in Peking's foreign policy line during the PRC campaign to criticize Confucius and Lin Biao. Chiang Kai-shek and other Nationalist leaders were once again severely criticized. Peking stopped calling for the peaceful liberation of Taiwan and stressed instead China's willingness to use military force to liberate the island. While maintaining circumspection toward U.S. policies, PRC media renewed harsh criticism of alleged Soviet and Japanese efforts to block Peking's control of Taiwan.

Zhou Enlai's January 13, 1975, report to the Chinese National People's Congress signaled the return to a more moderate phase in Peking's public approach to Taiwan. Zhou emphasized Peking's confidence that "fellow countrymen" in Taiwan would play a major role in what was now seen as a long-term struggle to liberate the island. At the same time, PRC propaganda began to play down the PLA's possible role in Taiwan's liberation. Peking's new stress on encouraging liberation from within received added impetus following the death of Chiang Kai-shek in April 1975, when Peking propaganda argued that the new regime of Premier Chiang Ching-kuo was far weaker and urged that the people on Taiwan intensify their struggle against the "tottering clique."

Peking's conciliatory overtures to Taiwan were emphasized in 1972 and 1973. During the early 1970s, a steady succession of nations extending recognition to the PRC rapidly eroded the international position of the Taipei administration and prompted growing confidence in Peking about international support for its claim to Taiwan. PRC propaganda maintained that developments such as the October 1971 UN General Assembly vote admitting the PRC into the United Nations, Nixon's February 1972 visit to the PRC, and the normalization of Sino-Japanese relations in September 1972 had delivered a "hammer blow" to those trying to block Taiwan's reunion with the mainland. Peking therefore halted its previously routine media charges that the United States, the Soviet Union, Japan, and other countries were trying to keep Taiwan from

PRC control. Attempting to capitalize on its improved international prestige and on Taipei's isolation and disarray, Peking undertook a series of gestures designed to overcome Taipei's traditional distrust of the mainland government and to prepare the ground for a major PRC initiative—a proposal for peace talks with Taiwan, put forth in February 1973.

Peking's new policy toward the Nationalist government prompted PRC media to halt abusive personal attacks on Chiang Kai-shek and to revive favorable comment about Sun Yat-sen, the founder of the Republic of China, after a hiatus of several years. During an October, 1972, PRC National Day reception in Peking, CCP Politburo Member Ye Jianying extended a highly unusual invitation to "Taiwan compatriots" to tour the mainland and visit relatives. Stressing sentiments of patriotism among Chinese on both sides of the Taiwan Straits, Ye declared that all Chinese patriots belong to "one big family" and that no distinction would be drawn between "those who come forward first and those later." He assured Taipei officials that even "those with wrongdoings in the past" were welcome to join the patriotic family.

Peking's official proposal for peace talks with the Nationalists came in a speech by a former Kuomintang general Fu Cuoyi at a February 28, 1973, meeting in Peking commemorating the 1947 Taiwan uprising against Nationalist rule. Addressing a "few words to the military and administrative personnel" on Taiwan, the general claimed that Peking's recent diplomatic successes and Taipei's isolation demonstrated that Taiwan's unification with the mainland was the "trend of the times," which "no force whatever can obstruct or undermine." He warned Taipei leaders that they should no longer cherish "illusions" about support from the United States or other powers, claiming that the United States recognized one China and would oppose any effort by Taipei to seek support elsewhere. Stressing that "this situation cannot be changed," he called for talks: "We are all Chinese. Why couldn't we talk for the sake of the sacred cause of unifying the motherland?" Citing the example of Mao's negotiations with Chiang Kai-shek during 1945, he said that the two sides should come together and talk, "the sooner the better." He did not mention any preconditions for the negotiations, claiming that Peking was willing to have either formal or informal discussions, and promised that the PRC would keep the talks secret if the Nationalists so desired. (Peking had not officially raised the possibility of peace talks with the Nationalists since the 1950s. A January 30, 1956, report by Zhou Enlai to the Chinese People's Political Consultative Conference had called on Nationalist officials to negotiate with the PRC in order to bring about the "peaceful liberation" of Taiwan.)

The possibility of peace talks was not raised in subsequent PRC public statements, but the concept of "peaceful" liberation of Taiwan did appear in scattered low-level media comment over the next year. While it was never authoritatively endorsed by PRC leaders, Taiwan's peaceful liberation was alluded to by Ye Jianying on July 23, 1973, when he urged a group of Chinese "patriots" from Hong Kong and Macao to contribute to the cause of the "peaceful reunification of the motherland." Judging by the NCNA account, Ye did not explicitly mention Taiwan, but the dispatch noted that the meeting took place in the "Taiwan hall" of the Great Hall of the People in Peking. Subsequently, low-level Peking radio commentaries beamed to Taiwan repeatedly called on officials and the people in Taiwan to work for "peaceful reunification" and "peaceful liberation" of the island.

Peking's approach to the Taiwan problem hardened at the end of 1973. PRC comment over the next year renewed harsh criticism of Chiang Kai-shek, revived shrill warnings of Chinese resolve to block suspected foreign efforts to "interfere" in Taiwan, and pointedly raised the specter of a military liberation of Taiwan. The new line may have been prompted by the failure of Peking's forthcoming overtures to elicit a positive response from Taipei, but it also reflected a general hardening of China's foreign policy during the anti-Confucius campaign.

An article in the February 1974 edition of *Red Flag* launched the first major Chinese attack on Chiang Kai-shek in several years. In keeping with the anti-Confucius campaign, the article attacked Chiang primarily because of his long-standing admiration for the ancient Chinese sage. Subsequent Peking comment began—for the first time since 1971— to use epithets such as "traitor" and "political mummy" to describe Chiang.

Chinese criticism of alleged foreign interference in Taiwan focused on Soviet and Japanese policies; Peking remained circumspect about U.S. policies toward Taiwan. A December 14, 1973, NCNA article, for the first time in over a year, harshly condemned Soviet contacts with the Taipei government. NCNA reportage and a February 2, 1974, *People's Daily* article also sharply criticized the Seirankai, a right-wing political group in Japan that was allegedly "incessantly entertaining the ambition of seizing the Chinese territory of Taiwan."

Fu Cuoyi's keynote speech at the February 1974 anniversary reception in Peking underlined the new militancy in Peking's approach. Whereas Fu had confidently predicted the previous year that the PRC's growing international stature would compel Taiwan to agree to peace talks, this time he emphasized that Taiwan's reunion with the mainland would result from Chinese determination and the preparedness of the PLA. He pointedly raised the possibility of the forceful liberation of Taiwan.

Noting the army's readiness, he stressed that Peking reserved the right to choose the "means by which we liberate Taiwan," and he raised an ominous "cry of warning" that "the Taiwan Straits are today no longer an obstacle to the liberation of Taiwan."

With the conclusion of the anti-Confucius campaign in late 1974, there was a tapering off of shrill polemics concerning Taiwan. Although subsequent PRC comment continued to note routinely the PLA's "preparedness" to liberate Taiwan, Peking media did not repeat warnings that the PRC would strike across the Taiwan Straits. The propaganda stressed instead that Peking anticipated that the people of Taiwan, through their "protracted struggle," would overthrow the Nationalist regime and bring about the reunification of Taiwan with the mainland.

Signaling the start of the new PRC line on Taiwan, Zhou Enlai's January 13, 1975, report to the National People's Congress laid special stress on the role of the people of Taiwan. Zhou called on "fellow countrymen in Taiwan" to work together with the people of the whole country to bring about Taiwan's liberation. PRC Overseas Chinese Affairs expert Liao Chengzhi underlined Zhou's call during an address before the February 1975 Taiwan anniversary celebrations in Peking. Liao avoided Peking's warnings of the previous year on the possible use of PRC military power to liberate Taiwan, and he praised the "compatriots in Taiwan province" who were struggling against the Chiang Kai-shek administration to bring about the liberation of Taiwan. Liao voiced Peking's "firm support" for their struggle and expressed confidence that no "reactionary force whatever can thwart the struggle of the people in Taiwan province to liberate Taiwan and unify the motherland."

Chiang Kai-shek's death in April 1975 prompted an intensification of Peking propaganda encouraging resistance in Taiwan. Chinese comment claimed that increasing disarray had beset the Taiwanese administration, and it encouraged compatriots there to intensify their fight against the newly "weakened" regime under Chiang Ching-kuo. Speaking at the February 1976 Taiwan anniversary celebrations, Liao Chengzhi charged that the Chiang Ching-kuo administration was "unprecedentedly enfeebled and isolated" as a result of acute internal "bickerings and rivalries." He claimed that Taipei is "tottering," noted that the struggle of the people in Taiwan "has been going on wave upon wave with growing momentum," and added that people on the mainland "pin our hopes on the people of Taiwan province" to liberate the island.

Peking also began a new series of gestures toward Taiwan following a hiatus during the anti-Confucius campaign. In 1975 Peking announced the release of almost 300 former Nationalist "war criminals" in March, 144 Nationalist "secret agents" in September, and 72 former Kuomintang military and political leaders in December, noting in each case that those released would be given PRC aid to return to Taiwan if they wished.

Comment after 1974 occasionally noted alleged foreign interference in Taiwan but avoided the shrill polemics common during the anti-Confucius campaign. From time to time, Peking criticized the United States, as well as the Soviet Union and Japan, for alleged "schemes" concerning Taiwan—a departure from Peking's almost total silence on U.S. policy toward Taiwan following Nixon's 1972 visit. In April 1975 Peking issued its first authoritative criticism of U.S. policies toward Taiwan since 1972—a low-level PRC official statement decrying the previously mentioned U.S. opposition to a PRC entertainment troupe's inclusion of a song about Taiwan's liberation in its repertory during a planned tour of the United States. A year later, a March 21, 1976, NCNA attack on a statement about Taiwan made in Congress by Senator Barry Goldwater represented the first PRC criticism of a U.S. official on the Taiwan issue in recent years. The United States was also mildly criticized, in contrast to harsher attacks on the USSR, in PRC comment attacking the superpowers' alleged efforts to foster a "two Chinas situation" at the July 1976 Olympic games. Japan also came under attack in July when NCNA publicized sharp Japanese domestic criticism of the Japanese foreign minister for a statement he allegedly made urging the United States to slow its departure from Taiwan.

Peking's media coverage of the Taiwan issue did not reflect Senator Hugh Scott's disclosure that PRC officials had been particularly uncompromising on the Taiwan question during a July 13, 1976, meeting in Peking with a U.S. congressional delegation led by Scott. Peking also maintained its standard silence on developments in the U.S. election campaign, giving no hint of U.S. disapproval of the pledges by President Ford and Governor Carter regarding U.S. commitments to Taiwan.

American Debate over China Policy on the Eve of U.S.-PRC Normalization

Following the election of President Carter, the death of Mao, and the arrest of the Gang of Four in late 1976, the new leaders in both capitals took steps to restore momentum to the stalled normalization process. PRC leaders reaffirmed their desire to maintain a good political relationship with the United States, showing more interest in developing closer economic and technical ties with the United States and other capitalist countries. In early 1977 Peking discussed with the Carter administration a settlement of the issue of Chinese assets frozen in the United States during the Korean War—a step that would facilitate Sino-American trade.[1] Peking also began sending delegations abroad to discuss purchases of advanced technology from the West, moved fairly rapidly away from the autarchic economic policies that had characterized the PRC's past development, and favored closer economic ties with the developed world.

The Carter administration reaffirmed its intention to work for the full normalization of U.S.-PRC relations, although it remained concerned over the security of Taiwan and sidestepped comment on a timetable for normalization.[2] Secretary of State Cyrus Vance's trip to Peking on August 22–26, 1977, was marked by over a dozen hours of talks with Chinese leaders. Vance repeatedly emphasized that his visit—the first by a high-level Carter administration official to China—was "exploratory" in nature, designed to give U.S. leaders a firsthand look at the PRC's post-Mao leaders and to familiarize them with U.S. policies on a broad range of international issues, including Sino-American relations.

Although PRC media described the visit positively, neither side offered any indication that there had been significant forward movement on the key question of Taiwan. President Carter said in welcoming

Secretary Vance back to Washington on August 27 that the PRC leaders had sent him word that the talks with Vance had been very fruitful from their point of view and added that the visit represented "a major step forward" in normalizing U.S.-PRC relations.[3] Ten days later, Deng Xiaoping indirectly contradicted the president when he told visiting U.S. journalists that reports of progress on the normalization issue during Vance's visit were wrong.[4]

The Carter administration resumed deliberations over China policy in preparation for Dr. Zbigniew Brzezinski's visit to Peking in May 1978—a visit that initiated the negotiations leading to the announcement of the normalization agreement between Washington and Peking in December of that year. Although the deliberations leading to the agreement were held in secret and their importance was apparent only after President Carter's surprise announcement on December 15, 1978, of the establishment of U.S.-PRC diplomatic relations, Congress took several steps to clarify the state of play in the continuing discussion of China policy in the United States. Most notably, the House International Relations Subcommittee on Asian and Pacific Affairs held a major set of unusually comprehensive hearings in late 1977 dealing with the implications for the United States of U.S.-PRC normalization.[5] The testimony of twenty-two witnesses—including several members of Congress and other prominent Americans—underscored other recent signs in the press, opinion polls, and elsewhere demonstrating that U.S. leaders had agreed on several important questions regarding U.S.-PRC relations, although U.S. officials remained strongly divided over some issues—notably Taiwan—that continued to block progress toward normalization with the PRC.[6]

In particular, a number of experts in and outside government argued that rapid movement toward the establishment of formal U.S. diplomatic relations with the PRC was needed to maintain and enhance cordial Sino-American relations. That would necessitate a break in U.S. diplomatic and defense ties with the Republic of China on Taiwan and a withdrawal of U.S. forces from the island. Other experts opposed any rapid policy changes, arguing that Peking would be patient about the development of U.S.-PRC diplomatic relations. They claimed that Peking's primary concern was that the United States remain strategically strong vis-à-vis the Soviet Union to offset what Peking perceived as heavy Soviet pressure against the PRC. Many experts of this persuasion maintained that the current state of relations between the United States and the PRC would suffice until the advantages and costs to the United States of improved relations became more satisfactorily balanced.

Points of Agreement

The hearings, press comment, opinion polls, and other data showed that a large majority in the United States had come to favor the establishment of full U.S. diplomatic relations with the PRC.[7] It was clear that at this point no major constituency in the United States opposed establishing relations with the Peking government. Rather, attention focused on the questions of how quickly and under what conditions normalization should take place.

There was little agreement on these latter issues: some Americans supported rapid normalization in accord with Peking's preconditions; others thought that the United States should continue its existing relations with the ROC as the ruling government on Taiwan while seeking the establishment of relations with the PRC as the administration controlling mainland China. The majority, however, favored a continuation of close U.S. ties with Taiwan, even after U.S.-PRC normalization. None of those testifying at the hearings favored a policy that would be likely to lead to a violent takeover of Taiwan by PRC military forces. As Harvard University professor Jerome Cohen, an advocate of normalization on terms consistent with PRC conditions, said in testimony on September 21, 1977, "No one is talking about abandoning Taiwan."[8] Opinion polls also showed that the American people continued to view Taiwan not just favorably but more favorably than the PRC. Thus, the question of whether the United States should "sacrifice" Taiwan to establish full relations with the PRC—a question that enjoyed wide currency in past discussions on normalization—no longer appeared relevant.

There remained serious differences over what kind of ties the United States should maintain with Taiwan after U.S.-PRC normalization. Some observers, like Robert Barnett of the Asia Society, believed that U.S.-Taiwan relations could be maintained through unofficial arrangements, which would comply with Peking's demands for the termination of all official U.S. political and defense ties with the Taipei government.[9] They claimed that U.S. trade and arms sales to Taiwan could continue under unofficial arrangements, similar to those used by the Japanese in continuing their extensive trade with Taiwan following Tokyo's break in official relations with Taipei and establishment of full diplomatic relations with Peking in 1972. Some of these observers, such as Harvard University China specialist Ross Terrill, added that the United States could replace the U.S.-Taiwan defense treaty with a unilateral U.S. statement affirming an American intention to "defend the region in which Taiwan is located."[10] In contrast, other observers, including

Pennsylvania State University professor Parris Chang, saw such unofficial arrangements as a weak foundation on which to base Taiwan's security and continued U.S.-Taiwan relations.[11] They favored continuing official U.S. political and defense relations with Taiwan.

As a third point of general agreement, it was repeatedly affirmed that legal obstacles to normalization, while potentially troublesome, could be overcome—provided that the president, in close consultation with Congress, made a firm political decision to proceed toward the establishment of U.S.-PRC relations. Thus, for example, legal experts testifying at the House Asian Affairs Subcommittee hearings concluded that tenets of international law and U.S. domestic law did not preclude the United States from establishing relations with the PRC and breaking official ties with the ROC, while maintaining unofficial contacts with the Taipei government.[12]

Several legal details concerning the normalization process were subject to dispute, however. For one thing, there was considerable disagreement over whether the Shanghai Communiqué was an official document requiring the United States to work toward the normalization of relations with the PRC. Some held that the communiqué was equivalent to a press release issued by a past U.S. administration and therefore no longer binding on the United States,[13] while others insisted that the communiqué was an important U.S. document that had provided the fundamental basis of the China policy of every U.S. administration since 1972.[14]

More important disagreement prevailed concerning whether the president had the right to terminate unilaterally the U.S.-Taiwan defense treaty. Legal experts testifying at the hearings seemed to agree that the president could end the treaty on his own; but others, including Senator Barry Goldwater and other congressional leaders, maintained that since the treaty was formally approved by the Senate, the approval of Congress was required for its termination.[15]

Considerable discussion also focused on whether other U.S.-Taiwan treaties could remain in force after a break in U.S. political relations with Taipei and the establishment of ambassadorial relations with the PRC. Harvard's Jerome Cohen strongly maintained that all U.S. treaties with Taipei would automatically lapse under those circumstances.[16] Stanford University Professor Victor Li held, however, that international law did not require the treaties to lapse in such a case. It was his opinion that the United States would be required to take some sort of formal action either to retain or to terminate all existing treaties with the ROC.[17]

It was generally held that the United States would have little difficulty meeting the first two of Peking's three preconditions for normalization—

withdrawing U.S. armed forces from Taiwan and breaking U.S. diplomatic relations with Taipei. It was the third condition—the demand that the United States end its security guarantee for the ROC under terms of the U.S.-Taiwan treaty—that posed the greatest problems for U.S. interests, both at home and abroad, and was therefore the major impediment to U.S.-PRC normalization.[18]

Finally, U.S. leaders thought that problems caused by the existence of a government in Taiwan in opposition to the government in Peking were not likely to be settled quickly and would probably persist for years, if not decades. Former Senator Hugh Scott and other spokesmen indicated that the United States should use its influence to encourage peace talks between Peking and Taipei, as well as to maintain stability in the Taiwan area and to support Taiwan's security vis-à-vis the mainland.[19] Because of the protracted nature of the Taiwan issue, U.S. experts usually judged that the United States should not wait for a reconciliation between Taipei and Peking before proceeding with U.S.-PRC normalization.

Issues in Dispute

Agreement on these questions of U.S.-PRC normalization did not eliminate differences of opinion in the United States over whether U.S. interests would be well served by normalization along Peking's terms. Strongly divergent schools of thought emerged on this issue and reinforced the difficulties faced by leaders in the Carter administration and Congress as they determined how quickly and in what ways the United States should try to normalize with the PRC.

The task was made more difficult by Peking's relatively inflexible demands for conditions that had to be met for the normalization of diplomatic relations: that the United States withdraw all military forces from Taiwan, break diplomatic relations with the ROC, and terminate the U.S.-Taiwan defense treaty. The Chinese strongly implied that the United States would be required to follow the example of Japan's normalization of relations with the PRC in September 1972. That so-called Japanese formula would have had the United States end diplomatic relations with the ROC, recognize Peking as the sole legal government of China, and express "respect" for Peking's claim that Taiwan is part of the PRC.[20] Although the U.S.-Taiwan defense treaty would have been automatically terminated, U.S. economic relations with Taiwan could have continued unhindered, and political relations could have been maintained through private offices staffed by career foreign service officers who were officially "retired," "separated," or "on leave."[21]

Opponents of Peking's terms for normalization argued that establishing relations in accord with Peking's conditions would seriously damage U.S. interests. In particular, U.S. withdrawal from Taiwan would undermine significant American strategic and trade interests in East Asia and tarnish seriously the image of the United States as an advocate of morality and justice in international affairs. Supporters of the establishment of U.S.-PRC relations in accord with Peking's conditions maintained with equal vehemence that U.S. interests would be best served by Sino-American normalization. As in most debates on policy alternatives, the majority of U.S. observers occupied positions somewhere between these extremes. Typically, they saw major advantages for the United States in normalizing relations with the PRC, but they were also concerned about the future security of Taiwan. The conflicting arguments made by opponents and proponents of normalization were divided into four categories: U.S. strategic interests, American moral principles, U.S. economic concerns, and questions of PRC leadership stability.

U.S. Strategic Interests

Relative Importance of Taiwan and the PRC. Opponents of normalization on PRC terms maintained that a U.S. withdrawal from Taiwan would have a detrimental impact on U.S. strategic interests in East Asia.[22] Some argued that the United States would lose access to Taiwan—a long-standing ally that occupied an important position astride the major communication lanes in the western Pacific and provided the United States with essential bases for military operations in Asia. Because of its location and relatively strong military power, Taiwan also served U.S. strategic interests by preventing the PRC from exerting heavy, and potentially troublesome, influence in the western Pacific. If Taiwan were to come under PRC control, the busy sea traffic in the area would be more vulnerable to interdiction by the PRC, and Peking's capability for military use of the seas would be substantially enhanced. Although most U.S. experts saw little likelihood of an immediate PRC military take-over of Taiwan, even if the United States withdrew from the island, some noted that Peking was technically capable of such an assault. They cited the opinion voiced by Central Intelligence Agency Director Stansfield Turner during a July 17, 1977, interview with the *Boston Globe* in which he said that the PRC could militarily take over Taiwan after a U.S. withdrawal, but it would incur great loss of life and seriously upset its relations with the United States and noncommunist Asian nations.[23]

Proponents of normalization stressed that the easing of U.S. tensions with the PRC over the past decade had reduced the need for American bases on Taiwan. Many claimed that there was little likelihood that the PRC would soon be exerting direct military control around Taiwan. Citing limited PRC sea-lift capabilities and relatively strong defense forces on Taiwan, they noted that U.S. experts generally agreed not only that Peking was unlikely to attack Taiwan directly but also that the communists would have great difficulty engaging in a successful military blockade of the island.[24]

Other proponents of normalization pointed out that Peking's enormous power in East Asia was far more important to the United States than was Taiwan's relatively small strategic capability. They added that the United States should take prompt, vigorous measures to cement a favorable relationship with the PRC, including breaking U.S. ties with Taiwan.[25] To underline their case that Peking was of great strategic use to the United States, these spokesmen noted that since the signing of the Shanghai Communiqué in 1972, Peking had worked closely with the United States to ensure that important areas of East Asia did not fall under the influence of the Soviet Union. For example, Peking strongly encouraged Japanese leaders to solidify defense and political ties with the United States to offset growing Soviet political and military pressure in northeastern Asia. Peking also encouraged noncommunist states in Southeast Asia to maintain cordial relations with the United States to help block Soviet penetration of the region. Advocates of normalization acknowledged that Peking's reliability as a supporter of U.S. strategic interests in East Asia was not as well proven as was Taipei's, but they predicted that the United States and the PRC were likely to continue close cooperation in East Asia to deal with the future growth of Soviet power there.

Opponents of normalization maintained that Peking's current cooperation with the United States in East Asia was a clear and understandable tactical maneuver that could well be short lived and not worth the cost of breaking U.S. relations with Taiwan.[26] They expected that as Peking grew in military power over the next decade, China might be better able to deal with the Soviet Union on its own and therefore would have less interest in cooperation with Washington. In this situation, the Chinese communists could begin to challenge directly the interests of the United States and other Western-aligned countries in Asian affairs.

Chance of Conflict over Taiwan. Both opponents and proponents of normalization agreed that the outbreak of an armed conflict over Taiwan would seriously compromise the U.S. aim of maintaining a stable balance of power in East Asia. Senator William Roth and other foes of normalization on PRC terms predicted that a continuation of the status quo in U.S.-Taiwan relations was unlikely to lead to serious conflict over the island.[27] They noted that the Chinese communists had recently shown little urgency about the Taiwan issue, and they judged that Peking would be unlikely to endanger its relations with the United States by launching a military attack on Taiwan. Many suggested that a U.S. pullback from Taiwan and a break in the U.S. security treaty with the ROC might even increase the likelihood of conflict over the island. For example, Peking might be tempted to gain control of the island by force following a U.S. withdrawal, particularly if the communists perceived that Taiwan—devoid of U.S. support—might try to develop nuclear weapons or align with the Soviet Union.

In contrast, advocates of normalization saw little likelihood of an immediate PRC attack following U.S. withdrawal from Taiwan, claiming that the real danger of conflict over Taiwan lay in the future.[28] They said it was foolhardy for the United States to expect Peking's patience over Taiwan to last for long, warning that the longer Taiwan remained outside PRC control, the more tenuous would become Peking's claim to be the island's rightful ruler. As a result, it would not be surprising if Peking eventually decided that it had little alternative but to build up its power in the Taiwan area so it could assert its claim to the island by force. If the U.S.-Taiwan defense treaty were still in effect, the United States would then become directly involved—on the side of the weaker party—in a major armed confrontation of the Chinese civil war that the American people might be unwilling to support.[29]

Implications for Sino-Soviet and U.S.-Soviet Relations. Most observers agreed that the emergence of the Sino-Soviet dispute over the past two decades had added to U.S. leverage in international affairs and that the United States should try to follow policies that did not stimulate a major easing of Sino-Soviet relations, which would be detrimental to U.S. interests. Promoters of normalization claimed that the establishment of U.S.-PRC relations would reduce the chances of such a Sino-Soviet rapprochement.[30] Peking in recent years had relied on the United States to help block Soviet expansion in Asia—something that China could not accomplish on its own. Without dependable support from the United States, some of these observers warned, Peking might feel compelled to accommodate the Soviets and might even try to revive the Sino-Soviet alliance. The United States could help preclude such developments by normalizing relations with the PRC, thereby demonstrating to the Chinese communists that the United States was a reliable friend that fully intended to support China against the USSR.

Pro-normalization spokesmen maintained that establishing U.S.-PRC relations would also help increase U.S. leverage against the Soviet Union in areas outside East Asia. They claimed that improved Sino-American relations over the past few years had caused the Soviets to feel less secure in international affairs and had made Moscow more willing to compromise with the United States over such important issues as strategic arms limitation and disarmament in Europe.[31]

Foes of normalization disputed these claims, arguing that a rapid move by the United States toward China might prompt serious suspicion in Moscow over U.S. intentions toward the Soviet Union.[32] Thinking that Washington was determined to side with Peking against Moscow, the Soviets might be inclined to resist U.S. initiatives on SALT and other issues.

At the same time, these officials doubted that the establishment of U.S.-PRC diplomatic relations would significantly affect prospects for Sino-Soviet rapprochement. They stressed that Peking's hatred of the Soviet Union was based largely on Chinese ideological and national interests that had little to do with the United States.[33] Some emphasized that even though Peking expected the United States to remain a strategically strong power that would resolutely help it offset the Soviet "threat," PRC leaders would not necessarily see the establishment of Sino-American relations as a demonstration of such U.S. resolve. In fact, some foes of normalization argued that Peking might have seen U.S. acceptance of the Japanese formula as an indication of further U.S. withdrawal from Asia—a sign of "weakness," which might have caused China to question U.S. strength vis-à-vis the USSR, reassess its strategy toward the two superpowers, and adopt a more accommodating stance toward the Soviet Union.[34]

Japanese Concerns. Most American experts agreed that the U.S.-Japan alliance represented the foundation of recent U.S. strategic policy in East Asia and thought that the United States should avoid unnecessary complications in its relations with Japan. Foes of normalization on PRC terms stated that a U.S. break with Taiwan would adversely affect U.S.-Japan relations.[35] They maintained that the Japanese government had become worried in recent years about the determination of the United States to remain actively involved in Asian affairs and to continue safeguarding Japan's security. Tokyo's concerns had grown, especially after the United States failed to prevent the defeat of pro-U.S. regimes in Indochina in 1975. These American opponents of conformance to PRC terms claimed that Japanese concern was graphically illustrated in mid-1976 when the Japanese foreign minister privately informed Senator Mike Mansfield that Tokyo was urging the United States to slow normalization with the PRC. Japanese concern was increased by the official U.S. plan, announced in 1977, to withdraw U.S. ground forces from South Korea by 1981 and by speculation in the Western press that the United States intended to pull back from its bases in the Philippines.

Against this backdrop, it was argued that U.S. withdrawal from Taiwan might cause Japan to reassess its traditional close relationship with the United States and to attempt to strengthen Japanese security by other means in the changing balance of power in East Asia. For example, Tokyo might reduce its dependency on the United States and become more accommodating toward the other major powers in the region—the Soviet Union and the PRC—or it might transform its massive economic strength into military power, leading to a large increase in the size of Japanese self-defense forces and the development of Japanese nuclear weapons. Another possibility was that Tokyo's perception of declining U.S. interest in Asia might lead to political instability in Japan and paralysis in the foreign policy decision making of the Japanese government, prompting reduced business confidence in Japan and, possibly, a serious economic downturn there.

Proponents of normalization emphasized that Tokyo could not reasonably object to the United States following the Japanese formula in establishing U.S.-PRC relations. They added that even though Japanese leaders might have been worried about U.S. support for Japan in the wake of U.S. withdrawals from Taiwan and South Korea, the United States could reassure the Japanese in other ways. The United States could increase U.S. naval and air strength in the region, expand U.S. military facilities in Guam and other islands in the western Pacific, and reaffirm the U.S. commitment to abide by the U.S.-Japan mutual security treaty. Some proponents of normalization, who claimed that only a minority of Japanese politicians actually opposed U.S. normalization with the PRC, asserted that even within the ruling conservative party in Japan there was considerable support for the United States rapidly establishing relations with the Chinese communists.[36]

Stability in Korea. U.S. policy makers also generally agreed that the maintenance of stability in Korea was an important element in U.S. policy in Asia, as it had been since the 1950–1953 Korean War. Continuing U.S. defense ties with the Seoul government and similar Soviet and Chinese ties with Pyongyang meant that the outbreak of armed conflict on the peninsula could trigger a great-power confrontation there. Opponents of normalization argued that U.S. withdrawal from Taiwan to establish diplomatic relations with the PRC might increase tension in Korea.[37] South Korean leaders—already faced with the prospect of the withdrawal of U.S. ground forces from their country by 1981—probably would have seen the move as a sign of U.S. weakness and might have felt compelled to adopt new measures to guarantee their security. This could have involved a major South Korean arms buildup, perhaps including the development of nuclear weapons—events that would almost certainly have prompted a strong North Korean response and greatly increased tension on the peninsula.

The North Korean authorities might also have seen the U.S. withdrawals from both Taiwan and South Korea as signs of American weakness and might have responded with increased pressure against the South. Both Moscow and Peking recognized that supporting such North Korean action would seriously complicate their respective relations with the United States, but both communist powers were competing for favor in Pyongyang and might have felt constrained to continue supplying the North Koreans with military and economic supplies to avoid loss of influence in the region and to maintain their adversary credentials as leaders of the world communist movement.

In contrast, proponents of normalization saw little danger that U.S. withdrawal from Taiwan would increase chances for conflict in Korea. They judged that the United States could continue to guarantee South Korean security while it was withdrawing forces from both South Korea and Taiwan, adding that the maintenance of U.S. air forces in Korea following the 1981 deadline for withdrawal of U.S. ground forces would reassure South Korea of U.S. intentions.[38] Washington could also assuage possible South Korean fears by maintaining a strong naval presence in the region and by increasing U.S. matériel and training support to South Korean armed forces.

Some advocates of normalization also pointed out that improved Sino-American relations had served in the past to curb PRC support for aggressive North Korean actions and would probably do so in the future.[39] Chinese leaders had helped dampen enthusiasm in Pyongyang in spring 1975—coincident with the defeats of pro-U.S. regimes in Indochina—for a more aggressive North Korean policy toward the South. Some U.S. observers claimed that the establishment of U.S.-PRC relations might even cause the Chinese to exert pressure on North Korea to permanently settle the Korean problem in a manner agreeable to the United States. Of course, this claim was countered by the argument that Chinese communist ideology and rivalry with the USSR for influence in North Korea would preclude any significant PRC contribution to a permanent settlement that was contrary to North Korean interests.

Arms Control. In the early 1960s the United States had begun making great efforts to advance international arms control and disarmament, emphasizing in particular the need to control the spread of nuclear weapons and to limit nuclear testing. The U.S. efforts had been particularly stymied by the PRC, which had opposed U.S.-sponsored nuclear disarmament measures far more stridently than had any other nuclear power.

Proponents of normalization maintained that the establishment of U.S.-PRC diplomatic relations could help the United States encourage the PRC to accept arms control plans.[40] They said that U.S. normalization with the PRC would establish an atmosphere of trust between Washington and Peking, an essential element if the United States was to obtain a positive Chinese response to its proposals on sensitive issues like nuclear proliferation and curbing atmospheric nuclear tests.

Opponents of normalization, in contrast, saw little likelihood that normalization would have any effect on Peking's hostile attitude toward arms control. They noted that the PRC had consistently rebuffed arms control proposals and had rapidly expanded its armed forces. Until the PRC saw a reduction in the threat of outside attack—especially by the USSR—or was more confident of its ability to deter any such attack, Peking was unlikely to agree to any substantial arms control programs.[41]

Moral Considerations

U.S. observers also disagreed over whether normalization was consistent with U.S. efforts to promote democratic political practices, individual freedom, and human rights in world affairs. A few U.S. leaders argued that a U.S. break with Taiwan represented a morally unjustifiable "sacrifice" of the security of the people of Taiwan for the sake of improved U.S.-PRC relations. A far larger group opposed any U.S.-PRC agreement that would not leave room for continued U.S. support of Taiwan against possible PRC attack.

Opponents of normalization argued that if the United States ended its security commitment to Taiwan, it might be subjecting the people there to military pressure and possible attack from the mainland.[42] The people on Taiwan had remained allies of the United States for almost thirty years and were said to deserve better treatment—at the very least, the United States should allow them to decide their own future. If the people on Taiwan were given a choice, surely they would reject PRC control. In fact, some opponents declared that even though the Nationalist authorities in Taipei might eventually agree to reunite the island with the mainland, the majority of people on Taiwan would strongly object to such a settlement and might respond to it by openly rebelling against the Nationalist authorities.

Opponents of normalization also maintained that the United States would be sanctioning a major setback for the cause of international human rights if it allowed Taiwan to come under PRC control. Taiwan was said to be an example of successful U.S. efforts since World War II to encourage the development of democratic principles, the promotion of individual freedom, and the growth of a free enterprise economic system in the developing world. These spokesmen also cited the findings of nonpartisan organizations such as Freedom House, which consistently gave Taipei a better human-rights rating than Peking. They said that the PRC was a restrictive, totalitarian regime with a poor record in support of basic human rights.[43]

Some foes of normalization pointed out that a U.S. withdrawal from Taiwan might lead to rapid decline in human rights on the island, even if Peking did not assert control there. Faced with the threat of military attack from the mainland, the Nationalist government might well impose stern measures limiting any form of dissidence or political opposition that the Chinese communists could view as a sign of weakness. These opponents added that after the United States withdrew from the island, it would almost certainly be unable to exert much influence to encourage Taipei to moderate its policies.

Proponents of normalization strongly rejected these arguments, stressing that a U.S. break with Taiwan would not involve sacrificing Taiwan's security because Peking was unlikely to attack the island.[44] They noted that PRC leaders had repeatedly pledged to try to settle the Taiwan issue by peaceful means and that armed PRC attack against the island was also improbable for at least four reasons: (1) it would seriously complicate Peking's improved relations with the United States; (2) it would alarm other important Asian states, especially Japan, over PRC intentions in the region; (3) it would meet a strong response from the well-trained and -equipped ROC armed forces; and (4) the limited sea-lift capability of the PRC navy would make a successful attack extremely difficult.

Pro-normalization advocates added that the U.S. commitment to Taiwan was obsolete and should be broken to bring U.S. policy into line with the "reality" of communist China's role in Asian affairs.[45] The 1954 U.S.-Taiwan mutual security treaty—the cornerstone of Washington's commitment to Taipei—was part of U.S. efforts at the height of the cold war to block suspected PRC expansion with a "containment" policy in Asia. Since containment of the PRC had now been abandoned in favor of Sino-American cooperation, ending the defense treaty with Taiwan was said to be reasonable.

Other arguments for ending the defense treaty included the claim that the United States had fulfilled (and even surpassed) its commitment to the ROC by providing it with economic and military aid for over thirty years. Moreover, some proponents of normalization asserted that it was morally wrong and deceptive for the United States to maintain the defense treaty with Taipei, inasmuch as recent polls indicated that the American public had no intention of intervening in a Chinese civil war in order to protect Taiwan's security. They added that the United States could better ensure Taiwan's security by ending the defense treaty, establishing normal relations with Peking, and entering into a tacit understanding with the PRC leaders that would either preclude PRC attack against Taiwan or permit continued U.S. arms assistance to Taiwan forces. Their arguments for ending the defense treaty were given greater strength by the U.S. commitment to normalize relations with the PRC, made in the 1972 Shanghai Communiqué.[46]

On the human rights issue, advocates of normalization expressed doubt that Taipei's record was superior to that of Peking, noting that the Nationalist regime had maintained a monopoly of power in Taiwan for thirty years and had a long history of forcefully suppressing political dissidence and procommunist sympathizers on the island. Although they acknowledged that the PRC was a communist dictatorship that limited human rights, pro-normalization advocates pointed out that the vast majority of people on the mainland were economically better off than when the Nationalists ruled there and that political participation for the mainland Chinese people was far greater than it had been at any time in Chinese history.

Some proponents of normalization also maintained that the establishment of U.S.-PRC diplomatic relations was necessary to open China to Western influence, which would presumably help soften some of the harsh and authoritarian features of the PRC government. They pointed to the example of the moderating influence that increased Western contact had on the authoritarian communist regimes in Eastern Europe over the previous three decades, adding that U.S.-PRC exchanges would increase following normalization, allowing the two sides to learn more of each other's technical accomplishments and sociopolitical systems. The process presumably would expose the PRC leaders and people to more of the good points of the West, thereby increasing Chinese aspirations for a more moderate and free system. Such claims, of course, ran counter to the argument that the Chinese communists intended to strictly control exchanges with the United States after normalization— just as they had done with other Western countries that had normalized diplomatic relations with them. According to this view, Peking fully intended to guard against exposing the Chinese people to what it saw as ideologically corrupting or politically subversive foreign contacts.[47]

Economic Issues

Some American business leaders with interests in Taiwan argued strongly against unconditional U.S. acceptance of PRC terms for normalization.[48] They claimed that normalization would probably harm U.S.-Taiwan trade, which amounted annually to several billion dollars— several times the amount of U.S. trade with the PRC—and would likely endanger extensive U.S. investments on the island. They also contended that normalization was unlikely to lead to U.S. investments in the PRC or to a significant increase in U.S.-PRC trade, since Peking's policies of economic self-reliance tended to limit Chinese interest in foreign trade and preclude direct foreign investment in the country.

Those business leaders asserted that if the PRC eventually gained control of Taiwan, it would probably confiscate U.S. investments there. In 1978 private U.S. banks had lent $1.5 billion to Taiwan, and the U.S. government-owned Ex-Im Bank had extended another $1 billion in credits. Other American investments in Taiwan amounted to about $500 million. In view of these interests, the United States should—at a minimum—maintain some form of security guarantees for Taiwan and ensure that the island continued to receive trade and economic benefits from the United States. Particularly important were most-favored-nation (MFN) status for Taiwanese exports to the United States; U.S. duty reductions for Taiwanese exports; insurance coverage for American investments in Taiwan under OPIC (a U.S. government institution); and U.S. sales of nuclear fuel to power plants in Taiwan.

Proponents of normalization countered by stating that U.S. investments and trade on Taiwan would not be adversely affected because the PRC was unlikely to gain control of the island following U.S.-PRC normalization.[49] Even if Peking did gain control of Taiwan, U.S. economic interests on the island would remain secure because PRC officials had repeatedly promised to respect U.S. investments and other foreign economic concerns in Taiwan following the communists' "liberation" of the island.

Advocates of normalization added that the establishment of U.S.-PRC diplomatic relations was likely to increase U.S.-PRC trade over its moderate level. Although Peking officials had made no explicit promises of increased trade following normalization, other Western countries had seen their trade with the PRC increase after they established diplomatic relations with Peking, and PRC leaders had repeatedly emphasized over the previous year that they wanted to expand their nation's trade with the major capitalist countries, including the United States.

PRC Leadership Stability

Foes and proponents of normalization disagreed strongly over whether the unstable political situation in Peking, seen in the major changes in PRC leadership since 1976, should cause the United States to slow down or speed up its efforts to establish formal diplomatic relations with China. Even those who favored rapid U.S.-PRC normalization argued that it would be foolhardy for the United States to normalize on Peking's terms without first engaging in extensive, high-level negotiations with the recently installed Chinese leaders.

Since 1976 the PRC had seen the deaths of Zhou Enlai and Mao Zedong; the purge and subsequent reinstatement of Zhou's protégé, Vice Premier Deng Xiaoping; and the arrest and purge of Deng's chief adversaries—the notorious Gang of Four. Many experts, like Harold Hinton of George Washington University, questioned whether the United States could be sure that normalization agreements reached with the current Chinese leaders would continue to be honored by future leaders in Peking. They warned that since the United States had little assurance that the present leadership in the PRC would prove to be any more stable than its recent predecessors had been, Washington should delay normalization until more firmly established PRC leaders emerged. Because the current officials in Peking remained preoccupied with domestic political difficulties stemming from the recent leadership changes, they were said to be unwilling to make any major changes in PRC foreign policy—such as a shift against the United States—that would seriously complicate Peking's already extensive problems. Thus, Peking would probably continue cordial relations with the United States, whether or not Washington met its conditions on normalization.

In contrast, some proponents of normalization maintained that the unstable leadership situation in China should prompt the United States to speed the pace of normalization efforts, thereby showing support for the current pragmatic, moderate leaders in Peking, who were following policies more agreeable to the United States. If Washington delayed normalization, it ran the risk of alienating the new Peking leaders and subjecting them to pressure from other PRC officials who distrusted the United States and favored a more militant line against both the United States and the Soviet Union. By promptly normalizing relations with China, the United States would provide the moderates in Peking with a major diplomatic success—something that would enhance their efforts to consolidate power and offset potential rivals for power.

Alternative Proposals for Normalization

The debate over China policy at this time clearly demonstrated that there was no formula for U.S.-PRC normalization that would be advantageous to the United States, acceptable to the PRC, *and* welcomed by the majority of Americans. Although quite a few experts favored having the United States follow the Japanese formula in normalizing with Peking, many others opposed normalization without conditions set by the United States. In general, the latter observers demanded that the United States set conditions for normalization that would maintain the security of the people on Taiwan and safeguard U.S. economic interests on the island. Some of their proposals contained vaguely worded conditions that probably would have been acceptable to the PRC, inasmuch as they conformed generally with the three main conditions set forth by Peking: (1) withdrawal of U.S. forces from Taiwan, (2) breaking U.S. diplomatic ties with the ROC, and (3) termination of the U.S.-Taiwan defense treaty. Other proposals, however, contained strict conditions that severely impinged on Peking's claim to Taiwan and therefore were likely to meet with strong objections from the PRC.

Proposals Probably Acceptable to the PRC

A number of U.S. leaders urged that the United States adopt the Japanese formula, with an added formal U.S. declaration of strong opposition to the settlement of the Taiwan issue by other than peaceful means.[50] For the present, the declaration would reassure the people on Taiwan of continued U.S. interest in the island's security, while in the future, if Peking threatened to use force against Taiwan, the United States could respond with warnings and military deployments justified on the basis of the U.S. declaration. The statement could be issued in the name of Congress or the president or both.

If the U.S. statement referred explicitly to Taiwan, Peking might have objected strongly, accusing the United States of interfering in China's "internal affair." However, the U.S. statement need not have referred to Taiwan; it could have declared U.S. opposition to the use of force to settle problems in "the western Pacific along the rim of East Asia"—a general formula that would clearly include Taiwan but would have avoided directly affronting the PRC. (Harvard University professor John K. Fairbank was associated with this view.) Other experts suggested that the U.S. declaration be made after the formal establishment of U.S.-PRC diplomatic relations, when Peking would be unlikely to bear the onus of breaking relations over the issue.

One variation of this approach called for Congress to support a U.S. declaration against the use of force regarding Taiwan with an amendment of the War Powers Resolution.[51] Such an action would have increased the president's freedom to deploy military forces for the protection of Taiwan and would have provided a sort of security guarantee for Taiwan without the formal aspects of a defense treaty, which was offensive to the PRC.

Another variation emphasized that the United States should demand that Peking allow continued U.S. arms sales to Taiwan as a precondition for normalization.[52] The United States could use the arms sales to enhance Taiwan's ability to defend itself against possible PRC attack and to tangibly remind Peking of Washington's continued interest in the island's security. Of course, Peking was likely to object to any explicit agreement with the United States on this subject, but PRC leaders were thought to be willing to turn a blind eye to continued arms sales, provided that the United States strictly adhered to the communists' three major conditions for normalization.

Other experts proposed that the United States underline its continued interest in Taiwan by having the president and members of Congress visit the island soon after relations with Peking were normalized.[53] Although such visits would be largely of symbolic importance, they would reassure the people on Taiwan of the United States's continued interest in their security and welfare and would also show the PRC that Washington remained strongly opposed to the use of force against the island. If the U.S. visits were of a private, unofficial nature, it seemed likely that Peking would find little basis for objecting to them.

Proposals Probably Unacceptable to the PRC

Several American leaders predicted that unilateral U.S. declarations opposing the use of force on Taiwan, high-level U.S. visits to the island, and continued U.S. arms sales after normalization would not be sufficient to guarantee Taiwan's future security and prosperity. They urged the United States to set more strict conditions for normalization, even though those conditions would be officially rejected by Peking as unacceptable prerequisites for the normalization of relations.

Some observers claimed that the United States should insist as a condition of normalization that Peking formally renounce the use of force against Taiwan, maintaining that such a declaration represented the bare minimum needed to guarantee Taiwan's security following U.S. withdrawal from the island.[54] Of course, Peking claimed that its right to use force over Taiwan was an "internal matter" in which foreign powers had no right to interfere. Others advised that the United States should not break its ties with Taiwan and should insist that normalization with the PRC conform with the "reality" of the two governments existing on Chinese soil.[55] Thus, the United States should continue its political, defense, and economic ties with Taiwan and should establish relations with Peking as the ruler of mainland China. This "one China-two governments" plan was said to be similar to the policy the United States followed toward Germany—acknowledging one German nation but maintaining diplomatic relations with both West and East Germany.

Congressman Lester Wolff suggested that the United States support self-determination in Taiwan—a move that would encourage the Taiwan government to declare itself an independent country with no claims on the mainland.[56] The United States could then legally sustain ties with Taipei as the government of Taiwan while recognizing Peking as the sole government of China. Although the rulers in Taiwan had long opposed any plan that would reject their claim to the mainland, it was claimed that if they were faced with the prospect of total U.S. withdrawal and almost certain control by Peking, they might become more favorable toward the independent Taiwan option. Of course, Peking had repeatedly rejected any proposals for normalization that involved "one China–two governments" or an "independent Taiwan," insisting that they were inconsistent with its claims that Taiwan was part of China and that Peking was the sole legal government of China.

Another alternative, which represented a less direct challenge to Peking's claim to Taiwan, was that the United States refuse to acknowledge explicitly the PRC claim to Taiwan as part of normalization.[57] That would leave open the possibility of the United States maintaining some form of official presence on the island, perhaps in the form of a consulate or a liaison office similar to the one it maintained in Peking in the 1970s.[58] Continued official U.S. ties with Taiwan would serve to deter Peking from attacking Taiwan, even after the withdrawal of U.S. forces from the island and the termination of the defense treaty. The ties would also be a useful point of official contact for U.S.-Taiwan economic relations and possible continued U.S. military sales to Taiwan. This plan was reportedly suggested by Senator Henry Jackson during a visit to the PRC in 1974 but was rejected by the Chinese communists as an unacceptable "two Chinas" proposal.[59]

A variation involved U.S. refusal to acknowledge the PRC claim to Taiwan and continued—albeit indirect—official U.S. contacts with the ROC. Following U.S.-PRC normalization, U.S. and ROC diplomats could be stationed in the embassies of third countries in Taipei and Washington, or U.S. and ROC diplomats could maintain official contacts through a permanent forum for negotiations in some third country. The former situation would have been similar to the arrangement between the United States and Cuba in 1977, in which U.S. diplomats were stationed at the Swiss embassy in Havana and Cuban envoys were posted at the Czechoslovakian embassy in Washington. The second option would have been similar to the ambassadorial talks between U.S. and PRC envoys, which were carried out first in Geneva, Switzerland, and then in Warsaw, Poland, from 1955 until 1970.[60]

Partial Measures

In addition to formulas designed to complete the normalization process, some proposals were designed to move normalization forward partway, without establishing full U.S.-PRC diplomatic relations. Congressman Les AuCoin proposed in 1977 that the United States take several steps to improve prospects for U.S.-PRC trade. He called for an amendment of the Ex-Im Bank charter to allow U.S. exporters credit for ventures in the PRC, a change in the so-called Jackson-Vanik amendment to the Trade Act of 1974 that would "unlock" Ex-Im Bank credits to the PRC, and a reduction of tariffs on imported silk fabric, an important product of PRC cottage industries.[61] Selig Harrison of the Carnegie Endowment for International Peace proposed that the United States make official its current informal policy of not allowing U.S. oil companies to exercise Taiwan-granted concessions in areas away from the island itself. This policy would have favored PRC offshore oil claims in the South and East China seas, enhancing PRC relations with the United States.[62]

Other officials—notably former Senator Hugh Scott—saw renewed peace negotiations between Peking and Taipei as a way to expedite progress in U.S.-PRC normalization.[63] They urged the United States to encourage Taipei to respond favorably to PRC calls for peace talks to help ease tensions in the region and allow for an eventual U.S. withdrawal from Taiwan. Professor Victor Li of Stanford University proposed that the United States recognize the PRC as the legal government of China, withdraw its forces from Taiwan, and lower its diplomatic representation on Taiwan. He affirmed that the United States should maintain the defense treaty in force until a firm substitute for Taiwan's security could be worked out between Peking, Taipei, and the United States. While acknowledging that his plan was an interim measure that was unlikely to meet with Peking's full approval, Li judged that the plan would enhance forward movement and break the impasse in U.S.-PRC relations.[64]

Legal Implications of Normalization

U.S. leaders in the Carter administration and Congress also devoted considerable attention to the possible implications of U.S.-PRC normalization for U.S. law, especially laws governing relations with Taiwan and the PRC.[65] It seemed obvious that if the United States broke ties with the ROC to establish full diplomatic relations with the PRC, it would no longer be extending *de jure* recognition to the government in Taipei. This posed problems in terms of general U.S. laws and specific U.S. treaties with the Taipei administration.

As Victor Li pointed out in an authoritative review of the problem, a number of important statutory schemes involving economic and military relations and aid applied to so-called friendly countries—a category that in the past included the ROC. These programs included military sales and assistance, OPIC, sales of U.S. agricultural surplus on credit terms or for foreign currency by the Commodity Credit

Corporation, loans to small farmers of predominantly rural countries, and expenditures of funds pursuant to the Agricultural Trade Development and Assistance Act of 1954. Although nowhere in these statutes was the term *friendly* defined, withdrawal of recognition was seen as possibly being interpreted as a loss of friendliness, which in turn might have precluded the application of programs under these statutes to the Taipei government.

Also, several laws imposed sanctions upon countries with which the United States had severed diplomatic relations. The Foreign Assistance Act, which affected both economic and military aid, included a blanket provision to this effect, and some laws placed restrictions on dealings with "communist countries." If Taiwan were considered part of a communist country after normalization, then the Ex-Im Bank, the generalized system of preferences (GSP), and tariff rates might be affected to the detriment of U.S.-Taiwan ties.

Professor Li suggested that these difficulties could be overcome and obstacles to maintaining existing economic, cultural, and other ties with Taiwan could be removed by legislation that would have affirmed the Taiwan authorities *de facto* control and "friendly" status and would have removed possible restrictions on dealings with "communist countries" or countries with whom diplomatic relations were severed. (It was this kind of planning that laid the foundation for American determination to pass the Taiwan Relations Act, which would govern U.S. interchange with Taiwan after the establishment of U.S.-PRC diplomatic relations.)

A second area of concern involved important U.S. treaties with the ROC: the mutual defense treaty, trade and navigation treaty, air transport treaty, treaty on civilian uses of atomic energy, and agreements on quotas for Taiwan's exports of certain commodities, such as textiles, to the United States. Some experts—like Jerome Cohen—felt that these treaties would lapse after the United States recognized the PRC, prompting the need for new mechanisms for unofficial U.S. relations with Taiwan. Other experts, including Li, maintained that the legal effect of withdrawing recognition in such circumstances was unclear, and Li added that the United States had the choice of either formally terminating or continuing the treaties after normalization. (Li's interpretation became the official U.S. view following U.S.-PRC diplomatic normalization.)

Regarding U.S.-PRC relations, many U.S. officials judged that after U.S.-PRC diplomatic relations were established, Peking probably would step up its demands for MFN nondiscriminatory tariff treatment by the United States. In the Trade Expansion Act of 1962, as amended, section 231 provided for mandatory continuation of the prohibition against MFN tariff treatment for countries under communist rule. This provision was still in effect, through the Trade Act of 1974, though that law also provided a mechanism by which MFN tariff treatment for China could eventually be restored. However, under terms of the Jackson-Vanik amendment, MFN status was not to be extended to any non–market economy nation that denied its citizens the right or opportunity to emigrate or that imposed more than nominal exit fees or taxes on documents or individuals—provisions that seemed to apply directly to the PRC.

Settlement of the issues of PRC assets blocked in the United States and U.S. private claims against the PRC was seen as required before certain steps in U.S.-PRC commercial relations could be taken. Those issues stemmed from the blocking by the United States of PRC dollar-denominated accounts and other assets on December 17, 1950, after PRC military forces entered North Korea and from the subsequent Peking decree of December 29, 1950, announcing the seizure of U.S. public and private property in the PRC. In 1978 claims by private U.S. citizens and corporations totaled about $197 million, while the value of PRC assets held by the United States was put at $76.5 million. In addition to the private claims of U.S. nationals, there were potential public claims arising from Ex-Im Bank loans, from large Lend-Lease loans of money and equipment during the Sino-Japanese War, and from other obligations of previous Chinese governments.

Moreover, the Trade Act of 1974 included a section that was potentially troublesome where the settlement of outstanding claims was concerned. Section 408 required a claims settlement, previously negotiated with Czechoslovakia by the State Department, to be renegotiated and submitted for congressional review on grounds that the settlement reached was unfair to U.S. claimants. The PRC was not mentioned in the section, but any eventual settlement negotiated with Peking was at least potentially liable to a similar congressional "veto."

In the wake of normalized U.S.-PRC diplomatic relations, legislation might be needed to ease restrictions on the provision of U.S. aid and credits to the PRC. Provisions of Public Law 480 prohibited assistance provided for in the law from being granted to communist countries. The Foreign Assistance Act of 1961 also limited the furnishing of almost every type of assistance provided for in the act to "friendly countries," although the act did not explicitly define the term. There was a specific ban on furnishing any assistance covered by the act to a communist country unless the president issued a very narrowly defined waiver. Also exempt, upon presidential waiver in the national interest, were programs administered by OPIC, which provided investment guarantees to U.S. firms investing abroad. Similarly, the Export-Import Bank Act of 1945 as amended prohibited the bank from entering into any credit transaction directly or indirectly involving a communist country, unless the president determined that such a transaction was in the national interest.

4
Congressional-Executive Friction over China Policy, 1978–1980

President Carter attempted to cut boldly through the maze of the various arguments, alternatives, and legal complications that hindered the forging of a new, closer U.S. relationship with the PRC. In broad terms, his administration's goals were consistent with those of the two previous administrations:

1. to position itself favorably in the U.S.-Soviet-PRC triangular relationship;
2. to use improved relations with Peking to help stabilize Asian affairs, secure a balance of forces in the region favorable to the United States and China, and foster a peaceful, prosperous future for Taiwan;
3. to build mutually beneficial economic, cultural, and other ties with the PRC; and
4. to work more closely with the PRC on internationally important issues such as world food supply, population control, and arms limitation.

As the Carter administration moved toward a decidedly more anti-Soviet position in its foreign policy, however, it increasingly viewed the PRC as an important global and regional power in the Third World. The president and his advisors thought that China could work closely with the United States and its allies in the developed world and help counter what they came to see as the major U.S. strategic problem over the next decade—the containment of expanding Soviet military power and influence in world affairs.

The administration followed the December 15, 1978, announcement of U.S.-PRC diplomatic relations with a series of major initiatives made as high-level U.S. officials visited China during the next two years. It also worked hard to build a consensus behind those initiatives within the executive branch, in Congress, and among the public at large. Thus, scores of officials in the State, Commerce, and other departments were mobilized to lobby on Capitol Hill and throughout the country for the new policy. Supporting these efforts were Chinese Vice Premier Deng Xiaoping's widely publicized tour of the United States in early 1979 and China's increasingly positive public approach toward the United States. As a result, the administration was remarkably successful in moving U.S.-PRC relations forward, but it was less successful at consensus-building. The new approaches to Peking aroused strong opposition, especially in Congress.[1]

Heavily influencing that congressional opposition was the fact that the Carter administration had shifted from a cautious approach toward the PRC (seen in Secretary Vance's visit to Peking in August 1977) to the bold approach of 1978–1980 without major pressure from U.S. constituencies, China, or other international forces. There had been no domestic consensus demanding that the administration move ahead on Peking's terms, as demonstrated by the continued debate in the United States over normalization. Indeed, U.S. public opinion remained particularly opposed to the total official break with Taipei that Peking required as a condition for improved U.S.-PRC diplomatic relations.[2] Meanwhile, China continued to show its interest in maintaining good relations with the United States, despite the absence of formal diplomatic recognition. (Those U.S. experts who warned that Sino-American relations might seriously retrogress if the United States refused to meet Peking's terms for normalization could point to few signs of current impatience in the PRC over the U.S. delay. Instead, their forecasts were generally based on predictions of *future* Chinese actions.)

According to senior Carter administration officials, pressure for change in China policy came almost exclusively from within the administration.[3] Two factors were said to be uppermost in the minds of the president and his advisors as they decided to push ahead with improved relations with the PRC. The first concerned the administration's commitment, made in private policy meetings after the 1976 election, to seek normal relations with Peking. Achieving that goal had been delayed when Secretary Vance visited China, partly because the administration had to devote its major efforts to the Panama Canal treaties if it hoped to secure their passage by Congress. The ratification of the treaties in spring 1978 opened the way for new efforts to normalize diplomatic relations with China.

The second factor related to a shift in the administration's attitudes and policy toward the Soviet Union. Until early 1978, President Carter remained generally committed to the view—associated with Secretary

Vance—that relations with China should not be allowed to complicate seriously U.S. efforts to reach an understanding with the Soviet Union over strategic arms limitation. Continued Soviet expansion in the Third World, a growing American perception of reduced U.S. ability to halt such expansion, and a perceived decline in U.S. strength vis-à-vis Moscow's growing strategic and conventional military might combined to gradually shift the administration away from Secretary Vance's approach. Instead, the top leaders in the administration increasingly favored a policy associated with Brzezinski in which the United States would attempt to develop relations with a wide range of countries that could cooperate in a global effort to confront Soviet expansionism. With its stridently anti-Soviet foreign policy and its strategic position along the long, hard-to-defend Soviet Asian frontier, China became a growing and important element in that newly perceived strategic equation. In addition, after the PRC was formally recognized, international and domestic events—notably, the Soviet-backed Vietnamese invasion of Cambodia in December 1978, the holding of U.S. hostages in Iran from November 1979 to January 1981 (with the perception of American weakness that followed), the congressional debate over U.S. military preparedness during deliberations on the SALT II treaty in 1979, and the Soviet invasion of Afghanistan in December 1979—acted to solidify further the consensus within the administration behind those officials who would use relations with the PRC to help the United States contend with Soviet global power.[4]

Because the new approach to the PRC was formulated in great secrecy, the president's announcement of U.S.-PRC normalization surprised all but a handful of U.S. leaders. Congressional officials with important responsibilities in foreign affairs reported that they had been kept in the dark about the administration's plans until only a few hours before the decision was announced.[5] Although it marked the start of a dramatic new era in U.S. China policy, the recognition of the PRC also began one of the most contentious periods in congressional-executive relations over that policy.

Several implications of the change in China policy concerned members of Congress and many of their constituents; yet, according to both congressional and administration sources, the president and his aides never offered any real consultations on the shift in policy.[6] Thus, congressional officials were unclear how the new policy would fit in with U.S.-Soviet relations and with U.S. interests in Taiwan and the rest of Asia. They were also uncertain of the new policy's possible political repercussions inside the United States. They judged that the president's action was a serious affront to their position and prerogatives in forming U.S. policy in this important area, especially since they had gone on record earlier in the year expressing their interest in being consulted before any major changes were made in relations with the PRC and Taiwan.[7]

Administration officials acknowledged that the tight secrecy compounded their problems in dealing with Congress after the normalization agreement was announced, but they insisted that there were several good reasons for keeping Congress in the dark. Few in the administration were prepared to answer the deluge of congressional and other queries about the new approach, and some misinformation was passed to Congress by administration briefers who were unaware of the full details of the new policy. Because of the secrecy, the administration was unable to formulate promptly the legislation needed to protect future U.S.-Taiwan relations, and that caused Congress to feel under excessive pressure to pass the bill before official U.S. ties with Taiwan lapsed.

The passage of the Taiwan Relations Act in April 1979 temporarily eased congressional-executive friction over China policy. Later in the year, however, new disputes arose over the administration's handling of U.S. agreements with the Taipei government, over the transfer of U.S. arms to Taiwan, and over suspected efforts by the administration to use improved relations with the PRC as a source of leverage against the USSR. Many congressional officials thought they had been misled by the administration into thinking that all U.S. agreements with Taiwan, except for the defense agreement, would remain in effect after normalization. In fact, the administration planned to phase out many of those official accords—an intention that did not become widely known until August 1979.[8]

In 1980 congressional members complained that the administration had misled them about U.S. policy on military ties with China.[9] Although Carter officials repeatedly denied that they had any interest in playing the Chinese card, many congressional officers judged that the administration was being more vigorous than any previous U.S. government in its pursuit of closer strategic cooperation with China against the USSR. By mid-1980 congressional members and staff most closely associated with Asian affairs were among the most suspicious and critical of the president's policy, reflecting serious, mutual misunderstanding and disrespect that had emerged between some administration officers and some members of Congress. Officials on each side were increasingly defensive of their prerogatives in foreign affairs in the face of what they saw as repeated challenges from those on the other side.

Impact of the Normalization Announcement

President Carter's announcement that, as of January 1, 1979, the United States would establish diplomatic relations with the PRC, break its diplomatic ties with the Nationalist Chinese administration on Taiwan, and terminate its defense treaty with Taiwan one year later, presented Congress with a wide variety of legal, economic, and strategic concerns about future U.S. relations with the PRC and Taiwan. In general, these issues focused on the following three questions:

1. How would the United States continue commercial (including arms sales), cultural, and other forms of interchange with Taiwan after the break in official relations?
2. What legislative actions would be required to normalize commercial and other interchanges with the PRC following the normalization of diplomatic relations?
3. What should be the direction of future U.S. policy toward the PRC, and what effect would changed relations with Peking have on important U.S. foreign and defense concerns?

President Carter made clear that the United States would meet Peking's three conditions and that it would follow, with few modifications, the Japanese formula on normalization. The United States did not terminate the U.S.-Taiwan defense treaty immediately. Instead, Washington gave Taiwan a one-year notice that the mutual defense treaty would be terminated, in accord with the treaty's provisions. In addition, the United States publicly announced that it expected the Taiwan issue to be settled peacefully. Administration officials told the press after the president's announcement that the United States would continue during 1979 to deliver military equipment already contracted for to Taiwan and that even after formal military ties ended, the United States would continue to make available to Taiwan "selected defense weaponry" on a "restricted basis."[10]

The administration subsequently prepared a package of legislation to govern future relations with Taiwan and submitted it to Congress in January 1979.[11] As expected, the bill's provisions for continuing unofficial political ties with Taiwan were similar to the Japanese formula. The proposal called for the establishment of a nonprofit private corporation, to be called the American Institute in Taiwan (AIT), that would carry out programs, transactions, and other relations previously conducted by the U.S. embassy. The institute would receive government funds to carry out its functions and would be staffed by personnel separated from government service but eligible for reinstatement with full career benefits after their employment with AIT ended.

The proposed Taiwan Relations Act also provided that the Taiwanese would not be denied eligibility for U.S. programs that legally required the maintenance of diplomatic relations with the United States; specified that laws, regulations, and orders referring or relating to "foreign governments" would continue to apply to Taiwan; and provided for dealing with the people on Taiwan through an instrumentality established in their behalf. These provisions confirmed Taiwan's continued eligibility under the Arms Export Control Act, the Export-Import Bank Act, the Foreign Assistance Act of 1961, and other legislation.

Congressional reaction to the administration's decision and proposed legislation was mixed. An overwhelming majority of members of Congress judged that special congressional efforts were needed to change several aspects of the administration's new policy toward the PRC and Taiwan. Few members opposed the establishment of diplomatic relations with Peking, since most agreed with the administration's argument that this was a goal that had been widely accepted in the United States since Nixon's trip to the PRC in 1972. Rather, they were concerned over what they saw as inadequacies in the administration's handling of the normalization question. In their view, the more important issue was what some members called the "practical implications" of normalization—questions about the timing and method of normalization and especially about its impact on Taiwan and broader U.S. foreign policy issues. In these respects, the members of Congress thought that the administration had not done a good job.[12]

The Congress used deliberations and legislative action during the debate on the Taiwan bill to register its dissatisfaction and to make numerous amendments and changes. Although the congressional actions focused on future U.S. relations with Taiwan, they also showed concern over U.S. policy toward the PRC and Asia in general and over the problems and prospects of congressional-executive interaction in the conduct of American foreign policy. Many members of Congress were especially critical of the Carter administration's "haste" and secrecy in coming to an agreement with the PRC. The administration's lack of consultation especially concerned some of them, since only a few months earlier Congress had passed an amendment to the International Security Assistance Act of 1978—Public Law 95-384—expressing its sense that the president should consult with Congress before he made any policy changes that might affect the mutual defense treaty with Taiwan.[13]

Some members became even more irritated with the administration when its representatives implied at hearings on the Taiwan bill that Congress should complete work on the bill quickly, before March 1, 1979, because at that time official ties between the United States and Taiwan would be cut off completely after a two-month adjustment period, and without the new legislation those ties would have no secure basis for continuing.[14] This was especially unsatisfactory, inasmuch as the administration did not submit its proposed bill to Congress until late in January. House Foreign Affairs Committee Chairman Clement

Zablocki remarked to his colleagues that they were working "under the gun" of this administration-imposed deadline.[15] Meanwhile, several congressional officials were irritated when President Carter repeatedly warned them that he would veto the Taiwan legislation—and thereby risk disrupting relations with Taipei—if Congress altered the administration-proposed bill in a way that the president judged to be inconsistent with the agreement he had reached with the PRC.[16]

Against this background of congressional-executive friction, Congress set to work to modify several substantive aspects of the Taiwan Relations Act. In broad terms, Congress thought that the bill gave too little attention to U.S. security interests in Taiwan and the western Pacific, failed to treat adequately future U.S.-Taiwan economic relations, slighted several important legal questions regarding relations with Taiwan, and avoided providing for strong congressional oversight of U.S.-Taiwan ties.[17]

Security Issues

Congress was particularly concerned that the official U.S. break with Taiwan might be misinterpreted in Asia and elsewhere as part of a continuing American withdrawal from commitments in East Asia after the failure of U.S. efforts in Indochina in the mid-1970s. Some of its members judged that the Carter administration's failure to consult closely with U.S. allies in Asia before it announced the normalization decision could have given the impression that the United States was not concerned with the fate of its friends in the area and could not be counted on for future security support.[18] Thus, after heated discussion and consideration of several different proposals in both houses, Congress decided to add language to the Taiwan Relations Act that would demonstrate more clearly the U.S. commitment to support the security of people on Taiwan and to maintain an active interest in backing U.S. allies elsewhere in the region. In sections 2 and 3 of the bill, Congress added several policy declarations affirming, among other things, that it was the policy of the United States:

> To declare that the peace and security of the Western Pacific are in the interests of the United States;
> To make clear that the United States expects that the future of Taiwan will be determined by peaceful means;
> To consider any nonpeaceful effort against Taiwan—including boycotts and embargoes—as a threat to the peace of the Western Pacific and of grave concern to the United States;
> To provide Taiwan with enough defensive arms to maintain a sufficient self-defense capability; and

> To maintain the capacity of the United States to resist any resort to force or other coercion that would jeopardize Taiwan's well being.[19]

To assure that this policy was fully carried out, Congress specified that it, along with the president, would determine the types and quantities of defensive arms and services to be provided to Taiwan and required the president to inform the Congress promptly of any threat to Taiwan's well-being.

Economic and Legal Questions

In view of the speed and secrecy surrounding the administration's final decision on normalization, many in Congress concluded that most executive-branch officials knowledgeable in Chinese affairs were caught unprepared to deal with the complicated economic and legal questions involved in future U.S. relations with the PRC and Taiwan.[20] During hearings on the Taiwan Relations Act, several members of Congress showed particular concern that the administration had brought in only belatedly, if at all, American economic leaders and legal experts with extensive experience in dealing with the PRC and Taiwan to help it establish a mechanism for maintaining stable economic and legal ties with Taiwan after diplomatic normalization with the PRC.[21] After hearing the opinions of those leaders and experts, Congress adopted numerous changes in the legislation designed to place U.S.-Taiwan ties on firmer legal ground.

To help safeguard U.S.-Taiwan economic relations, Congress added provisions that allowed American investors in Taiwan to continue receiving guarantees from OPIC, even though Taiwan's annual per capita income of about $1,300 surpassed the $1,000 ceiling normally imposed by OPIC. Congress also inserted language that specifically continued the transfer of nuclear power supplies and technology to Taiwan, added the previously noted wording specifying U.S. opposition to embargoes and boycotts of Taiwan, and specified that the end of U.S. official ties with Taiwan should not be seen as a basis for supporting the exclusion of Taiwan from continued membership in international financial institutions or other international organizations.

In addition, to protect legal ties with Taiwan, Congress added provisions explicitly affirming Taiwan's ability to sue and be sued in U.S. courts, specified how Taiwan should be treated under terms of the Immigration and Nationality Act, and set forth in more detail the services to be provided by the AIT to U.S. citizens in Taiwan. Congress also asked the president to grant Taiwan's counterpart to the AIT—known as the Coordinating Council for North American Affairs (CCNAA)—the same number of offices in the United States as the

Taipei government had had before January 1, 1979, and authorized the president to grant privileges and immunities to CCNAA personnel in the United States equivalent to those granted AIT personnel in Taiwan. Congress held that the U.S. switch in recognition should not be seen as affecting Taiwan's assets in the United States—a provision that governed the sensitive issue of Chinese diplomatic property in the United States. And, to strengthen the Taiwanese government's standing under U.S. law, Congress added a precise definition of the term "Taiwan" to include the governing authorities on the island recognized by the United States prior to January 1, 1979.

Finally, since the issue of human rights in Taiwan was repeatedly mentioned during the course of the hearings and deliberations on the bill, Congress added a provision to section 2 of the act reaffirming American interest in the human rights of the inhabitants of Taiwan and asserting that nothing in the act should be seen as opposing that interest.

Security Treaty

Several members of Congress, led by Senator Barry Goldwater, took particular issue with President Carter's legal claim to the right to terminate the mutual security treaty with Taiwan without the approval of Congress. Filing suit in federal court in Washington, D.C., the senator and other plaintiffs were successful in their case before Judge Oliver Gasch, who ruled on October 17, 1979, that President Carter had acted unconstitutionally in deciding to end the security treaty without the approval of either two-thirds of the Senate or both Houses of Congress.[22] The ruling included an order prohibiting Secretary Vance from taking the formal actions necessary to end the treaty. Administration leaders warned that the ruling could have the effect of seriously upsetting the normalization agreement reached with Peking, and the official PRC press duly criticized the judge's decision.

The Carter administration promptly filed an appeal in the U.S. court of appeals, hoping to have Judge Gasch's decision overturned before January 1, 1980, when the treaty with Taiwan was scheduled to end under terms of the normalization agreement with Peking. The court of appeals overturned Judge Gasch's decision on November 30, 1979, but lawyers for Senator Goldwater appealed the matter to the Supreme Court. On December 13, 1979, the Supreme Court granted certiorari, vacated the judgment of the court of appeals, and ordered the district court to dismiss the complaint as either not ripe for judicial review or a political question, thereby opening the way for the termination of the treaty at the turn of the year.[23]

Congressional Oversight

Concerned by the administration's previous failure to consult fully with Congress and by the absence of specific references to Congress's role in future U.S.-Taiwan relations in the administration's proposed legislation, Congress added several amendments that explicitly gave Congress a strong role in the oversight and supervision of U.S.-Taiwan relations. Not only did Congress add language requiring the president to promptly inform it of any threat to Taiwan, but it also set up other reporting procedures. Thus, for example, section 12 of the act said that agreements made by the AIT would be subject to congressional notification, review, and approval procedures and that the secretary of state would be required to make semiannual reports to Congress on the status of U.S.-Taiwan relations for two years after the act became effective. In addition, the president was required to report to Congress any rules and regulations he might formulate for carrying out provisions of the Taiwan Relations Act during a three-year period following the start of the act. Section 14 added that the House Foreign Affairs Committee, Senate Foreign Relations Committee, and other appropriate committees should monitor the implementation of the act, the affairs of AIT, U.S.-Taiwan economic relations, and U.S. security policies in the western Pacific.

Post-Act Developments

After passage of the Taiwan Relations Act, many members of Congress disputed the administration's handling of commercial and other agreements with Taiwan, as well as its policy regarding arms sales to Taiwan.[24] Vice President Walter Mondale disclosed in Canton, China, in August 1979 that the administration planned to end some commercial agreements with Taiwan, replacing them with unofficial arrangements. To many observers in Taiwan and the United States, including several members of Congress, the vice president's disclosure was a reversal of the administration's repeated assurances (given at the time of U.S.-PRC normalization) that all treaties and agreements between the United States and Taiwan, with the exception of the defense treaty, would remain in effect after normalization. Administration officers countered that Congress was told during deliberations on the Taiwan Relations Act that existing agreements with Taiwan would have to be altered over time, especially as they expired or became obsolete or irrelevant to U.S.-Taiwan relations. In response to congressional criticism on this issue, the administration clarified its position in late 1979, affirming that it did "not have a policy to convert or terminate all the treaties and agreements we maintain with Taiwan," would adjust each agreement "as the circumstances require . . . on a case-by-case basis," and would "maintain close contact with Congress on this subject."[25]

Meanwhile, the Defense Department notified Congress in July 1979 that a package of military equipment, mostly aircraft and missiles worth about $240 million, was being forwarded to Taiwan. (Although the normalization agreement with Peking required that no new arms deals would be made with Taiwan during 1979, existing U.S. commitments were allowed to move ahead.) And in January 1980 the Defense Department informed Congress of a package of new weapons—worth about $280 million—that it would be selling to Taiwan during the year.

Even though some sophisticated weapons were contained in the package, some in Congress were critical of the administration not only because the package allegedly did not go far enough to meet Taiwan's defense needs but even more because the administration chose to ignore the congressional statement in the Taiwan Relations Act that it wished to work closely with the executive branch in determining what U.S. arms would be sold to Taiwan. Congressional critics judged that this provision made it clear that Congress ought to have been involved in consultations on the arms transfers policy before the Defense Department notification. Administration representatives countered that they had complied with all legal requirements in dealing with the arms transfers to Taiwan and that the Taiwan Relations Act did not require special efforts for consultations with Congress on this matter.[26] The dispute persisted into June 1980, when seven members of the Senate Foreign Relations Committee sent a letter to President Carter asking that U.S. companies be permitted to move ahead with plans to discuss the sale of advanced fighter aircraft—the so-called FX—to Taiwan. The administration acquiesced to this proposal later that month.[27]

U.S.-PRC Economic Relations

Congress faced an entirely different set of questions regarding economic relations with the PRC as a result of Vice President Mondale's trip to the PRC in August 1979. At that time the administration decided to supplement its normalization of diplomatic relations with China by adopting several measures designed to improve U.S.-PRC economic ties. Specifically, it put aside a barrier in U.S. law to provide official American technical support, pledged to work with Congress to provide expeditiously MFN tariff treatment and Ex-Im Bank loans, and promised to provide U.S. government guarantees to American businessmen investing in China. Congress began formal deliberations on the MFN issue after the administration submitted the Sino-American trade agreement to it on October 23, 1979, but it delayed final approval until it reconvened in January 1980. The issue of Ex-Im Bank loans and investment guarantees occupied congressional attention later in 1980.[28] (See discussion in Chapter 7.)

Congress not only assessed the impact of these initiatives on U.S.-PRC bilateral relations but also examined their broader implications for U.S. foreign policy, especially concerning the Soviet Union. In particular, it observed that the Carter administration's moves to improve economic relations with the PRC were not accompanied by similar efforts vis-à-vis the USSR but coincided with a serious downturn in U.S.-Soviet relations over such sensitive issues as SALT and the presence of Soviet combat troops in Cuba. As a result, serious debate developed in Congress and elsewhere over the future direction of what heretofore had been a declared U.S. policy of "evenhandedness" toward the USSR and the PRC.

Observers on one side of the debate argued that the Carter administration's gestures to China were a misguided departure from its previously balanced policy in dealing with the PRC and the Soviet Union. They warned that a U.S. "tilt" toward Peking and away from Moscow could result in unforeseen Soviet actions and might seriously undermine U.S.-Soviet relations. These opponents of the president's initiatives were especially critical of what they saw as efforts by some officials in the administration and Congress to "play the Chinese card"—building closer U.S. political, economic, technical, or military ties with the PRC to gain greater U.S. leverage against the Soviet Union.[29]

Analysts on the other side of the issue applauded the Carter administration's efforts to improve economic and political relations with the PRC. They urged the United States to go further to provide the PRC with sophisticated technology, including equipment with military applications, and to cooperate more closely in defense planning and foreign policy strategy with the PRC against the USSR.

Meanwhile, administration officials argued in private discussions with congressional and other critics that the United States had not abandoned its past evenhanded policy toward the PRC and the Soviet Union. They maintained that such a policy did not require that the United States strictly provide every benefit to one communist power that it provided to the other. They also asserted that the administration hoped for forward movement in relations with both powers and that, although the United States generally applied the same criteria and standards in its dealings with either country, it was reluctant to allow the lack of progress with one power—the USSR—to hold up progress in relations with the other—the PRC.

Mondale's Trip to China

The debate came into sharper focus after Vice President Mondale's visit to the PRC in August 1979. Earlier in the year, U.S. leaders in Congress had focused primarily on the bilateral aspects of Sino-American relations, examining problems concerning future trade and other exchanges with the PRC and future U.S. dealings with Taiwan. The broader implications of U.S. China policy for relations with the Soviet Union tended to receive only secondary attention, especially since it appeared that the administration was trying to balance its forward movement on relations with China with a summit meeting and SALT agreement with Soviet leaders.

U.S. pledges to the PRC during Mondale's visit and the coincident decline in U.S.-Soviet relations over SALT and Cuba altered substantially—in favor of China—U.S. policy in the triangular relationship. (That policy seemed to change even further when the administration disclosed on October 1, 1979—simultaneously with President Carter's speech to the nation announcing U.S. military countermoves to the presence of a Soviet brigade in Cuba—that the United States, for the first time, was sending its defense secretary to the PRC to discuss matters of mutual concern. While noting the trip to China, administration officials still insisted that U.S. policy toward Peking and Moscow remained basically in balance.)[30]

During Vice President Mondale's trip to China, the administration unilaterally adopted four separate measures that significantly improved economic relations with the PRC, measures that were not to be applied to the USSR for the foreseeable future.[31]

Services to China. In August 1979, just before Vice President Mondale's departure for the PRC, administration officials informed the press that President Carter would now allow the PRC to receive U.S. technical services under the terms of section 607(a) of the Foreign Assistance Act of 1961, as amended. That decision allowed any agency of the U.S. government to furnish services and commodities on an advance-of-fund or reimbursement basis to Peking. The section limited such aid to "friendly" countries, but administration officials maintained that President Carter had determined that the PRC was a friendly country for the purpose of receiving such services.

Most-Favored-Nation, Nondiscriminatory Tariff Treatment. In remarks to PRC leaders in Peking, Vice President Mondale promised that the administration would soon submit for congressional approval the previously negotiated Sino-American trade agreement granting MFN tariff treatment to China. Under terms of the Jackson-Vanik amendment to the Trade Act of 1974, the granting of MFN status could not be extended to any non–market economy—that is, communist—country that denied its citizens the right or opportunity to emigrate or that imposed more than nominal exit fees or taxes on documents or individuals. Both these provisions applied to the PRC, but President Carter notified Congress in October 1979 that he was waiving them when he submitted the Sino-American trade agreement to Congress. Such waivers were authorized by law in certain circumstances, but the waiver authority was subject to annual congressional review and the possibility of a one-house veto. On January 24, 1980, after a delay that saw close congressional consideration of the implications of the U.S.-PRC accord for U.S.-Soviet relations, Congress approved the agreement granting MFN status to China.

Export-Import Bank Credits. Vice President Mondale pledged to the Chinese leaders that the United States would provide their country on a case-by-case basis with up to $2 billion in Ex-Im Bank credits over the next five years. Ex-Im Bank credit transactions (export credits and credit guarantees) were also subject to the Jackson-Vanik ban and required a waiver to be extended for non–market economy countries that curbed their citizens' right to emigrate. But President Carter's October 1979 waiver concerning the Sino-American trade accord also applied to Ex-Im Bank credits.

Investment Guarantees. Vice President Mondale also promised PRC leaders that the Carter administration would seek investment guarantees from OPIC for Americans wishing to invest in China. (The PRC appeared to make such investment more likely when it adopted a law on joint ventures in July 1979.) Such guarantees could not be applied to the PRC unless existing legislation were amended or the president issued the narrowly defined waiver specified in section 620(f) of the Foreign Assistance Act. The administration favored the former action and supported legislation introduced and passed by the Congress in 1980 to make OPIC programs available for U.S. investors in the PRC.

U.S.-PRC Strategic Cooperation

Even critics who argued that the Carter administration was now tilting toward China generally agreed that U.S.-PRC economic cooperation was less likely to antagonize the USSR and compromise other U.S. long-term interests than U.S.-PRC security ties were. Some asserted, however, that the administration had already taken several steps to complement developing Sino-American economic relations with closer strategic ties and that the administration's economic gestures toward the PRC were designed primarily to consolidate the bilateral relationship and lead to greater all-around cooperation with Peking, eventually including the sale of U.S. high technology and arms to the PRC.[32]

Not only did U.S. leaders repeatedly voice support of PRC security against Soviet "hegemony," but they also began in 1978 to stress U.S. backing for a "strong" as well as a secure PRC.[33] During 1978 American warships calling on Hong Kong—which Peking regards as part of China— began to receive Chinese communist officials for well-publicized visits.[34] The United States also began to adopt a more liberal attitude toward the transfer of sophisticated technology to China, allowing it, for instance, to purchase special U.S. geological survey equipment and nuclear power plant technology. Perhaps most important, the United States announced in November 1978 that it would no longer oppose the sale of military weapons to the PRC by West European countries.[35]

Several policy makers in the Carter administration and Congress advocated incremental increases in Sino-American technical and military cooperation. They called for the United States to sell arms to the PRC and to provide it with advanced technology in such areas as electronics, computer science, mining, and oil drilling. Many suggested that the United States could better protect its interests in Asia from Soviet "expansion" by working more closely in foreign policy and defense planning with China against the USSR. They judged that the United States, Japan, and other noncommunist Asian states should consult carefully with the PRC to build a common front to prevent the expansion of Soviet influence and power into such areas as Indochina, Afghanistan, the Indian Ocean, and the western Pacific.

Some of these policy makers (Senator Jackson and Brzezinski were prime examples) judged that such U.S. moves would not only shore up American strategic interests in Asia but would also prompt the Soviet Union to be more accommodating toward the West and more cautious in trying to gain advantage over the United States in other parts of the world. Several of them reportedly called for the United States to use the prospect of defense cooperation and the transfer of arms to China as a means of forcing the Soviet Union to reassess and perhaps pull back from its military involvement in Cuba. Some observers judged that Secretary of Defense Brown's visit to the PRC was disclosed by the administration in October 1979 with this motive in mind, although administration officials at the time publicly denied any such link between U.S. policy toward China and the USSR.

Meanwhile, opposing spokesmen, like Secretary Vance in the administration and Senator Adlai Stevenson in Congress, were less sanguine about China's intentions and were seriously concerned about possible Soviet countermoves to Sino-American strategic cooperation. Some of them, including Congressman Lester Wolff, were concerned that the

PRC appeared to be one of the most unpredictable major powers in world affairs, since it had shown in the past a notable willingness to use force, as well as conventional diplomacy, to achieve foreign policy objectives. The disunity of the PRC leadership was a major unpredictable element in Chinese foreign policy, and any major shift in the policies of either the Soviet Union or the United States might easily result in substantial changes in Chinese policies. Thus, for example, if the United States adopted decidedly pro-PRC policy and sold arms to Peking, the Soviets might take violent action against the weaker link in the Sino-American "alliance"—the PRC—seriously damaging the interests of the U.S., China, Japan, and other states important to the United States in the maintenance of stability and prosperity in Asia. Perhaps of more immediate importance, closer Sino-American strategic cooperation at a time when Chinese leaders were threatening to use force against Moscow's ally, Vietnam, only served to increase the likelihood of a major East-West confrontation breaking out in a part of Asia that was no longer considered vitally important to U.S. interests.

The demise of the evenhanded U.S. strategy toward the USSR and the PRC was confirmed in Secretary Brown's week-long visit to China in January 1980, following the Soviet invasion of Afghanistan the previous month. Although the full details of the visit are still unavailable, the United States strongly indicated that it would side closely with the PRC in common efforts to offset Soviet power in Asia. According to various press accounts:

1. The United States agreed to sell a ground station enabling China to receive data from U.S. satellites that might have military uses.
2. The United States offered to sell China an array of nonlethal military equipment, with a potential for more items in the future.
3. The United States and China closely coordinated their strategies in support of Pakistan and in backing other unspecified efforts—perhaps including support for anti-Soviet Afghan forces—to thwart Soviet expansion in southwest Asia.
4. The United States informed China that it would welcome the PRC's military help against Vietnam in whatever form Peking might choose, if Vietnamese forces crossed from Cambodian territory into Thailand.[36]

The American willingness to sell military equipment to the PRC came as a surprise to many congressional members and revived bad feelings over the Carter administration's lack of consultations over China policy. At hearings conducted by the House Foreign Affairs Subcommittee on Asian and Pacific Affairs in April 1980, Chairman Lester Wolff complained:

> I am convinced that the administration is moving incrementally but surely into a military relationship with the People's Republic of China.
>
> Moreover, I am concerned that once again China policy is being advanced without adequate consultations with the Congress and, in fact, almost in total disregard of Congress. A case in point is the decision to sell military-use equipment announced after Secretary Brown's January visit to the People's Republic of China.[37]

5
Conflicting Assessments of Congressional and Administration Officials over China Policy

The strong public reaction of congressional critics to Carter administration initiatives toward the PRC clearly testified to the wide differences between the two branches over Sino-American relations. But they failed to clarify what officials privately judged were the underlying causes of the disagreements. Press reports of the personal views of congressional and administration leaders, interviews with officials of both branches, and congressional studies on the subject of consultations over China policy have clarified the conflicting private views of the participants in congressional-executive interactions on that issue during the Carter presidency.[1] They have cast into sharper relief the misperceptions, misunderstandings, and failures in communication that plagued this episode in U.S. foreign policy and helped undermine efforts to establish a consensus in the United States over new directions in China policy.

The Normalization Decision

Congressional Concerns

The Carter administration publicly defended its record of consultations with Congress over the decision to normalize diplomatic relations with Peking, stressing that even though members of Congress were not informed of very much before the president's announcement, they had been told of the administration's intention to establish diplomatic relations with the PRC. Congressional observers agreed that they were well aware that President Carter wanted to normalize ties with Peking, but they stressed that the central question in China policy at that time related not to diplomatic relations with the PRC but to concern about how normalization would be handled by the administration. In particular, how would Taiwan be treated, how would the timing of the decision affect other U.S. interests at home and abroad, and how would the decision fit in with the United States's changing role in Asian and world affairs? These observers judged that the administration failed to provide anything close to adequate consultations on such "practical implications" of normalization. Administration sources privately agreed that no real consultations occurred on these important questions in late 1978.

Some congressional officers with important responsibilities in Asian affairs pointed out that the Carter administration's record on consultations over China policy had been relatively good until late 1978. They noted that at least some members of Congress with oversight jurisdiction for U.S.-Asian relations had been well briefed about the visits of Secretary of State Vance and National Security Advisor Brzezinski to China in August 1977 and May 1978, respectively. They also pointed out that there even appeared to have been some interchange between the administration and those members, with administration officials altering their policy plans to take into account congressional concerns over the possible future course of China policy.[2] They hastened to add, however, that administration officials had led Congress to believe that continued Sino-American differences over Taiwan meant that China policy could not be expected to move ahead very quickly.

Given this record of past consultations, congressional officials were all the more surprised and dismayed over the administration's unexpected announcement in December 1978. Very few congressional officials had been informed in advance of the administration's decision, and some indicated that, even though they knew that Sino-American negotiations were then in progress, they had been told that no breakthroughs appeared likely.[3]

Many congressional officials were also surprised by the absence of consultations with Congress because both houses had made clear before late 1978 that they expected to be informed of any possible changes in the U.S. approach toward the PRC and Taiwan. Thus, one source noted that Congressman Lester Wolff, chairman of the House International Relations Subcommittee on Asian and Pacific Affairs, said at hearings his subcommittee held on U.S.-PRC relations in 1977 that, "the Congress and the American people must have all the information they need to assess whether initiatives and advances may be made by the administration" in relations with the PRC. He pointedly warned of a "divisive debate" and the creation of "uncertainty and mistrust" in the United States if the administration went ahead to change China policy on its own without consulting carefully with Congress and without building support among the American people.[4]

Several others cited the amendment to the International Security Assistance Act of 1978 that specified that there should be consultations between the administration and Congress before there were any policy changes affecting the continuation of the U.S. defense agreement with Taiwan. This nonbinding resolution—known as the Dole-Stone amendment—was initially proposed by Senators Robert Dole and Richard Stone in somewhat stronger form, but it was weakened in the Senate. As a result, administration officials later felt free to ignore its provisions when they decided to end the security agreement with Taiwan. Congressional officials acknowledged that the administration was legally correct in asserting that the amendment was not mandatory, but they stressed that the main import of the amendment, which passed by wide margins in both houses, was that it underlined Congress's expectation that it would be consulted before a major change was made in policy affecting Taiwan's security.[5]

Congressional officials who had been influential in the handling of the amendment during the Senate debate pointed out that the amendment had been proposed because they had received reports in mid-1978 that the administration was planning a major shift in China policy. They wanted to be certain that there would be adequate provision for Taiwan's security and that Congress's intention to play a role in the formulation of new policy affecting Taiwan would be clearly highlighted. In addition, these congressional sources pointed out that even the members who had been influential in changing the language of the amendment to a less binding form still held very strongly that the amendment underscored the sense of Congress that it should be consulted before the administration undertook any major change in China policy.

Congressional sources offered several reasons why members of Congress were so concerned about being consulted before a shift in China policy. Several pointed to what they saw as vacillation and weakness in the Carter administration's policy in Asia up to that time. They judged that the administration had not clearly defined U.S. goals in Asian affairs; as a result, many in Congress saw the United States going too far in withdrawing from security commitments in the region (notably, by announcing a pullback of ground forces from Korea) and in trying to improve relations with former adversaries—in particular, by trying to normalize diplomatic relations with Vietnam. They were also sensitive to the repeated expressions of concern from long-standing U.S. allies and friends in Asia about the Carter administration's seemingly greater interest in establishing better ties with former adversaries than in maintaining close relations with old friends. These members of Congress wished to be sure that the administration was taking fully into account the worries of several important leaders of noncommunist Asian states about possible future shifts in U.S. policy.[6] Several members of Congress knowledgeable about U.S.-Asian relations judged that a pledge by the PRC—either in public or in private—that it would not use force against Taiwan ought to be a basic requirement for the United States to insure Taiwan's security after normalization. These members reportedly had informed the administration of their views before December 1978.

Some congressional officials stressed the Carter administration's poor record in consultations with Congress on other foreign policy issues. They noted not only the spectacular congressional-executive confrontation over the Panama Canal treaties during 1977 and 1978 but also other disputes, including those over the administration's announced intentions to sell arms to Saudi Arabia and to resume arms transfers to Turkey.[7] They added that consultation problems were made worse by the Carter administration's deliberate cultivation of a public image as an "anti-Washington" administration, determined to avoid the "parochial" practices of the past and to follow policies in accord with the national interest as interpreted by President Carter. This image reportedly put Congress on notice that it could expect resistance from the administration if it tried to influence foreign policy in unapproved ways— a development that they felt was obviously contrary to the creation of a smooth working relationship in the conduct of foreign affairs.

Meanwhile, many congressional officials were concerned about the sudden change in China policy because that policy had long been an especially emotional and contentious political issue in the United States. China policy reportedly was one of the few foreign policy issues—like the Panama Canal treaties—that had a strong impact on local constituencies, even if those constituencies generally showed little interest in foreign policy or Asian affairs. Polls in 1977 and 1978 had shown that while a clear majority of the American people favored establishing normal ties with the PRC, a majority of about the same size opposed a break in U.S. officials ties with Taiwan.[8] Thus, any U.S. decision to end official ties with Taiwan as a condition of normalization was likely to alienate a large portion of the American electorate. Even congressional officials who favored U.S.-PRC normalization on terms similar to those used by the Carter administration judged that the administration, at a minimum, should have carefully informed Congress of its shift in China policy so that the members could have prepared themselves adequately to meet what was expected to be a serious political storm over the new China policy.

Administration Views

Although administration officers were generally aware of these congressional concerns, a variety of countervailing judgments caused them not to seek consultations in late 1978. Several said that the recent record of congressional-executive disagreements in foreign policy in general and over Asia in particular had prompted them to keep the China policy secret.[9] To do otherwise could have resulted in strong counteractions by critics in Congress that might have upset the new opening to China. In particular, those in the administration who reportedly feared that the so-called China lobby had the power to block initiatives toward the PRC thought that the lobby had to be circumvented with secrecy, at least until the agreement with the PRC was completed and announced.

In contrast, others thought that the administration had little to fear from Congress. Some officials took time in late 1978 to analyze possible countermeasures by opponents of the new China policy in Congress. They concluded that opponents would have few ways to block the policy, particularly if President Carter retained the initiative by presenting Congress—without prior notice—with a fixed agreement with the PRC. Those in Congress opposed to the policy were assumed most likely to take steps to strengthen U.S. ties with Taiwan during congressional consideration of the legislation on U.S.-Taiwan relations that was expected to be needed after the switch in relations. The administration was considered to be capable of effectively controlling congressional actions in this area and avoiding a basic compromise in its overall China policy.

Some administration leaders did not fear congressional reaction, because they "naively" judged that since they had reached such a "good deal" for the United States and Taiwan in the negotiations with the PRC, opposition in Congress would come only from a few "diehards." Still others originally had intended to inform selected congressional leaders of the China policy switch once an agreement with the PRC seemed in view, but the intervention of Vice Premier Deng Xiaoping in the talks in early December sped the pace of the negotiations so markedly that agreement was reached before congressional leaders could be informed. Any consultations after the agreement with Peking had been reached, but before a public announcement was made, could have been perceived as "disingenuous" by Congress, so the decision was made to make the surprise announcement and endure Congress's inevitable critical reaction.[10]

Looking back at the experience with Congress over China policy in 1978–1980, several administration officers said that it was a mistake not to have given Congress at least a few days notice before the agreement with China was announced. They claimed, for one thing, that the administration grossly overemphasized the power of the China lobby in Congress. According to these sources, the reaction of the lobby to the normalization decision was much weaker than they had expected. Some of these observers speculated that administration leaders misjudged its power because they were heavily influenced by the past fierce congressional-executive confrontations over China policy, in which members of the China lobby in Congress conducted investigations, sometimes characterized as witch hunts, against State Department and other administration officials who were thought to be less than firm in their support for the Chinese Nationalist administration on Taiwan.

At the same time, administration sources claimed that policy planners had given insufficient consideration to the possible adverse reaction to the surprise China decision on the part of many conservative and moderate members of Congress. These members, who were not seen as being part of any sort of China lobby, viewed the administration decision as ill considered, ill timed, and a direct affront to Congress. Their criticisms stemmed not from association with special interest groups but from their views of U.S. concerns in Asia and world affairs and from the strong reactions of their constituents to the China decision.

Although administration representatives acknowledged these drawbacks in their consultations with Congress, they also sometimes strongly asserted that a reasonably successful U.S. China policy could not have been reached without cutting off most of Congress from the substance of the secret negotiations. They advised that the clearly positive results of the new China policy offset whatever negative consequences resulted from a lack of adequate consultations, stating that even though poor consultations over China clearly exacerbated congressional-executive friction over China policy during the rest of the Carter administration, such friction was probably inevitable anyway given the traditional division of power in the U.S. system of government.

Friction Before the Passage of the Taiwan Relations Act

The Carter administration's decision to move ahead quickly on U.S.-PRC normalization without reference to Congress almost immediately caused serious difficulties for congressional-executive interaction over China policy. For one thing, communications seriously broke down, largely because administration officials were not ready for the surprise announcement. Few officers, aside from those at the highest levels in the State Department and National Security Council, were aware of how rapidly the negotiations with the PRC were progressing in late

1978.[11] Many responsible officials had only a few hours' advance notice of the announcement, and simple communication within the executive branch regarding relevant elements of the decision and their policy implications was time consuming and confused. As a result, State Department officers were ill prepared to respond to the deluge of questions on the new policy from other executive agencies, Congress, the press, and the public. At the same time, they had to draft the major legislative proposal for future U.S.-Taiwan relations and prepare for the extensive public hearings on that proposal and on the overall thrust of U.S. relations with the PRC and Taiwan that were expected to begin soon after Congress reconvened in January 1979.

The State Department organized a special task force, known as the China Working Group, to handle these and similar issues. The members of the group received praise from congressional officials for their hard work and strong efforts to assist congressional-executive interaction during this transitional time in Sino-American relations, but it was widely acknowledged in Congress and the administration that the group—or the State Department as a whole—was incapable of handling the heavy demands for information and advice. The congressional-relations and legal officers at the State Department were particularly hard pressed.

As a result, even members of Congress with important responsibilities in U.S.-Asian affairs had to wait several days before they received briefings on the new policy. And in these briefings, there reportedly was a good deal of confusion. According to a few administration officials, effective communications were so lacking between the policy makers who had helped negotiate with China and the officers who were briefing members of Congress that misinformation was sometimes passed on to Congress. One of these officials characterized the situation as one in which "the right hand didn't know what the left hand was doing."[12]

Over the next few weeks, the situation improved as the administration prepared for the hearings on the Taiwan bill, which began in February. But even then, failures in executive-branch handling of consultations with Congress continued to occur. In particular, some administration officers noted that senior administration officials misrepresented U.S. policy regarding Taiwan when they indicated that, aside from the defense treaty, all U.S. agreements would remain in effect.[13] According to executive-branch officials, the administration had already told the PRC that it intended to replace those accords with unofficial arrangements. This failure of communications occurred in considerable part because the senior administration advisor on Taiwan matters, who was writing testimony for administration witnesses and providing answers to congressional questions, had not been given access to the relevant reports on the U.S. negotiations with the PRC. As a result, Congress was given the impression in early 1979 that the United States intended to keep all those agreements in effect and was later unprepared for the administration's disclosure in August 1979 that it wished to change certain agreements to an unofficial status—an announcement that further complicated congressional-executive relations.[14]

Friction over China policy increased as congressional officials saw the administration acting unilaterally and with seeming disregard for Congress. The administration not only had affronted members with its unilateral normalization decision but also had appeared to be directly challenging the prerogatives of Congress in the conduct of foreign policy. According to several congressional officials, by ignoring the Dole-Stone amendment, the administration prompted considerable suspicion in Congress over executive-branch intentions in China policy, causing speculation that the Carter administration had "something to hide" in its China policy—presumably something against the interests of Taiwan and U.S.-Taiwan relations. Frustration and anger over the lack of consultations added incentive to those in Congress who decided to file suit in federal court to block President Carter's decision to end the security treaty with Taiwan without considering the views of Congress.

Other complaints centered on the administration's failure to obtain a pledge from the PRC that it would not use force against Taiwan. Those moderate and conservative members of Congress who saw such a pledge by the PRC as a minimum requirement for the normalization of relations reportedly interpreted the Carter administration's failure to obtain such a pledge as an indication that executive-branch officials were decidedly "pro-Peking" and indifferent or hostile to the Chinese Nationalist government on Taiwan.[15] If the administration were not hostile to Taiwan, they asked, why did it not delay the normalization announcement until after elections in Taiwan, which were scheduled for late December 1978 but were canceled because of the normalization announcement? Furthermore, they prodded, if the U.S. officials were not indifferent to Taiwan, why did they provide so little advance warning to Taipei's leader Chiang Ching-kuo, causing him to be awakened in the middle of the night to be informed of the Carter administration decision only hours before the decision was publicly announced? And if the Carter administration was concerned with U.S.-Taiwan relations, why did it fail to consult closely with U.S. business leaders on possible problems in future U.S.-Taiwan economic relations before it submitted its Taiwan Relations Act to Congress?

Anger and suspicion over the new China policy were further aroused by the strict time limits the administration tried to impose on congressional consideration of the Taiwan Relations Act, by President Carter's threats to veto the legislation if Congress amended it in ways he deemed improper, and by the president's having made his decision when Congress was out of session and therefore less able to launch effective and well-coordinated responses to his initiatives.

A few congressional and administration officials also complained that the unilateral decision undermined what they saw as the broader U.S. interest in a SALT agreement with the USSR. Because of its quick decision, the administration temporarily upset the SALT agreement process, with the result that the Soviet Union postponed the signing of the accord for several months. Meanwhile, some congressional aides noted, the administration's haste in moving ahead with U.S.-PRC normalization did not even allow it to gain the significant domestic political support from those congressional officials who should have been the administration's allies on the issue—e.g., those who had all along been urging the United States to move closer to the PRC without regard to the Soviet Union or the SALT agreement. The failure of the Carter administration to garner such congressional support was seen by congressional officials as a reflection of its "incompetence" in dealing with Congress over foreign policy—a view that clearly added to congressional-executive difficulties in dealing with Chinese affairs.

Other Disputed Issues

Disagreements between Congress and the Carter administration subsided briefly after the passage of the Taiwan Relations Act in April 1979, as both sides appeared fairly well satisfied with the compromise that had been achieved. However, a series of issues arose later in the year that renewed friction between the two government branches and widened the gap of misunderstanding and distrust that President Carter's normalization decision had opened between them in December 1978. In themselves, those issues were less important than the original normalization decision had been, but they significantly added to friction between the administration and Congress because of the atmosphere of suspicion and distrust that still surrounded congressional-executive relations over China policy.

Agreements with Taiwan

As noted earlier, many congressional officials were under the impression that U.S. agreements with Taiwan, except for the defense treaty, would remain in effect after U.S.-PRC normalization. When Vice President Mondale disclosed in the PRC in late August 1979 that the administration intended to change its official civil air agreement with Taiwan to unofficial status to open the way for a U.S.-PRC civil air agreement, Taiwan's supporters in Congress—backed by many other congressional members who were suspicious of the administration's China policy—demanded prompt clarification.

This strong and quick congressional response caught administration officials unprepared and placed them on the defensive. They were forced to answer repeated congressional complaints that the Carter administration had deliberately misled Congress earlier in the year about the agreements with Taiwan, presumably to win passage of the administration's Taiwan Relations Act. Some administration officers claimed that they had made clear to congress during the course of the deliberations on that legislation that some agreements with Taiwan would have to be changed, and they pointed to language in the act that implicitly gave the administration the legal right to change the status of these accords.[16] Other administration officials acknowledged, however, that testimony before Congress and other statements by administration leaders earlier in 1979 clearly had given an impression that the status of these agreements would not be changed.[17]

In any event, congressional pressure forced the administration to give ground. Carter administration representatives were compelled to reassure congressional leaders in several public pronouncements that the executive branch had no intention of converting or terminating all treaties and agreements with Taiwan and that the administration would consult closely with Congress if a particular agreement were to be converted or ended.[18] Administration officers judged that such statements served at a minimum as a brake to slow further efforts to change the status of agreements with Taiwan.

Arms to Taiwan

Given earlier strong expressions of congressional interest in maintaining the security of Taiwan and in determining what kinds of American arms would be transferred to the island, some congressional officials thought that the administration should have consulted more closely with Congress about U.S. sales in 1980. They claimed that the administration chose to ignore congressional concerns and provided no consultations on this issue, merely notifying Congress of the arms to be transferred, as was required by the other laws governing all U.S. arms transfers abroad.[19] The timing of the administration's notification— shortly before the public announcement on January 4, 1980—also raised congressional suspicions, as some officers argued that there was a clear pattern in this and two other major administration initiatives on the PRC and Taiwan over the previous year (the December 1978 announcement of normalization and Vice President Mondale's disclosure in August 1979 on ending official agreements with Taiwan): all three had come while Congress was out of session. The officials speculated that such timing was part of an administration effort to outmaneuver possible congressional objections to those important moves in foreign affairs.

Some administration officers said such congressional complaints were unjustified, claiming that members and staffs in Congress were going too far in making demands on the executive branch for consultations over China policy; to the executive-branch officials it appeared that congressional officers wanted the administration to forfeit its legal rights in the conduct of foreign affairs for the sake of good relations with Congress. They added that the administration had followed all legal requirements in regard to arms transfers to Taiwan and that the Taiwan Relations Act did not require the extraordinary consultations with Congress called for by these dissatisfied congressional officials.

MFN Status for the PRC

Suspicions of the administration's China policy and concern over congressional prerogatives in foreign affairs were also seen in the initially skeptical attitudes of several moderate and liberal members of Congress toward the administration's proposal to waive the Jackson-Vanik amendment and grant MFN tariff treatment to China. President Carter notified Congress that he was waiving the amendment's provisions when he submitted the Sino-American trade agreement to Congress for approval on October 23, 1979. According to some congressional aides, several members of Congress with oversight responsibilities for foreign trade policy were concerned that the president's waiver had not been accompanied by evidence of any firm assurances he might have received regarding PRC emigration policy. This lack of data, combined with past congressional suspicions of the administration's intentions over China policy, reportedly prompted these members to raise a series of objections, which were overcome only by the intercessions of high-level administration leaders in private discussions with congressional members.[20]

The Chinese Card

By late 1979 several congressional leaders with direct oversight responsibility for Asian affairs voiced serious concern over the implications of recent U.S. initiatives toward the PRC for broader U.S. interests in Asian and world affairs, especially vis-à-vis the USSR. They called for public assurances that administration planners were not trying to use improved relations with the PRC in some sort of international strategy against the USSR that might provoke conflict between either China and Vietnam or China and the Soviet Union.[21]

Other congressional observers questioned the basic coherence of the administration's China policy in a different way. Unlike those who feared that the Carter administration was resorting to secrecy in China policy to hide a grand strategy for using the Chinese card against the Soviet Union, these observers speculated that the administration had refused to consult with Congress on this policy or to discuss it in public pronouncements precisely because it did not know what to say. They judged that the administration was trying to hide its having "lurched ahead" in relations with the PRC with no clear idea of how those closer relations would affect broader U.S. strategic interests or how they would fit in with U.S. planning in Asian and world affairs.

A final reflection of congressional friction with the administration over China policy at this time was seen in the reported determination of several members of Congress in late 1979 to add a provision to the SALT II treaty that would have required Senate approval before the treaty could be terminated. Congressional officials noted that several moderate and conservative senators were interested in such an amendment in large part because of the Carter administration's decision a year earlier to ignore congressional requests that Congress be consulted before the mutual security treaty with Taiwan was terminated.

Causes of Congressional-Executive Friction over China Policy

Administration Failings—The Secrecy Issue

When asked to explain what they judged were the causes of the administration's weak efforts in working with Congress over China policy, an overwhelming majority of congressional and administration aides pointed to the tight secrecy that surrounded the policy. They noted, for instance, that since the results of the U.S.-PRC negotiations on normalization were known to only a few administration officials before December 15, 1978, the administration was not prepared to deal adequately with Congress's subsequent requests for clarification. And although some legal preparation for the Taiwan legislation had been carried out in 1978, State Department legal experts could not have known what was needed in the bill until full details of the Sino-American negotiations and agreements were available. As a result, the submission of the administration's bill on Taiwan was delayed.

In addition, extreme secrecy within the executive branch reportedly caused administration officers to give congressional officials the initially erroneous impressions that there would be no termination of new arms sales to Taiwan during 1979 and that the United States would maintain all official agreements with Taiwan except the defense treaty. Were it not for secrecy in U.S. China policy, several officials averred, few in Congress would have seen administration planners as "pro-Peking" or "indifferent" concerning Taiwan's future. Several observers also claimed that the congressional-executive disputes over the Chinese card in U.S. foreign policy would have been reduced if the Carter administration had been more aboveboard about its policy toward the PRC.

Administration officers noted several reasons for the secrecy in China policy. Some stressed that it was carried out that way to follow the interests of Chinese leaders, who reportedly preferred dealing with the United States in private to acknowledging to the world in general, and to the Chinese people in particular, the extent to which they were willing to compromise and collaborate with what Peking used to call "American imperialism." Others noted that since the Nixon administration's opening to the PRC, U.S. China policy had always been highly secretive. They thus concluded that the "inertia" of past practice caused Carter administration officers to continue dealing with the PRC discreetly. Some officials added that U.S. officers who worked on China policy frequently had a tendency to identify closely with, and to follow the procedures of, the Chinese and, as a result, were "naturally" inclined to follow China's lead in using secrecy in the conduct of U.S.-PRC affairs. They sometimes argued that this was a common pattern of behavior, as other foreign-affairs specialists also tended to identify with the area or country of their concern.

According to some State Department officers, there were efforts earlier in the Carter administration to "open up" China policy by providing background briefings to the press on developments in U.S.-PRC relations. But those briefings reportedly were seen as having had an adverse effect on U.S. interests—the most notable case being the announcement by a senior administration officer that Secretary Vance's August 1979 visit to China had resulted in significant progress on the normalization of diplomatic relations, only to have PRC Vice Premier Deng Xiaoping describe the Vance visit as a "step backward."[22] According to these State Department aides, Deng's remarks were seen as a rebuke to the United States for "leaking" reports of the Vance negotiations; Deng's interview caused the administration, in the words of one official, to "circle the wagons" on China policy to avoid any further leaks.

Several officers in the State Department noted that the injunction against leaks was strongly felt there because the department was the administration's primary conduit of information on foreign policy to Congress and the press and because policy planners in the White House had long assumed it to be the source of unauthorized disclosures of information on sensitive issues. A few State Department officials resented White House pressure for secrecy on China policy. They complained that it ran counter to the need to keep Congress adequately informed about developments in China policy, and one official characterized White House aides as "obtuse" in their understanding of the need for the administration to consult with Congress on China policy.

Some administration and congressional sources claimed that White House pressures for secrecy led to unnecessary and unjustified friction between State Department officers working on China policy and their congressional counterparts. Because they were unable to be frank about China policy in talks with congressional officials, State Department aides were sometimes perceived as arrogant and dishonest by members of Congress. These sources claimed that the officers were seen this way because they were compelled by the White House to remain silent on the policy.

Among other reasons given for the covert approach in Chinese affairs, many officials said that without great discretion the normalization agreement might not have been successfully implemented. They stressed the need to resort to secrecy to avoid a head-on confrontation with the emotionalism that had surrounded the China issue in U.S. politics, the alleged power of the China lobby to block any attempt to reduce ties with Taiwan, and the broad unpopularity among the U.S. people of the requirement to break official U.S.-Taiwan ties.

Some congressional critics of the administration's handling of the normalization decision frankly admitted that they also would probably have conducted the negotiations in secret if they had been in the administration. They attempted to stake out a middle ground between tight secrecy and full disclosure, however, stressing that if they were in charge they would have been more careful to inform congressional members in private consultations before they made a public announcement of the normalization decision.

Some administration officials claimed that, even though the administration's unilateral announcement of normalization exacerbated congressional-executive tensions over foreign policy, such tensions would have been worse if the news of the negotiations had been reported prematurely. They judged that leaks would have prompted an exceedingly divisive debate and would probably have led to a failure in the administration's China policy, which in turn would have caused serious recriminations by both the administration and the Congress. They argued strongly that a wide body of authoritative opinion held that negotiations like those with the PRC *should* be conducted in secret.

Some administration aides and most congressional officials disagreed with that line of argument. Although they thought that premature disclosure might have been bad for the normalization policy, they judged that the administration's secrecy should not have involved keeping

Congress in the dark. By not at least informing congressional members beforehand of the details of the decision, the administration put itself in the position of having to ask members to support a policy they knew little about. As one officer put it, administration lobbyists were "asking members to walk the plank on China policy without giving them a good reason for doing so."

Several officials cited the Soviet factor—especially reputed Soviet concern over possible Sino-American "collusion" against USSR interests—as a reason for the administration's continued discretion on China policy. According to one view, U.S. secrecy was designed to hide close U.S.-PRC cooperation against the USSR from public view to avoid a complete alienation of the Soviet Union from the United States, a termination of prospects for East-West arms control, or a possible preventive Soviet military strike against the PRC. A contradictory view said that secrecy was designed to hide the purported fact that there was "more form than substance" in U.S.-PRC strategic relations. According to this view, secrecy in China policy allowed the United States to employ the image of close ties with the PRC to gain supposed leverage against the USSR. Since U.S. officials saw that as a useful political tool against the Soviet Union, they reportedly wanted to avoid public disclosure of how very limited the range of Sino-American strategic ties allegedly were.

Meanwhile, some administration aides emphasized that secrecy was needed so the United States could have as free a hand as possible in building a strong relationship with the Taiwan administration. These sources claimed that the PRC was more sensitive to public signs of U.S.-Taiwan interchange and more tolerant of secret contacts than others believed it was. Carter administration efforts to maintain close but discreet contacts with Taiwan leaders were jeopardized by calls from members of Congress for the administration to describe and clarify its approach to Taiwan during public hearings.

Finally, some congressional aides saw a more political and parochial need for secrecy. They claimed that some officials in the administration were trying to use their close involvement in the breakthrough in China policy for personal political gain and therefore did not want to share the "glory" of the China policy. In response, some administration officials said such charges reflected the jealousy of congressional aides who were trying to tarnish the reputations of officers who had achieved what they saw as a substantial foreign policy accomplishment.

Congressional Weaknesses

Heavy criticism of the administration's shortcomings in China policy was complemented by many administration officers and some congressional aides who pointed to a variety of failings on Congress's part. One common complaint centered on what many observers saw as the diffused nature of congressional responsibility over China policy. For example, administration employees argued that when they did begin to consult with Congress after the normalization decision in late 1978, their task was complicated by the difficulty of determining which members and staff to consult. Not only leaders of the full House and Senate needed to be contacted, but also leaders of the various congressional committees and subcommittees with oversight responsibilities for China. Meanwhile, additional consideration had to be given to possible interaction with members and staff of committees that in the past had expressed particular interest in China policy. Finally, inasmuch as the China issue was expected to have broad repercussions in U.S. domestic politics, it was assumed that many others would also want prompt and full information about the new policy. This enormous task was clearly beyond the capacity of the small number of officers available in the State Department and elsewhere in the administration for such liaison work.[23]

Some State Department officers suggested that their job would have been much easier if they could have worked directly with what they called responsible congressional leaders and their staffs, who in turn could have informed and consulted with others in Congress interested in China policy. It is interesting to note that they claimed that such an approach to congressional leaders was tried briefly, without a great deal of success, during early deliberations over the Taiwan Relations Act. According to these officials, the administration attempted to work closely with the chairman and ranking minority member of the Senate Foreign Relations Committee to reach compromise language on Taiwan's security and other contentious issues that would have been acceptable to the administration and that would have been "sold" by the leaders to the rest of the committee and, in turn, the rest of the Senate. (It was reportedly assumed that since the Senate was taking the lead in considering the Taiwan bill, the House would likely follow its example in most respects.)

These officials argued that the committee leaders failed to keep committee members fully informed of negotiations with the executive branch so that, when the leaders presented compromise language worked out with the administration, some members strongly objected and squelched the deal. In any event, administration officials disclosed that they had begun to have second thoughts about working so closely with the ranking minority member and his staff, who, they said, were exerting too strong a pro-Taiwan influence on the proposed legislation. The administration officials, therefore, were not seriously disappointed with the failure to reach a compromise.

The Senate Foreign Relations Committee was also criticized by some congressional aides for failing to share information about China policy with other interested members and staff. Congressional aides familiar with the workings of the committee countered that problems associated with security classification procedures and the rapid growth and turnover of Senate staff made committee representatives less than open in releasing policy information to members and staff they didn't know well.

Several administration sources and congressional aides emphasized that consultations would have been easier and more productive if they had been more of a "two-way street." They stressed the need for congressional members to make more clear what they expected in the way of consultations, and they added that if members and staff remained well informed on current issues, they were more likely to be able to ask for and receive the precise information they needed.

A well-informed member of Congress who would take the initiative in approaching the administration about concerns in China policy was also thought to be more likely to have a significant impact on the formulation of policy. Thus, for example, some administration officers noted in late 1979 that congressional members could have had a significant impact on issues associated with U.S.-PRC strategic cooperation. At that time, the administration was in the midst of deliberations over Defense Secretary Brown's visit to Peking in January 1980 and it reportedly had not yet achieved a consensus about how far Brown should go in offering strategic cooperation with the Chinese. These executive-branch officials maintained that congressional members, by weighing in with their views on the pros and cons of such cooperation, could have substantially altered the agenda the secretary was taking to Peking. They added that to their dismay few members of Congress were taking the initiative on this important issue. Instead, several members appeared to be waiting for the administration to arrive at a firm policy, after which they would be free to endorse or condemn the policy. The administration aides claimed that such a belated congressional approach was much less likely to change the policy than a congressional input before the establishment of a firm administration line would have been.

Some in the administration observed that congressional members and their staffs frequently could not be expected to deal with sensitive foreign policy information in a sober and careful way that would not run counter to broader U.S. interests. Rather, many legislators and their staffs could be expected to use such information for more parochial political concerns, sometimes engaging in "demagoguery," "political grandstanding," or newspaper "headline hunting" by using the information for personal advantage or that of their constituents. Thus, administration officials stressed that they had to make sure at all costs that China policy did not become subject to such "partisanship" and "factional interests" in Congress. From the perspective of these administration officers, it was understandable that they would deal most closely on Chinese affairs only with those few congressional members and staff they could "trust."

Several congressional aides predictably took issue with this view of the alleged irresponsibility of Congress. They judged that while some members and staff sought only narrow political interests in their concerns with China policy, many others were professional in their training and outlook and clearly able to take a broad view of important foreign policy issues. Some congressional aides added that administration complaints of irresponsibility in Congress were merely designed to rationalize keeping China policy secret from Congress so that the legislators would be unable to expose what they judged were the many "inadequacies" and "poor assumptions" underlying the Carter administration's approach to the PRC.

A final complaint voiced by some senior administration leaders was that the constant requests from Congress for consultations and information on China policy reflected part of a broader congressional effort during recent years to "chip away" at the authority of the president and the executive branch in the conduct of foreign affairs. They asserted that Congress had frequently been "unreasonable" in what it requested concerning China policy and that it was incumbent upon administration officials to resist or circumvent such congressional pressures, not only to help protect the administration's China policy but also to help preserve the constitutional rights of the executive branch and insure the future of the system of checks and balances in the American government.

Mutual Misunderstanding and Lack of Respect

The serious complaints over administration and congressional shortcomings in China policy underscored what several officials saw as one of the most important and potentially disruptive results of the new China policy: the widening gap in mutual understanding and respect between officials in the two branches of government. These officials judged that pressures imposed on both Congress and the administration because of the surprise decision on normalization and the subsequent rapid pace of U.S.-PRC-Taiwan relations exacerbated antagonism between congressional and administration officials to a point where officials of one side frequently viewed those on the other as adversaries—hostile forces whose opposition had to be overcome in the course of congres-sional-executive conflict over China policy. To underline their feelings of hostility, officials on both sides frequently gave blunt assessments of the personal shortcomings of officers on the other side. Thus, for instance, some State Department aides saw some of their counterparts in the Congress as ill prepared for their jobs, as "hopelessly naive" regarding the intricacies of China policy, or as "hardnosed S.O.B.s" who were determined to have their way on a policy issue even at the expense of broader U.S. interests.

Administration officials' lack of respect for, and hostility toward, members of Congress made those in the executive branch who were working on China policy more likely to view suggestions and require-ments from Congress as "obstacles" or "irritations" in the policy-making process rather than as useful contributions to the policy. Even congres-sional amendments to administration policy, passed by wide margins in Congress, were frequently seen as hurdles that the administration had to overcome. Thus, several aides recalled that the administration was pleased that the Dole-Stone amendment had been altered in the Senate to a nonbinding form, because it then allowed President Carter to move ahead with normalization with the PRC without consulting with Congress. They held this opinion despite their acknowledgment that Congress's clear intent in the amendment had been to underscore its desire to be consulted before any significant changes were made in China policy. Meanwhile, some other administration officials claimed that the many changes Congress made in the Taiwan Relations Act were unimportant and inconsequential and did not require the admin-istration to deal more closely with Congress on Taiwan policy than it would have done under the terms of the administration's original bill.[24]

In the process of circumventing or overcoming "obstacles" posed by Congress in China policy, administration officials sometimes said that they were constrained to be "disingenuous" in their discussions with Congress. A case in point was the Chinese card issue in late 1979. Some administration officials said that if Congress had asked in late 1979 whether the administration wanted to play the Chinese card, the administration would have denied it. They said that this denial would have been disingenuous because they noted that a number of high-level administration leaders were indeed interested in using better strategic relations with the PRC against the Soviet Union.

Some administration officers had no basic problem with Congress's role in U.S. foreign policy or the roles played by individual congressional members and staff, but because of the special pressures they were under to keep China policy secret and insulated from Congress, these officers felt compelled to try to bypass or offset congressional concerns.

For their part, congressional staff members frequently resented what they saw as a clearly condescending attitude toward them on the part of administration officers dealing with China policy. Many of these aides judged that they were treated as "intellectual inferiors" or "lesser brethren in the policy process" by the executive-branch individuals, and they charged that State Department and White House specialists on China policy were prone to having a "we know better" attitude in dealing with Congress. Thus, some congressional sources charged that administration specialists who had spent years studying and working on Chinese affairs and living in Asia felt that their backgrounds gave them a better grasp than Congress of what U.S. policy vis-à-vis China should be and that congressional members and aides should adhere to their "wisdom" and avoid "interfering" in the smooth functioning of their policy. A few congressional aides were particularly outspoken in their criticisms of these China specialists, accusing them of "arrogance," of "constantly lying" to the Congress, and of using their "entrenched bureaucratic position" to direct China policy in ways that were contrary to U.S. interests.

Congressional aides who claimed to have a smoother working relationship with administration officers dealing with China policy were much less critical of the latter's alleged arrogance. They sometimes acknowledged that administration specialists did indeed have a better understanding of China and China policy but still should have been more sensitive to the need to mix that knowledge with the mainstream of American opinion that they saw reflected in Congress. They also held out hope that a smoother working relationship and an effective division of labor could be worked out, particularly as the legacy of the normalization decision was moved further back in time.[25]

Even some of these officers, however, claimed frequently that a deep undercurrent in administration-congressional relations showed that administration officers felt superior and more competent than their congressional counterparts in dealing with Chinese affairs. Some congressional aides who worked regularly on East Asian matters were particularly irritated by this perception. On the one hand, they judged that they and other congressional colleagues frequently had professional training and competence in East Asian affairs equal to their counterparts in the administration. On the other hand, they thought that administration officers working on China policy had spent so much of their adult lives living in Asia and learning about China that they were frequently "out of touch" with what U.S. interests in China should be. These legislative staff members alleged that administration specialists were making policy in a "rarified atmosphere" in which they considered carefully the position of the Chinese government and people but failed to give adequate attention to the current interests of the American government and people. They added that congressional officials had to be responsive to the public mood to stay in office and were therefore more capable of providing this important complement to what was seen as the "narrow" China-oriented views of the administration specialists.

Debate over U.S. Military Sales
to China, 1980–1981

Continued progress in the development in U.S.-PRC relations and stability in U.S.-Taiwan ties helped to keep serious congressional-executive frictions over China policy from getting out of hand during the latter part of the Carter administration. Officials in the administration and Congress also began to make greater efforts to ease frictions and improve communications—a process facilitated by the passage of time and the fading of memories about disputes over the administration's normalization announcement and subsequent unanticipated initiatives. In effect, the two sides began to understand more clearly how far they could go in demanding consultations and cooperation from one another over China policy and became more aware of the likely consequences they would face if they ignored the interests of their colleagues in the other branch. Thus, for example, the Carter administration decided in mid-1980 to halt, at least until after the presidential election, further initiatives in U.S.-PRC relations, such as the granting of U.S. aid to China, in part because they realized that such proposals could ignite a new storm of controversy in Congress.

Meanwhile, the administration's China policy was slowed by strong and growing debate among members and officials in Congress about the wisdom of what many observers saw as the next logical step forward in U.S.-PRC relations—the sale of U.S. weapons and weapons-related technology to China. Rapid progress in U.S. political and economic relations with China had coincided with a budding military relationship seen notably during the visits of Secretary of Defense Brown to the PRC and Chinese military specialists to the United States during early 1980. In the course of those meetings, the United States had agreed to sell some military support equipment and civilian technology with military applications to the PRC. As PRC leaders pressed the United States to go further, notably to sell weapons and weapons-related technology to the PRC, some U.S. officials in both the administration and Congress argued that the sales would consolidate Sino-American political relations, increase the PRC's sense of security vis-à-vis the Soviet Union, and foster closer Sino-American cooperation in the face of Soviet expansion. Other U.S. officials in the administration and Congress, however, claimed that such cooperation would pose serious dangers for U.S. interests in East-West relations, stability in East Asia, and long-term cooperation with China. Receiving divided advice on the issue and facing a tough presidential campaign, the Carter administration decided to wait until after the November election before it considered whether to follow through with closer military ties.

The issue not only had military significance but also had broader political importance, including a direct impact on a central question in U.S. foreign policy—how far the United States should go in trying to move closer to the PRC to improve the U.S. international position against the USSR. Opinions ranged widely. Some authorities judged that the United States had already gone too far and should stop promptly; others generally were satisfied with the current policy but firmly resisted further development, at least for the foreseeable future; still others favored a gradual increase in U.S. military transfers to China as an important step toward a Sino-American mutual security arrangement against the Soviet Union.

Congressional interest in the debate was strong because existing law, notably the Arms Export Control Act (AECA), made the sale of arms and other military equipment subject to several restrictions directly involving Congress.[1] Interest in the debate grew after the election of a Republican administration that also received divided counsel on the issue of military transfers to China and the announcement during Secretary of State Alexander Haig's visit to the PRC in June 1981 that the United States was now willing to consider the sale of military weapons to China. The debate quickly subsided, however, as it became clear that U.S. military sales to the PRC would be blocked at least temporarily because of Peking's tougher policy toward the United States over Taiwan. In particular, China said it would not buy weapons from the United States until it received strong assurances regarding U.S. policy, especially arms sales policy, toward Taiwan.[2]

Background

Although debate over U.S.-PRC military ties began to receive prominent public attention in 1980, the roots of the debate went back to the Nixon administration, when the pros and cons of seeking U.S.-PRC security cooperation were considered before significant U.S. initiatives were made toward the PRC.[3] Those initiatives included the Nixon administration's decisions to sell the PRC a sophisticated ground station designed to pick up and transmit television signals via satellite and several Boeing 707 aircraft with attendant aeronautical technology. Also included were the Ford administration's approval of the sale to China of British Rolls Royce "Spey" aircraft engines and related technology for Peking's fighter aircraft program and its approval of the sale to China of a U.S. computer that had potential military applications. U.S.-PRC security contacts developed as Chinese and U.S. officials held frequent joint consultations on global and regional military issues, arms control, and other security matters and as U.S. leaders repeatedly voiced strong opposition to any Soviet effort to dominate or establish "hegemony" over China.[4]

Although the Carter administration continued this primarily symbolic interchange during visits of Secretary Vance and National Security Advisor Brzezinski to China in August 1977 and May 1978, respectively, it took other steps that appeared to increase Sino-American security ties incrementally. Not only did U.S. leaders repeatedly voice support for PRC security against Soviet "hegemony," but they also began to stress U.S. backing for a "strong" as well as a "secure" China. The United States also adopted a more liberal attitude toward the transfer of sophisticated technology to the PRC and indicated that the United States would no longer oppose the sale of weapons to China by West European countries.

Defense Secretary Brown underlined the strategic importance of Sino-American ties during his visit to the PRC in January 1980—one month after the Soviet Union invaded Afghanistan.[5] Headlines reporting on that visit and subsequent high-level interchange between military leaders of China and the United States spoke boldly of an emerging Sino-American "alliance" focused against the USSR. Indeed, the rapid decline in U.S.-Soviet relations at the end of 1979 and the increasingly strong perception in the United States of a growing Soviet military threat seemed to give impetus to U.S. interest in closer ties with the PRC, including security ties. Chinese leaders, for their part, stressed repeatedly their desire to develop a "long-term, strategic" relationship with the United States, adding on occasion their strong interest in obtaining weapons and other military equipment from the United States.

The United States followed Secretary Brown's visit with an announcement that it was willing to consider sales to the PRC of selected military items and technologies with military support applications. By mid-1980, the U.S. government had approved requests from several U.S. firms to make sales presentations to the Chinese for certain articles of military support equipment and dual-use technology (items primarily

of civilian use but with possible military applications). Carter administration spokesmen defined the limits of such U.S. military cooperation
with the PRC by noting that "the United States and China seek neither
a military alliance nor any joint defense planning" and that "the United
States does not sell weapons to China." But they repeatedly implied
that this policy could be subject to further change, especially if either
country faced a "frontal assault" on their common interests, presumably
from the USSR or its proxies.

The Carter administration's statements on the limits of the U.S.-
PRC security relationship departed from the past practice of the administration and its two Republican predecessors of avoiding public
explanations of the extent of Sino-American security relations or their
possible implications. Leaving the policy publicly ambiguous was thought
to be a useful way to increase the impact of the developing Sino-
American ties on the Soviet Union; it presumably would prompt the
USSR to be more forthcoming and accommodating in its relations with
the United States in order to discourage Washington from developing
even closer security ties with Peking.

Parameters of the Debate

Although debate between proponents and opponents of increased
U.S. military transfers to China ranged across a broad spectrum of
foreign policy issues, there were a number of common themes and
points of agreement. Consensus on these issues substantially narrowed
the scope of the debate, providing a framework for it. Public warnings
against U.S. military sales to the PRC were sometimes particularly
shrill and unrealistic, with some commentaries warning of the dire
consequences of a major U.S. effort to "rearm" China. In fact, even
strong advocates of closer U.S. military ties with the PRC saw insur-
mountable impediments in both the United States and the PRC to
such an effort, thereby effectively eliminating that as a realistic consideration in the debate, at least for the time being.[6]

Chinese Capabilities and Intentions

There was general agreement among U.S. officials knowledgeable in
Chinese affairs that the PRC did not face an immediate crisis in its
ongoing military confrontation with the USSR. The Chinese seemed
capable of resisting—albeit at great cost—a major Soviet conventional
attack, and a Soviet nuclear attack against the PRC appeared unlikely
because of the danger to the USSR of a Chinese nuclear counterstrike
against Soviet Asia. Clearly the weaker party militarily along the Sino-

Soviet border, China was likely to see its military capabilities decline relative to those of the USSR if existing trends continued.[7]

Although there was some disagreement over whether China had firmly decided what kinds of weapons and other military equipment it would like to obtain from the United States, the PRC had focused on obtaining the capability to produce such sophisticated equipment as fighter aircraft engines and radars, air-to-air missiles, and anti-tank missiles.[8] This accorded with the views of many Western analysts who stressed China's need for all-weather fighter aircraft, greater defensive capabilities against Soviet armor, and greater ability to provide air cover in nearby waters.

Chinese leaders were seen as pressing the United States to permit such military transfers, both to enhance China's military power against the USSR and to demonstrate the growing U.S. commitment to China's defense. Su Yu, a senior member of the PRC's Military Affairs Commission, told the Japanese press in March 1980 that the United States's willingness to move ahead with sales of military equipment to the PRC was seen by the Chinese as a key indication of the U.S. commitment to work with them in a common front against the Soviet Union. Vice Premier Geng Biao and Vice Foreign Minister Zhang Wenjin each subsequently told the Western media that they anticipated that the United States would sell weapons to China in the future.[9]

U.S. specialists generally agreed that PRC military forces were designed and deployed for the defense of China and were not well suited or positioned to project power far from that country's borders.[10] They did not agree, however, that the PRC would not use its existing forces to attack nearby areas. Indeed, some judged that prospects for a new PRC attack against Vietnam remained high, while others remained quite skeptical of PRC claims of "peaceful" intentions toward Taiwan.

Peking's ability to pay for and utilize large amounts of sophisticated weapons and weapons-related technology was also seriously limited, as the PRC's economic program actually called for a cut in the defense budget and promised to give defense modernization the lowest priority among the "four modernizations" (i.e., of agriculture, industry, science, and national defense) pursued by the post-Mao leadership.[11] The PRC's difficulties in using the relatively sophisticated aircraft engine technology of the Soviet MiG-21 and the Rolls Royce "Spey" were symptomatic of a broader PRC technical weakness that was severely exacerbated by the disruption of higher education and research in the PRC between 1966 and 1976.

Soviet Objectives

U.S. officials seemed to agree that the Soviet Union would remain insecure about its position in the Far East for some time to come.

Even if the PRC should alter its foreign policy and move toward a more evenhanded posture betwen the United States and the USSR, Soviet planners were likely to remain distrustful of China and intent on maintaining their own military power in the region to protect against possible Chinese incursions. Moscow saw military power as one of the few reliable sources of influence it could bring to bear against a PRC that was growing in economic and military power and consolidating relations with the other two major powers in the region, Japan and the United States. Protection and development of eastern Siberia, which USSR planners reportedly viewed as an important element in the future economic development of the USSR, required a firm policy toward the PRC. Substantial Sino-Soviet reconciliation allowing the USSR to lower its guard against China remained only a very remote possibility.[12]

Moscow's obvious desire to slow the development of Sino-American military ties was motivated by concern over growing Chinese power and worry about a possibly emerging U.S.-backed global system, including the PRC as well as the NATO countries and Japan, that would be directed against the USSR. Thus, Moscow was likely to view U.S.-PRC military ties not solely in the context of their impact on the Sino-Soviet military balance in Asia but also in the broader context of overall U.S. policy toward the Soviet Union.

U.S. Interests and Objectives

The United States favored a secure and independent PRC, but a radical change in Peking's defense policy toward a large-scale military buildup of Chinese forces was viewed as contrary to U.S. interests. It would upset the PRC's economic modernization program, could lead to political instability in the PRC, and might alter the regional balance of power in East Asia in ways adverse to U.S. interests.

Most U.S. leaders agreed that the United States would not likely offer free military assistance to the PRC under existing circumstances, and they acknowledged that Chinese economic and technical weaknesses precluded large-scale U.S. military transfers that would fundamentally affect the PRC's power projection capabilities in the near term. They focused on the political and symbolic repercussions of U.S.-PRC military ties, judging that ostentatious displays of U.S. military cooperation with China—if not backed by substance—were likely to risk misinterpretation at home and abroad and should be avoided in favor of more quiet interchange. Sino-American relations should mature for a few more years before they moved into the symbolically important area of military transfers.

Many recommended more clear articulation and management of U.S. policy toward the PRC.[13] Several claimed that Chinese leaders seemed to interpret past U.S. behavior as indicative that the United States would soon be willing to transfer significant military equipment to China, including arms, and they advised that the United States should avoid giving such impressions unless it had the intention—and the political support at home—to follow through with military sales. It was imperative, in their view, that the United States be able at some point to "draw the line" with the PRC, refusing pressure for military transfers without giving Peking the impression of a substantial decline in U.S. interest in close ties with China.

Increased U.S. military transfers to the PRC would probably reduce U.S. influence and enhance Chinese influence elsewhere in Asia because they would prompt uncertainty among long-standing U.S. friends and allies in Asia (with the possible exceptions of Pakistan and Thailand, which might welcome such ties). They would deepen the suspicions of India, Taiwan, and Vietnam toward the United States and would seriously reduce the chances for a more cooperative U.S.-Soviet relationship. (In light of recent U.S.-Soviet differences over bilateral issues, arms control, Poland, and competition in the Third World, such a relationship was generally thought to be a remote prospect in 1980.)

Implications for U.S. Policy

These commonly held views suggested a narrower range of dispute in the debate than appeared at first glance. They indicated that the United States need neither rush military transfers to the PRC to help it against military threat from the USSR, nor worry excessively about a possible breakthrough in Sino-Soviet relations that would substantially reduce Soviet military preoccupation with China in Asia. The PRC was likely to be quite selective in what it agreed to buy from the United States, since whatever the United States provided, it would probably take many years before the PRC markedly increased its strength against the USSR or its ability to project power far beyond its borders.

The main importance of U.S. transfers to the PRC would be political and symbolic. They clearly could have an upsetting—though not necessarily adverse—effect on U.S. relations with other Asian states, and the Soviet Union would view such transfers not only in the context of its competition with China but also with an eye toward broad U.S. intentions toward the USSR. Experts generally agreed that managing such a symbolically important and consequential relationship with China would require a more clearly defined perception of U.S. interests in the

PRC that would avoid serious misinterpretation of American intentions at home and abroad.

Differing Strategic Assumptions

U.S. officers interested in military transfers to China came down on different sides of the debate depending in large measure on their diverging assessments of an underlying broader stategic question in U.S. foreign policy: How far should the United States go in trying to improve relations with the PRC to strengthen the U.S. international position against the Soviet Union? Officials deeply concerned with U.S. military weakness vis-à-vis the Soviet Union and appreciative of the PRC's strong opposition to the USSR and support of the United States tended to back increased U.S. military transfers to the PRC. In contrast, those who were sanguine about U.S. power vis-à-vis the Soviet Union or who were skeptical of the PRC's reliability or strength tended to oppose such sales.

Soviet Expansion and Its Challenge to the United States

Many Americans saw the Soviet Union as an expansionist power that sought military, economic, and political preeminence in the world.[14] (Some added that the USSR was also anxious to promote revolution to gain international ideological preeminence.) Accordingly, the Soviets were seen as on the ascendancy in their efforts to establish overall international superiority over the United States, with recent trends favoring Soviet ambitions. Uncertainties and instability in the world were believed to offer the USSR fertile ground for exploitation. Although the Soviets suffered setbacks, they were not diverted from their ultimate objectives. Instead, they took a patient, long-term view of history, with their confidence bolstered by a sense of destiny.

Other Americans emphasized that even though Soviet leaders might strive for superiority and preeminence, circumstances unfavorable to the USSR profoundly affected their aspirations. World developments frequently ran counter to Soviet designs, as domestic and international setbacks limited the USSR's freedom to pursue its objectives. Aware that their ideological goals were presently unattainable, Soviet leaders were finding it necessary to adjust their policies to current realities. They strove to achieve superiority over the United States, but the Soviet Union qualified only militarily as a superpower.

A third group believed that the Soviet Union was far less expansionist than it had been, with Soviet policies being shaped primarily by the country's requirements for internal social and economic development and its historic sense of insecurity. According to this view, a more confident and secure Soviet leadership would be ready to act as a responsible participant in an increasingly interdependent world. Soviet military efforts were an unwanted drain on resources based on the (perhaps misguided) Soviet view of what was needed to maintain security. Since Soviet leaders understood that they were best served by international stability, their fundamental interests were reconcilable with those of the United States. The group of Americans with this view of Soviet policies and goals judged that it was shortsighted automatically to equate Soviet setbacks with Western gains and vice versa. They stressed that there were shared interests, dangers, and responsibilities between the superpowers in a number of areas and advocated a U.S. policy aimed at increasing the Soviet stake in international stability and providing the Soviet Union with incentives for continued cooperation with the West.

U.S. Ability to Deal With Soviet Power

Closely related to the differing views of Soviet power and intentions were diverging assessments of U.S. ability to deal with that power. On one side were those who thought that even though American abilities had declined somewhat from the time when the United States enjoyed dominant military, economic, and political influence in world affairs, they were nonetheless still quite adequate to handle emerging Soviet power.

Others stressed that U.S. power—especially military power—had declined steadily to a point where the USSR enjoyed basic superiority over the United States in both conventional and strategic weapons. They were generally optimistic, however, that the United States had begun to redress the military balance and would be able to catch up with the Soviet Union and close the so-called window of vulnerability by the end of the decade.[15] They sometimes added that projected Soviet economic and other internal difficulties by the end of the decade would restrict Moscow's ability to expand its military power as it had in the past, thereby enhancing the United States's ability to close the power gap.

Still other Americans were more pessimistic about U.S. military capabilities, which they saw as likely to decline further relative to the Soviet Union unless there were a major shock in U.S. foreign policy. Even though U.S. military capabilities might decline, the United States still had many more capable allies than did the USSR, and those allies presumably would assist in checking Soviet expansion. U.S. officers, however, stressed that the allies had been slow and halting in their efforts to redress what was seen as an emerging East-West disequilibrium. Thus, they judged that the balance in Northeast Asia had become more disadvantageous as U.S. forces were drawn down by the end of the Vietnam War and the diversion of forces to the Persian Gulf and Indian Ocean and as the Soviet Union continued to build steadily its air, naval, and ground forces in the area. They added that Japan—the largest and most capable U.S. ally in Asia—had been an inadequate help at redressing the balance over the past several years.[16]

Some officials offered similarly alarming views of the decline of the allied position in the face of Soviet or Soviet-backed expansionism in Southeast Asia. They argued strongly for closer relations with China as a means to sustaining a favorable equilibrium. As in the case of Northeast Asia, these leaders judged that it was fundamentally important that the United States increase military transfers to the PRC—not so much because they would increase Chinese power against the USSR but because they would consolidate U.S. relations with the PRC, thereby increasing the prospects that China would side with the United States if an East-West confrontation occurred in Northeast or Southeast Asia.

In contrast, some other American officers were less concerned by the changing military balance in East Asia. They emphasized Soviet logistical problems and other sources of military vulnerability, as well as Moscow's political isolation. In particular, the Soviet Union made few gains in expanding its influence as the United States pulled back its forces after the Vietnam War, and the two major regional powers—China and Japan—continued to work against Soviet interests in the region.

China's Utility in U.S. Competition with the USSR

China played an important and helpful role in U.S. global and regional strategic planning, especially vis-à-vis the USSR, according to many U.S. leaders.[17] Most agreed that China assisted the United States by tying down Soviet troops and resources that otherwise might have been focused against the West in Europe or the Middle East and by complicating Soviet defense strategy, notably by raising uncertainty in the USSR about the security of the Soviet Union's Asian front if conflict were to break out farther west.[18]

But within this context, there were wide-ranging views of China's utility in helping the United States in its competition with the Soviet Union. Some held that the PRC was a relatively weak source of leverage against the USSR, noting that China was so much weaker than the Soviet Union that it would be unlikely to cause serious concern for Moscow if there were East-West conflict elsewhere. A few held that the

PRC's commitment to an anti-Soviet foreign policy was less strong than it appeared, emphasizing that the PRC would likely arrange a modus vivendi with the USSR rather than risk being drawn into a U.S.-Soviet confrontation.

Others saw China as sufficiently strong militarily and reliable politically to represent a useful partner for the United States in efforts to curb Soviet expansionism. Still other officials stressed that while China might be effective against the USSR today, the growing disequilibrium between Chinese and Soviet forces along the border over the longer term could cause Peking to reconsider its anti-Soviet posture and reach an accommodation with Moscow contrary to U.S. interests.

Contending Schools of Thought

U.S. officials tended to identify with several discernible schools of thought about the PRC's potential role in the U.S.-Soviet rivalry that began to emerge in 1980. Members of the different groups were naturally inclined to stress some issues and softpedal others with an eye toward safeguarding the aspects of U.S. foreign policy that were particularly important to them.

Thus, for example, many U.S. military planners showed particular concern with what they saw as the relative decline of U.S. military power vis-à-vis the Soviet Union in recent years. Dissatisfied with allied efforts to help redress the balance, the planners viewed U.S. military cooperation with the PRC as a useful source of leverage that could help to remedy that decline.[19] In contrast, U.S. leaders interested in arms control with the USSR frequently were concerned with restoring enough trust in U.S.-Soviet relations to facilitate conclusion of important agreements on SALT and on conventional and nuclear force reductions in Europe. Members of this group, like former U.S. ambassador to the USSR Malcolm Toon, thought that U.S. military moves toward China were contrary to this objective and of marginal utility to the United States when compared to the importance of major U.S.-Soviet arms accords.[20]

U.S. specialists on the Soviet Union were divided into two general groups on this issue. Some, like former U.S. ambassador Raymond Garthoff, saw Sino-American military cooperation as contrary to what they judged should be the primary U.S. goal of establishing an international order based chiefly on a U.S.-Soviet modus vivendi.[21] Many others, like Ronald Reagan's foreign-policy advisor, Richard Pipes, saw the USSR as a newly emerging great power and believed that the United States should work closely with other sources of world power—including

China—to preclude more Soviet expansion and encourage the USSR to adjust to and cooperate with the status quo. They saw military cooperation with the PRC as useful in this context.[22]

China specialists were also divided. Many were concerned with the negative impact a U.S. refusal to transfer military supplies would have on Sino-American bilateral relations. Several judged that if the United States did not follow through with military supplies for the PRC, it might seriously disappoint Peking's leaders since they had been given the impression during visits and other exchanges that such equipment would be forthcoming. Some of these authorities on China added that supplying limited amounts of weapons and weapons-related technology would be an effective way to consolidate relations with the new Chinese leadership. Amicable Sino-American relations were seen as a very useful means to stabilize the situation in Asia in the face of possible internal and external challenges, including possible Soviet expansion. This view was held by several important China officers in the Carter administration but was not subject to much media attention.[23]

Many other Chinese affairs specialists worried that closer military cooperation with the PRC might have negative consequences for future Sino-American relations. Concerned about leadership instability in the PRC or anxious over Chinese intentions toward neighboring countries, they averred that U.S. military ties might identify the United States too closely with one group in China's leadership—a group whose tenure might prove to be limited and whose successors might not be as favorably disposed toward the United States. Reagan foreign policy advisor Ray Cline, who was critical of recent developments in U.S.-PRC ties, was one of the leaders closely identified with this group.[24] Other China specialists, including A. Doak Barnett of the Brookings Institution and Allen Whiting of the University of Michigan, stressed that the Chinese might come to rely too much on the United States or find U.S. military equipment inappropriate for their country's military modernization—developments that possibly could lead to a severe downturn in U.S.-PRC relations.[25]

Of course, not all views of U.S. arms transfers to the PRC were governed by the U.S.-Soviet-PRC triangular relationship. Many Asian specialists, for example, reflected the uneasiness of the countries of the region over U.S.-PRC military cooperation.[26] Their concerns focused on Peking's irredentist claims and its potential role as a destabilizing force in the region—factors that were seen as possibly more difficult to deal with if the United States seemed to defer more to the PRC's interests in Asian affairs. Those authorities with particular interest in Taiwan had an obvious strong interest in blocking military ties with the PRC. Meanwhile, U.S. leaders interested in increased trade with the PRC sometimes favored improved military ties as a means to show American good faith toward China, to insure a fruitful economic relationship with Peking, and to build the PRC's sense of security.[27]

Perceived Advantages and Disadvantages of U.S. Military Sales to China

Strategic Considerations

Some of the strongest arguments in favor of increased U.S. military transfers to the PRC centered on the effect they were said to have on Chinese and Soviet strategic planning. U.S. military transfers to the PRC would consolidate U.S. ties with an emerging great power in Asia, further insuring that China would remain on Washington's side against the USSR during the period of U.S. strategic vulnerability in the years ahead. The U.S. military moves could also pave the way to what some saw as a desirable and necessary Sino-American mutual security arrangement in northeast Asia—an alliance system that they thought should also include Japan.[28]

U.S. military supplies would increase China's sense of security vis-à-vis the Soviet Union, reduce the chance that the USSR would be able to intimidate or otherwise pressure it into a more pro-Soviet foreign policy stance, and establish enough Chinese confidence in the world balance of power that the PRC might be willing to join in serious discussions on limiting nuclear arms development. Although the U.S. transfers would not substantially alter the PRC's ability to project power against the USSR, they might complicate Soviet military plans in Asia. Moscow would have to devote more resources to countering whatever limited improvements were made in PRC forces and would also have to worry more about conflict along its Asian front in the event of an East-West confrontation over Europe or the Middle East.

Some U.S. officials worried that the Soviet Union might redeploy westward forces in Asia if there were a crisis with the West in Europe and added that such redeployments would be less likely under circumstances of closer Sino-American military cooperation. Better ties with the PRC could also give the United States the option of using Chinese facilities (air fields and ports, for example) during a major confrontation with the USSR, thereby placing Soviet central Asia and the Far East under increased pressure.

A few officials thought that closer military ties with the PRC could help ease U.S. frustration with the slowness of the Japanese defense development. Because the United States feared alienating its most important ally in Asia, it had seemed unable effectively to pressure

Japan into strengthening its military capability. U.S. ties with Peking, however, could allow Washington more latitude in pressuring the Japanese to do more in defense against the USSR and could increase Japan's sense of vulnerability—thereby prompting Tokyo to give defense a higher priority.

Opponents of U.S.-PRC military cooperation were not impressed by these supposed advantages and pointed to a variety of strategic disadvantages they saw associated with closer U.S.-PRC military ties. Since the PRC's nuclear strategic capability was potentially threatening to the United States, U.S. aid to China's conventional forces could have the drawback of allowing Peking to devote more attention to developing strategic weapons. China was said to be likely over the longer term to pose a threat to U.S. interests in Asia. As it became stronger with U.S. support, the PRC might well act more independently and assertively, coming into conflict with some of its neighbors—like Taiwan—whose interests were close to those of the United States.[29] Closer military cooperation with Peking might lead to such negative consequences as even more Soviet military pressure on the PRC[30] or a punitive Soviet strike along the Chinese border,[31] which, if successful, could undercut China's relatively pro-Western leadership and discredit those Chinese officials who linked their country's defensive strategy to close association with the United States.[32]

The USSR could react to U.S. transfers of military supplies to the PRC with countermeasures involving Vietnam or India, perhaps including stepped up efforts to establish Soviet military installations in Southeast and south Asia. Not only would such moves help the USSR encircle China and curb Chinese influence in Asia, but they also would seriously challenge the ability of the United States to defend sea lines of communication in those important areas. U.S. moves toward military ties with China could seriously dampen Soviet interest in arms control with the United States, upset existing East-West understandings for these negotiations, and, because of Chinese nuclear forces, prompt Moscow to be more insistent in demanding compensation in any disarmament proposal—something the United States had rejected in the past.[33]

Political-Economic Factors

Perhaps the strongest political argument for going ahead with limited military transfers to the PRC was that U.S. leaders had apparently already given Chinese officials the impression that they would do so. As a result, for the United States to reverse its course at that stage could have led to serious complications in Sino-American relations. The transfers would have shown American "good faith," built support for and established U.S. influence with the relatively pragmatic leaders governing China, and promoted important channels of communication with segments of the Chinese military leadership who might otherwise have remained skeptical of their country's recent tilt toward the United States.[34] Preparing such a solid foundation for Sino-American ties was essential to enable the relationship to withstand future difficulties over such issues as Taiwan,[35] U.S.-Soviet arms control, and human rights.

Military transfers to the PRC were also said to provide the United States with a "Chinese card" useful in prompting more positive Soviet behavior toward the United States or in compensating the United States for Soviet gains made elsewhere in the Third World. They reportedly had indirect advantages for U.S. trade with the PRC, which was said to be likely to give business people associated with its major military backer more advantageous treatment than their competitors from other countries.[36] Closer military ties with China could have reduced U.S. dependence on Japan and increased U.S. leverage over the Japanese on a variety of issues, including U.S.-Japanese trade disagreements.[37]

Opponents of military transfers raised a host of possible political and economic disadvantages to such ties, stating that they could lock the United States into an anti-Soviet posture in international affairs at a time when the United States might have more to gain from cooperation than confrontation with the USSR. Those disadvantages could occur even if the United States wanted only a limited military relationship with the PRC, because such relationships, once started, develop rapidly and prove difficult to stop. The transfers could link the United States closely with the Chinese side of the Sino-Soviet dispute in Asia, notably reducing prospects for more independent U.S. policies vis-à-vis Vietnam or India; could promote a view that the United States perceived China, rather than Japan, as its main ally in Asia, thereby leading to an erosion of the U.S.-Japanese alliance; and could signal a loss of U.S. influence in Asia,[38] as well as a loss in influence over China's future behavior.

Even some analysts who favored arms transfers to the PRC argued that such sales should be seen only as a supplement to, not as a substitute for, U.S. power in the region. Otherwise, they warned, the United States would become too dependent on China to protect U.S. interests in the region. Others favoring Sino-American security ties judged, however, that it was unrealistic to expect the United States not to use China as a substitute for U.S. power in East Asia. They emphasized that the United States needed to consolidate its forces to deal with the USSR in other important areas, notably the Persian Gulf, and that it should use China as a strategic bulwark in East Asia. Some noted that the United States in effect had already started this kind of approach in Southeast Asia, where China—and not the United States—was seen as the main strategic guarantor of U.S. interests in Thailand against military pressure from Soviet-backed Vietnam.

In view of China's history of political instability, it was possible that a new leadership less favorable to the United States could emerge in the PRC over the next few years. The example of Soviet military cooperation with the PRC in the 1950s was also not reassuring, since it seemed to prompt unrealistic Chinese expectations that the USSR was unwilling to fulfill. That led to a serious downturn in relations— a pattern that could be followed in Sino-American relations during the 1980s if the Chinese military leaders and other PRC officials came to rely too heavily on American supplies and support.[39]

China was also seen as gaining much more than it gave in its new relationship with the United States. Some stressed the contrast between the risks the United States would take in increasing military ties with the PRC and the fact that the Americans would still have no guarantee that China would be any more likely to side with the United States on issues important to U.S. interests vis-à-vis the Soviet Union and elsewhere.

The Economic Factor in the Evolution of U.S. China Policy, 1971–1981

Since the signing of the Shanghai Communiqué, a few members of the American business community have actively promoted closer relations with China as a means to increase the U.S. share of China's growing foreign trade and of foreign investment in the PRC. Issues in U.S.-PRC commercial relations—such as the settlement of the claims-assets dispute in 1979 and the negotiation and passage of the U.S.-PRC trade agreement in 1979–1980—have preoccupied U.S. policy makers for months at a time. U.S. media periodically have flagged the China market as an area of great potential for U.S. exporters and investors. The PRC media have reciprocated by offering sometimes idealized accounts of U.S. material accomplishments in an apparent effort to encourage the Chinese people to cooperate more closely with the United States in economic areas of mutual benefit and to learn from U.S. management and development techniques.

In general, however, economic relations with the PRC have remained largely of secondary importance in the evolution of U.S. China policy. The conflict and confrontation that developed between the United States and China in the 1950s and 1960s had little to do with economics, although the United States did impose a trade embargo against the PRC to "contain" the possible spread of Chinese communism. The initial decisions by Mao Zedong and Zhou Enlai in Peking and Nixon and Kissinger in Washington to improve bilateral relations were motivated by strategic and political—not economic—factors, even though both sides used the lever of trade policy to demonstrate their good intentions to one another. Carter administration spokespersons similarly judged that improved U.S. economic ties with the PRC were primarily important for the overall effect they would have on China's strategic orientation toward the United States, its Asian neighbors, and the USSR.[1] Recent trends suggest that political and strategic considerations will continue for the foreseeable future to determine the course of Sino-American relations, with economic and business contacts playing a subordinate role.

The American business community generally has not exerted a major influence on the course of recent U.S. China policy and did not push strongly for rapid forward movement in normalization of relations with the PRC, which presumably would have led to improved U.S. economic opportunities in the PRC. In the past, most business representatives seemed to share the overall anti–Chinese communist hostility of the 1950s, although a small number opposed the U.S. trade embargo against the PRC and wanted increased contact and trade long before the embargo was officially lifted in the early 1970s. Subsequently, many business people sought to visit China, presumably for their commercial interests but also because of personal curiosity. Many were fascinated—as were other Americans—by the mystery of a "New China" and by the drama of a new era in U.S.-PRC relations. However, with the notable exception of the National Council for U.S.-China Trade, a private, nonprofit organization formed in 1973 to promote U.S.-PRC economic relations, U.S. business interests have not played a prominent role in trying to change U.S. China policy; they also have not been particularly active in helping to build a stronger consensus in the United States supportive of improving U.S.-PRC ties and overcoming continued obstacles such as the Taiwan problem.

Business representatives have tended to be more reactive, adopting a low-key posture that reflects important U.S. business considerations regarding the PRC. Most notably:

- U.S. business leaders—on the whole—have been cautious about trade and investment prospects in China. They have recognized that economic relations with the PRC are, at best, of only moderate, potential importance to overall U.S. commercial development. They have also noted that prospects for development in China have been, and are likely to remain, subject to rapid change depending on political and economic variables in the PRC that are poorly understood in the United States and hard to predict.
- Many American companies have also held back from pressing for rapid development of U.S. relations with the PRC for fear of jeopardizing their major business interests in Taiwan. This is not to say that U.S. businesses attempted to block a gradual U.S.

normalization with the PRC. On the contrary, so long as their Taiwan interests were secured, they tended to welcome slow and steady improvement in U.S.-PRC relations as a major stabilizing influence beneficial for all American companies involved in trade and investments among the rapidly expanding noncommunist economies throughout the rim of east Asia.

U.S.-PRC Trade, 1971–1977

U.S.-PRC economic relations emerged in the early 1970s as the Nixon administration began to dismantle the trade embargo against China and other impediments to U.S.-PRC trade. Most observers expected that trade would increase only gradually and would remain relatively small, but trade through 1974 rose at a very rapid rate, reaching over $900 million that year. The balance of U.S.-PRC trade was heavily in the United States's favor, with U.S. exports amounting to over $800 million in 1974; agricultural goods commonly made up about four-fifths of U.S. exports.[2]

Two major reasons appeared to account for the rapid growth in trade:

1. The PRC in the past had redirected trade for political reasons and appeared to be using purchases of U.S. goods to accelerate the process of normalization of U.S.-PRC political relations.
2. Because of poor harvests and a tight global grain market, China had little alternative but to turn to the United States as a supplier for large amounts of needed grain.

The rise in trade encouraged considerable optimism in the United States about further growth in U.S. development of the China market, but in 1975 the PRC cut off most U.S. grain purchases and total trade declined by over half. Several factors led to Peking's actions:

- an improvement in Chinese domestic grain production;
- Chinese complaints about the quality of U.S. grain shipped to China;
- a growing concern among PRC leaders about their country's rising trade deficits and shortage of hard currency to pay for foreign grain;
- a slowdown in the process of normalization of U.S.-PRC political relations following the resignation of President Nixon; and

- political debate in the PRC over the wisdom of using foreign purchases to assist Chinese economic development.

For the next two years, trade stagnated around 1975 levels.

The sharp rise and fall in U.S.-PRC trade affected American perceptions of the China market. Experts on Sino-American economic relations, such as University of Michigan economist Alexander Eckstein, concluded in 1975 that for Sino-American trade to be restored to its peak 1974 level or to develop beyond that point would require either a "supreme political leap" leading to the establishment of full diplomatic relations or a "step-by-step approach" gradually removing the technical, institutional, and economic barriers standing in the way of free U.S.-PRC commerce. Judging that the Ford administration would likely follow the step-by-step approach, Eckstein predicted a continued impasse in U.S.-PRC economic relations, asserting in reference to the Chinese that "barring some quite unusual and unforeseen circumstances, they will not permit a significant rise in trade with the United States short of formal diplomatic relations."[3]

Even such long-standing active proponents of increased U.S.-PRC trade as San Francisco attorney Stanley Lubman advised that "historical animosity" had combined with Peking's "uncertain economic development policies" and limited foreign trade to place "strong constraints" on developing Sino-American commercial relations. Lubman added that the growth of Sino-American trade would depend partly on whether the will existed on both sides to clear away at least part of the web of trade-related policies that impeded bilateral commerce and also on whether deep uncertainties in political relations between the two countries were resolved. Judging that neither country needed the other's trade so badly that commercial interest alone could propel the two closer together politically, he concluded that "in the absence of dramatic developments, trade will most likely develop slowly, with China making selective purchases—the amount probably varying with the intensity of the overall relationship—and U.S. buyers seeking out products which they can import profitably through the intricacies of the discouraging U.S. tariff and non-tariff barriers."[4]

Initially, the death of Mao Zedong and the arrest of the Gang of Four in late 1976 was not widely seen in the United States as likely to change substantially China's attitude toward foreign trade with capitalist countries like the United States. In 1977 Harvard University economist Dwight Perkins advised Congress that even with the establishment of normal U.S.-PRC diplomatic relations, "the prospects are that trade between the United States and the PRC will rise, but not in any dramatic way." Perkins added that "there are no comparable prospects for private investment in China."[5]

Chinese Economic Reform and the U.S. Response, 1978–1981

With the rehabilitation of Vice Premier Deng Xiaoping in mid-1977 and the start of a series of pragmatic political and economic reforms associated with him in 1978, China's approach to foreign trade changed substantially. Launching a highly ambitious economic modernization campaign by early 1978, Chinese leaders seemed poised for a major increase in imports of industrial products, advanced technology, and food grains and other raw materials from capitalist nations, including the United States. Perhaps more significant, PRC leaders seemed willing for the first time to finance imports with longer-term credits from Japanese and Western banks, raising the prospect that the PRC would purchase more goods than its current balance of payments and hard currency reserves would appear to allow. By the end of the year, reports indicated that Western European and Japanese governments and private banks had extended billions of dollars worth of credits to China.

Recognizing that they were clearly trailing behind Japanese and European competitors who were already fairly well established in the Chinese market, many U.S. firms became anxious to cash in on the new commercial opportunity. The resumption in 1977 of U.S. agricultural purchases by the PRC after a hiatus of two years also increased U.S. interest in the China market and pushed U.S. exports to a level that was 27 percent over 1976. By the year's end, about $60 million in cotton, soybeans, and soybean oil had left U.S. ports. Another $80 million in American cotton was scheduled to be sent to China by mid-1978, and new wheat contracts by that time totaled $300 million.

Meanwhile, prospects appeared particularly good for U.S. exports of certain industrial equipment, notably machinery for petroleum exploration, drilling, and production on- and off-shore and for petroleum refining and petrochemical plant technology. Aluminum, iron and steel scrap, pulp and paper, chemicals, fertilizers, mining and construction equipment, machine tools, electronic items, and scientific equipment were other potentially promising areas.[6]

As unprecedented numbers of U.S. business representatives traveled to China in 1978 for discussion of possible business deals, the Chinese signed protocols or letters of intent with U.S. firms for several large transactions: U.S. Steel signed a $1 billion agreement with the PRC, Bethlehem Steel concluded a deal for more than $600 million, Kaiser signed a protocol, and Fluor Corporation concluded an $800 million arrangement for a copper project. Both Hyatt and Intercontinental hotels negotiated agreements in excess of $500 million each, Kellogg sold a plant to the Chinese, and Peking ordered three Boeing 747 SP jets, with an option to purchase two more, a deal worth more than $200 million.[7]

Press reports of these negotiations reflected a decidedly upbeat assessment of the prospects for U.S.-PRC trade and investment, with many articles speculating about a "China trade boom" and the "awakening" of the "eastern giant" to trade opportunities with the United States.[8] President Carter's December 1978 announcement of the decision to establish normal U.S.-PRC diplomatic relations added to optimism in the United States. In subsequent weeks, the Bureau of East-West Trade in the Department of Commerce was deluged with over three hundred calls and letters a day, was forced to double the size of its staff to handle all the new China queries, and quickly exhausted its supply of twenty thousand copies of the bureau's report, "Doing Business with China." As a senior bureau official put it, there was a "sweeping" American interest in China and the "potentially enormous new market for American firms."[9] Deng Xiaoping's triumphant tour of the United States in January and February 1979 further highlighted U.S. business interest in the PRC as Deng went out of his way to visit with American commercial leaders in such important business centers as Atlanta, Houston, and Seattle.

Despite such widespread attention to the seemingly vast potential for U.S.-PRC trade and investment, many specialists and business leaders in the United States remained cautious about the prospects for economic cooperation with China. *Forbes* and *Fortune* ran important articles in early 1979 warning that "American businessmen would be wise not to expect too much soon from trade with China,"[10] and that "many of the seemingly big corporate deals are nothing more than vague agreements with Peking; the hard bargaining over money is still to come."[11] On January 15, 1979, four cabinet level officers in the Carter administration tried to convince five hundred U.S. business executives that they could have increasing trade with the PRC and still continue to trade with Taiwan under the normalization of relations arrangement worked out with Peking. The session, however, reportedly did little to reassure the executives about the major question on their minds: How would the Chinese pay for the many products and technical assistance they were seeking? Administration representatives were also frank in acknowledging that the United States still would have to overcome major legal hurdles—like the claims-asset dispute and the absence of MFN tariff treatment for Chinese imports into the United States—before trade would reach its full potential.[12]

The Carter administration set to work to overcome these problems and solved many of them during 1979–1980.

Blocked Assets and Private Claims

Settlement of the issues of Chinese assets blocked in the United States and U.S. private claims against the PRC was required before certain steps in U.S.-PRC commercial relations could be taken. These issues stemmed from the blocking by the United States of Chinese dollar-denominated accounts and other assets on December 17, 1950, after PRC military forces entered North Korea and from the subsequent Chinese decree of December 29, 1950, announcing seizure of U.S. public and private property in the PRC.[13]

In 1966 Congress amended the International Claims Settlement Act of 1949 to authorize the Foreign Claims Settlement Commission to undertake an evaluation of claims by U.S. nationals for losses due to PRC nationalization of property and other assets after October 1, 1949. Claims by private U.S. citizens and corporations adjudicated by the commission totaled about $197 million.

The Treasury Department, responsible under the Foreign Assets Control Regulations for maintaining control over the blocked Chinese assets, undertook a second census of those assets in June 1970. Since the first census of 1951, many changes in assets had occurred. The completed census placed the value of the assets in June 1970 at $76.5 million.

Unsettled, these issues prevented direct shipping and direct airline connections by the flag carriers of the PRC. Private claimants might have sought redress through the courts by attaching ships, aircraft, and other PRC property that came into the United States. Direct banking was forestalled for the same reason, and the resultant need to work through third-country correspondent banks was cumbersome for U.S. traders. The sending of Chinese trade exhibitions to the United States was virtually precluded. In addition, since the PRC had nationalized and expropriated U.S.-owned property, it was precluded from obtaining other U.S. trade benefits, notably preferential tariff treatment under the generalized system of preferences.

Treasury Secretary Michael Blumenthal reached agreement with PRC leaders on the settlement of U.S. claims during his visit to Peking in March 1979. Under the agreement, which was officially signed during Commerce Secretary Juanita Kreps's visit in May 1979, the Chinese agreed to pay 41 cents on the dollar for a total of $80.5 million. Some $330 million was to be paid to U.S. claimants on October 1, 1979. It was also agreed that the United States would unblock Chinese assets in the United States as of October 1, 1979. On September 30, 1979, Peking announced that the United States and the PRC had "recently" decided to delay implementing the claims agreement until January 31, 1980, presumably to allow Peking more time to prepare its legal case to claim assets in the United States that were disputed by other claimants and whose ownership would probably be determined through the courts.

MFN Tariff Treatment for the PRC

Under terms of the Trade Act of 1974, MFN status could be granted to the PRC through a Sino-American bilateral commercial agreement valid initially for three years after approval by Congress. The agreement had to, among other things, contain safeguards against market disruption, include procedures for settling commercial disputes, make provisions for bilateral consultations, and secure protection for the individual property rights of U.S. nationals equivalent to those contained in the Paris Convention for the Protection of Industrial Property. The Sino-American commercial accord, which the Carter administration signed with PRC leaders in July 1979 and which it submitted to Congress for approval in October 1979, met those requirements.

Moreover, since the granting of MFN status could not be extended to any non–market economy nation that denied its citizens the right or opportunity to emigrate or imposed more than nominal exit fees or taxes on documents or individuals, President Carter notified Congress that he was waiving those provisions when he submitted the Sino-American trade treaty to Congress in October 1979. The Congress endorsed the president's action, and on January 24, 1980, it approved the trade agreement granting MFN tariff treatment to the PRC.

Restrictions on Possible U.S. Investment Insurance and Export Credits to the PRC

The Foreign Assistance Act of 1961 limited the furnishing of almost every type of assistance provided for in the act to "friendly countries." Although the act did not explicitly define that term, it specifically banned furnishing any assistance covered by the act to any communist country unless the president issued a narrowly defined waiver.

Programs administered by OPIC were considered assistance under U.S. law. At the same time, the Export-Import Bank Act of 1945 as amended prohibited any credit transaction by the bank directly or indirectly involving a communist country, unless the president determined that such a transaction was in the national interest. Moreover, Ex-Im Bank credits in general could not be granted to nonmarket countries that curbed their citizens' right to emigrate.

In August 1979 Vice President Mondale told the Chinese that the Carter administration was prepared to establish Ex-Im Bank credit arrangements for the PRC on a case-by-case basis, up to a total of $2 billion over a five-year period, and that the administration would seek congressional authority to provide the guarantees and insurance of OPIC for Americans investing in China. By approving the U.S.-PRC trade agreement in January 1980, Congress in effect endorsed President Carter's waiver of the emigration issue in considering Ex-Im Bank financing for the PRC. In August 1980 Congress also passed special legislation amending the Foreign Assistance Act of 1961 to allow operations by OPIC with the PRC.

Chinese Economic Retrenchment

While these legal changes were underway, U.S.-PRC trade doubled to $2.3 billion in 1979 and doubled again in 1980. Events in the PRC began to show, however, that the initial bright outlook of many observers at the time of U.S.-PRC diplomatic normalization for growth in Chinese trade with the United States and other countries had been overly optimistic. Most notably, Peking was compelled to put aside the ambitious goals of its Ten-Year Economic Plan (1976–1985) that were announced in March 1978 as the PRC began an arduous process of drafting a new economic program. As a first step in correcting sectoral imbalances, low productivity, and a poor hard-currency position, the Third Plenum of the Eleventh Central Committee of the CCP decided in December 1978 to reorder economic priorities. In the process, investments for agriculture and light industry were expected to increase at the expense of heavy industry, while the slower approach to modernization was also expected to restrain the growth of, and lead to some cutbacks in, the PRC's imports of foreign—including U.S.—equipment in the 1980s.[14]

In addition to providing the basis for China's goal of achieving by the year 2000 the "four modernizations," the ambitious Ten-Year Economic Plan marked a sharp departure from Peking's past commercial dealings with the West. The Fifth Five-Year Plan (1976–1980) was to have been the springboard for the PRC's modernization drive. After a poor start caused by political turmoil, unfavorable weather, and a major earthquake in North China in 1976, the five-year plan was incorporated into the Ten-Year Economic Plan. Because of the plan's heavy reliance on imports—particularly Western technology and equipment—the PRC dropped ideological constraints on the use of foreign credits and began actively seeking joint ventures with the West, including equity arrangements. The new plan also gave more prominence to developing agriculture and light industry than had been given in the past, but it still continued to favor industrial growth. Agriculture and light industry in 1978 accounted for only 11 and 5 percent, respectively, of state budget–financed investment spending, compared with 55 percent for heavy industry. Some 120 large-scale projects, which heavily depended on imports of Western machinery and technology, were scheduled to be completed or at least under way by 1985. In addition, the ten-year plan set unrealistic 1985 production targets for key commodities such as oil, coal, and steel.

After assessing the PRC's economic situation and realizing the size of the gaps that existed between its capabilities and its ambitious ten-year plan, the Chinese government in late 1978 began making substantial changes to the 1976–1985 program. Besides being saddled with a large number of uneconomical and technologically backward plants, the economy suffered from an overcommitment of resources to capital construction projects, imbalances between sectors, and low productivity. As a first step toward solving the country's economic problems, the Third Plenum called for the reordering of planning priorities. Because of their key roles in meeting rising consumer expectations and supplying hard currency exports, agriculture and light industry were given renewed emphasis, and planned state investment spending for those two sectors was increased at the expense of heavy industry, particularly iron and steel. Within heavy industry, lagging areas—coal, electric power, petroleum, transport, and building materials—that constrained the PRC's economic growth continued to receive high priority.

In an effort to concentrate resources on the development of light industry and lagging sectors, Peking in early 1979 decided to scale down, postpone, or cancel many of the 120 projects called for in the original 1976–1985 plan. Priority was given to projects that required less foreign exchange, provided a quicker return on investment, and offered potentially greater export earnings. In addition, shorter construction lead times were stressed, and the upgrading and expansion of existing facilities were given precedence over new ventures.

In June 1979 the government formally announced a ten-point readjustment program for China's economy. The program, initially scheduled to run through 1981, incorporated the reordering of planning priorities and the new capital construction policies. Implicit in the retrenchment program was a slower pace for the modernization drive. Peking subsequently extended the readjustment period through 1982 and 1983 and then to 1985. The government also indicated that several ambitious production goals set for 1985—in particular, targets for oil, coal, and steel—were to be put off until much later.

The Third Plenum shifted the underlying theme of PRC domestic policy to that of economic productivity and consumer welfare are closely interrelated, and the many changes in economic policy that followed that plenum were aimed at productivity gains. Those changes included increasing material incentives for production and hence incomes of workers and peasants, installing new systems of rewards and penalties for individual managers and economic entities, and experimenting with new and more efficient forms of industrial organization.

Resource allocation policies were shifted to support the new policy course. While maintaining its interest in acquiring foreign equipment and technology and continuing to enter into selected undertakings on favorable credit terms, the PRC leadership suspended or postponed several planned purchases from abroad. Its domestic construction program was also cut back, eliminating poorly planned projects and those requiring long lead times. A drive to alleviate long-standing constraints on industrial production—electric power, coal, building materials, and transportation—was made one of the top priorities of China's economic managers.

The adoption and implementation of innovative economic policies—many on an experimental basis—increased throughout 1979 and 1980. Collectively, they involved a sweeping package of economic reforms that could be called the PRC's version of Lenin's New Economic Program, adopted in the 1920s in the USSR. Problems with the economy, however, continued to plague the PRC leadership. For example:

- Import demand generated by the original Ten-Year Economic Plan grew, pushing the foreign trade deficit to slightly more than $1 billion in 1979 and to almost $2 billion in 1980. (These deficits were small by international standards but were seen as extraordinarily and dangerously large by autarky-minded PRC leaders.)
- Relaxation of restrictions on personal travel led many youths, who previously had been sent down to the countryside, to rejoin their families in the cities, pushing the number of the urban unemployed to more than 20 million.
- A budget deficit of over $10 billion in 1979 led to a substantial increase in the money supply and serious inflationary pressure.

By late 1980 Chinese leaders acknowledged that although the new economic policies were successful in many ways, they had led to such negative consequences as budget deficits, inflation, foreign trade deficits, declining growth rates, persisting large pockets of poverty in the rural areas, and more urban unemployment. Those officials also said that the goal of putting the economy back on the track of self-sustained economic growth in three years would require an additional two years.

Some critically needed commodities, notably energy, experienced an absolute decline in 1980. The planned budget deficit for 1980 was exceeded by 50 percent, which led to further overdrafts from the central bank, an increase in currency in circulation, and persisting inflation.

In 1981 PRC leaders announced stern countermeasures to reduce the projected budget revenue and expenditures by 9.1 and 13.2 percent, respectively, and to provide a balanced budget. A large cutback in spending was to be achieved through a 45 percent reduction in the planned capital construction target for 1981. This caused a sharp reduction in PRC plans to purchase foreign industrial equipment. Additional restrictions were made in planned expenditures for national defense and government administration. The officials also decided that further experimentation with economic reform should not be extended beyond those enterprises where it had already been introduced and that a "consolidation" of experiments with those reforms was necessary.

In a major government report on December 1, 1981, Premier Zhao Ziyang disclosed that:

- The PRC would need at least until the mid-1980s to complete the economic readjustment originally scheduled to end in 1982.
- The economy would not grow very fast in the 1981–1985 five-year plan period. (No specific plan for the period had yet been announced.)
- A 4 percent growth rate in industrial and agricultural output was targeted for 1982, a slightly higher goal than the 3 percent announced for 1981.
- Heavy industrial production would fall 5 percent while light industry would rise by 12 percent in 1981.[15]

Meanwhile, the growth of China's hard-currency-merchandise exports—the country's major source of foreign exchange—was expected to slow in the 1981–1985 period, largely because of Peking's effort to improve living standards, a slower growth of oil output, and, to a lesser degree, sluggish economic activity in the West. In particular:

- *Foodstuff exports* in 1981–1985 were thought unlikely to rise substantially above the 1975–1979 annual rate of 9 percent because of growing domestic demand. Although the revised Ten-Year Economic Plan called for increased investment in agriculture, the focus of overall economic policy was on import substitution and boosting domestic consumption.

- Because of rising domestic demand and the expected substantially slower growth in oil production, the growth of petroleum export earnings was likely to depend mainly on world oil price increases. Production from China's older onshore fields such as Daqing, the country's first and largest oil field, had begun to level off, and even under the most optimistic conditions, production from off-shore fields was not expected to begin before 1985. Furthermore, growing domestic demand was likely to limit the volume of oil exports despite the PRC's conservation program and the push to use alternative energy sources such as coal and hydropower.
- Output of *manufactures*—particularly textiles—was expected to register substantial gains over the next several years because of increased investment spending for light industry. But rising consumer demand stemming from Peking's efforts to improve living standards, coupled with sluggish economic growth in the West and its accompanying protectionism, was expected to limit the growth of manufactured exports.

The PRC seemed likely to gain some increased revenues from remittances of Chinese who permanently resided abroad, tourism, and other commercial activities. However, the combination of the government's recently more restrictive policies regulating foreign loans and the limited potential for PRC exports over the near term led to a generally accepted picture of moderate expectations in the United States for the potential of the Chinese market, at least in the near future.

Prospects

Typical of the prevalent mood even among some of the strongest supporters of closer U.S.-PRC relations, A. Doak Barnett of the Brookings Institution argued in *China's Economy in Global Perspective,* his landmark work on the Chinese economy published in 1981, that the United States might well derive more political than strictly economic benefit from increased trade and economic cooperation with Peking. Barnett judged that increased U.S. sales to the PRC were "the most apparent, though not necessarily the most important" benefits to be derived from closer economic links with China, adding that while this would assist U.S. agriculture and industry, "the potential of trade with China should not . . . be exaggerated."[16] Underlining a point made by many other specialists, Barnett noted that even if the present volume of $4.5 billion in U.S.-PRC trade were to double, and then double again, it would still amount to only a tiny fraction of U.S. foreign trade. The trade would remain of particular importance only to selected groups of U.S. producers, notably grain farmers, rather than the country as a whole.

Reflecting a trend seen in U.S. China policy since the beginnings of Sino-American reconciliation, Barnett and others argued strongly that the United States should continue to use advances in economic relations with Peking to stabilize and advance the overall U.S.-PRC relationship. Even though closer economic links could not guarantee friendly political relations, it was claimed that, on balance, they would enhance prospects for good relations in general. "To the extent that U.S. cooperation, both private and government, helps Peking achieve its development goals, this should contribute to political stability in China, increase the chances that Peking will continue to pursue pragmatic, growth-oriented policies at home, and reinforce the trend toward more moderate cooperative Chinese foreign policies," Barnett concluded.[17]

Persuaded by these kinds of arguments, the Reagan administration and the Ninety-seventh Congress began to take small steps to strengthen the institutional framework of U.S.-PRC economic relations and to remove remaining U.S. legal and administrative impediments to those relations—a process begun by President Carter. Results were slow in coming, however, as the United States faced combined influences of stringent budget constraints and very busy legislative schedules focused on U.S. domestic issues. As a result, it appeared likely that it would be well into 1982 before the United States took further steps to improve economic relations with the PRC. Among the suggested options were:

- negotiating additional agreements governing U.S. grain and other commodity exports to China;
- granting preferential tariff treatment to PRC imports under terms of the GSP;
- granting U.S. food aid to China under the Public Law 480 program;
- granting other concessional aid to China that was blocked by provisions of the Foreign Assistance Act;
- easing U.S. administrative and legal restrictions on the transfer of high-level technology to China;
- providing adequate funding for U.S. government agencies (e.g., the Ex-Im Bank) to follow through on pledges made to China during the previous administration; and
- opening U.S. markets to more Chinese manufactured goods, notably textiles.

8
Conclusion:
Options for the United States

When the United States commemorated the tenth anniversary of President Nixon's historic 1972 opening to China, Americans focused, in large part, on the remarkable accomplishments of the Sino-American reconciliation. The United States has established effective communication with one of the most important Asian countries, one that in the past had been viewed as the greatest source of instability and threat to U.S. interests in the region. Trade, cultural, and tourist interchange has grown rapidly, exceeding even optimist expectations of only a few years ago. The parallel strategic interests of the United States and the PRC have pushed the two countries into closer cooperation against the Soviet Union, involving consultations and planning to offset Soviet and Soviet-backed expansion in Southwest and Southeast Asia, the establishment of a U.S. intelligence monitoring station in the PRC aimed at Soviet missile tests, and the beginnings of a U.S. military sales relationship with China. Even in areas of dispute in Sino-American relations, both sides have often sought to avoid confrontation in the interest of preserving and fostering a mutually beneficial relationship.

Recently, however, it has become clear to most Americans that below the surface of these major accomplishments lie complicated dilemmas in contemporary U.S. China policy concerning Taiwan, U.S.-PRC military and economic relations, and the covert nature of U.S. China policy. These dilemmas, which are based on persisting and fundamental American leadership differences over China policy, have deep historical roots. They have evolved along with U.S. China policy since President Nixon traveled to the PRC to begin the Sino-American reconciliation. At times, U.S. leaders have been able temporarily to put these problems aside in the interests of fostering closer U.S.-PRC relations, but the difficulties have later reemerged to complicate and jeopardize the progress in Sino-American relations.

Until a strong consensus on these questions is established in the United States, its China policy will remain subject to sharp dispute and possible abrupt change. Since U.S. leaders vary widely in their views of China policy and the American electoral process results in frequent changes in U.S. leadership, it is quite conceivable that U.S. leaders could emerge who would radically change or reverse the recent course of Sino-American relations.

Indeed, such an abrupt shift appeared at hand at the start of the Reagan administration. The president had a close affinity for Taiwan and had pledged in the campaign to improve relations with Taipei, even though it might risk undermining the new U.S. relationship with Peking.[1] Faced with strong PRC pressure and the danger of a substantial setback in U.S.-PRC relations, however, the Reagan administration— as of 1982—has followed a more cautious policy on Taiwan. It also has generally not pursued the abrupt advances toward the PRC that characterized the Carter administration's policy and prompted intense disputes within the administration and with Congress.

The slowdown in U.S.-PRC relations—caused largely by strong PRC differences with Reagan administration policy toward Taiwan—had the effect of easing, at least for a brief time, the major internal political frictions that had troubled U.S. China policy. This relatively quiet interlude in the formation of U.S. China policy was also influenced by several other factors. Ronald Reagan entered office with strong credentials as a supporter of Taiwan, thereby reassuring U.S. leaders who had been sharply critical of what they saw as the cavalier treatment of Taiwan by the Carter administration.[2] At the same time, however, by avoiding precipitous actions to upgrade U.S. relations with Taiwan or to supply arms to the island, Reagan administration officials reassured U.S. leaders who thought that U.S. interests with the mainland should override U.S. interests on Taiwan.

The administration did prompt considerable controversy by agreeing during Secretary Haig's visit to China to consider the sale of arms to Peking. But the main argument against such sales—that they could lock the United States into an anti-Soviet posture that would preclude meaningful U.S.-Soviet cooperation—seemed less than potent at a time when U.S. relations with the USSR were already at their lowest point since the cold war.

The administration's relations with Congress over China policy were relatively smooth, in part because conservative members seemed generally to agree with the president's approach. While some may have wished for greater support for Taiwan, they found it difficult to argue that Ronald Reagan could be anything but favorable in his policy toward Taiwan.

Meanwhile, Democratic leaders in the Senate and House committees and subcommittees who had been sharply critical of Carter administration policy on China were removed as a result of the 1980 elections. The Republicans put in charge of the Senate Foreign Relations Committee were less likely than their predecessors to take issue with the new administration. Chairman Lester Wolff of the House Foreign Affairs Subcommittee on Asian and Pacific Affairs, perhaps the most active public critic of the Carter administration's China policy, was replaced by another liberal New York Democrat, Stephen Solarz. Congressman Solarz also had a reputation of not being reluctant to advocate a policy approach different from administration guidelines,[3] but his subcommittee's actions and recommendations on China were generally supportive of administration policy.

Despite this period of relative quiet in the China debate in U.S. domestic politics, U.S. policy makers have faced a series of hard decisions in the period ahead that are likely to reflect the major divisions in the United States that continue to complicate China policy. At present, PRC pressure has forced Americans to focus attention on the Taiwan issue. When and if Peking were to reduce pressure on this question and allow for greater development in U.S. cooperation with the PRC in military, economic, and other areas, dilemmas concerning U.S. defense ties and assistance to China, as well as the covert nature of U.S. policy, would likely come to the fore.

Taiwan

Americans sympathetic with Taiwan's interests against the mainland tend to favor what they call the "full" implementation of the Taiwan Relations Act that would include improved unofficial contacts between Taiwan and U.S. representatives, the opening of more Taiwanese offices in the United States, and most important, the provision of U.S. weapons for sale to Taiwan.[4]

The United States could go further and formally recognize the "reality" of Taipei as one of two governments existing in China—an option favored by some of the most outspoken supporters of Taiwan in the United States.[5] This action would presumably involve the reestablishment of some sort of official ties with Taiwan. Another option that favors Taiwan against the mainland would involve efforts by the United States to use its growing leverage with Peking to obtain a PRC commitment not to use force in dealing with Taiwan.[6]

The main advantages of these options are that they would help to discharge honorably the U.S. commitment to Taiwan, would underline U.S. reliability and dependability in support of long-standing allies and friends, and would enhance U.S. ideals of peace and nonuse of force in international affairs. They also would clearly win great favor with Taiwan.

The main disadvantage concerns the likely reaction of the PRC. Probably any sustained U.S. effort to demand a renunciation of force agreement from the PRC over Taiwan or to reestablish official contacts with Taiwan would rapidly lead to an unraveling of the Sino-American reconciliation of the past decade. U.S. implementation of provisions of the Taiwan Relations Act is also offensive to the PRC, but it is hard to judge what countermeasures or retaliation Peking would adopt. Thus far, PRC leaders have shown more sensitivity to the possible U.S. sale of weapons to Taiwan than to any other interchange for which the act called.[7] A major setback in U.S.-PRC relations, of course, could easily become a significant issue in U.S. partisan politics.

In contrast, U.S. leaders could follow options that favor PRC interests vis-à-vis Taiwan. They could try to reduce or eliminate the Taiwan issue as an impediment in U.S.-PRC relations by gradually cutting back U.S. support, especially military support, for Taiwan. That would represent an indirect but unmistakeable signal to Taipei leaders that they should adjust to the new situation in U.S.-PRC relations and begin efforts to achieve an accommodation with the mainland. U.S. leaders could speed this process by adding political pressure on Taipei leaders to come to terms with the PRC, perhaps establishing the United States in a formal mediating role between the two Chinese sides.[8]

The main advantage of this approach is that the United States would ease tensions with the PRC and thereby open the way to smoother cooperation in U.S.-PRC relations. A solution of the Taiwan issue would remove the most serious impediment to closer U.S.-PRC relations. The disadvantages of this approach are that it could be seen as a victory of expediency over principle in U.S. foreign policy, with the United States "selling out" Taiwan for the sake of U.S. interests vis-à-vis the mainland, and that it might so alienate Taipei leaders that they would take actions to undercut any deal with the mainland. Thus, Taipei might move to establish relations with the Soviet Union, develop nuclear weapons, or declare Taiwan an independent state.

U.S. policy makers have agonized for years over the proper approach to the Taiwan issue, and they appear no closer to a solution today than they were in the past. Since the normalization of U.S.-PRC diplomatic relations, and the passage of the Taiwan Relations Act, they have conducted a delicate balancing act between approaches favored by Peking and Taipei (and their respective supporters in the United States). Although as a presidential candidate Ronald Reagan attempted for a brief time to voice authoritative and definitive statements on

Taiwan policy, soon after he moved into the White House he reverted to the practice of previous presidents in adopting a lower public posture and avoiding pronouncements that would likely antagonize either Peking or Taipei. When statements have been made, U.S. policy makers have tended to couch them in ambiguous terms that attempt to sidestep issues sensitive to either Chinese group.

There seems to be no good alternative to a continued ambiguous U.S. policy on Taiwan, at least for the near future. Rather than confront either Peking or Taipei with one of the options noted above, U.S. leaders could strive to maintain the status quo and wait for possible changes in the PRC, Taiwan, or the United States that could make future decisions easier. Thus, for example, the passage of time could reduce the communist-nationalist historical antagonism and improve prospects for a reconciliation acceptable to both sides. The agreement announced in 1981 among Peking, Taipei, and the International Olympic Committee on Chinese representation in the world body,[9] and the recent growth in trade and other contacts between the mainland and Taiwan may be precursors to such a trend. Meanwhile, U.S. memories of the political battles over China policy could fade over time, leaving U.S. decision makers with more flexibility in the years ahead.

The FX Decision

Unfortunately, these changes will probably take a long time to develop, and U.S. leaders will be required to make some important decisions on Taiwan policy in the interim. A major recent test case was seen in the U.S. debate over whether to sell new, sophisticated fighter aircraft—popularly called the FX—to Taiwan.[10]

Before U.S.-PRC diplomatic relations were normalized, the United States followed a cautious policy regarding arms sales to Taiwan. The United States did not sell arms to Taiwan that would disrupt the process of normalization in U.S.-PRC relations, upset the ratio of military forces then prevailing in the Taiwan Straits, or contribute to Taipei's offensive military capability against the mainland. Renewed fighting between Peking and Taipei and the outbreak of serious political or social instability in Taiwan were seen as detrimental to U.S. interests. Carefully limited U.S. arms transfers to Taiwan were designed to enhance the military equilibrium in the Taiwan Straits, strengthen stability on Taiwan by affirming continued U.S. military support for the government and people of Taiwan, and avoid the transfer of powerful weapons likely to prompt a strongly hostile reaction from the PRC.

In this context, the U.S. State Department and Defense Department recommended in mid-1978 that the United States allow Taiwan to coproduce, with the U.S. Northrop Corporation, a new fighter aircraft, designated the F-5G. The plane was to be manufactured in Taiwan, after the completion in 1980 of an existing U.S. agreement with Taiwan involving coproduction of Northrop's F-5E fighter for Taiwan's air force. Presumably unwilling to jeopardize the ongoing secret talks on normalization with the PRC by selling a more modern fighter to Taiwan, President Carter turned down the State-Defense recommendation in favor of a policy that allowed for the coproduction of several dozen more F-5E fighters in Taiwan from 1980 to 1983.

When President Carter announced the establishment of U.S.-PRC diplomatic relations in late 1978 (with its provisions that the United States would end the mutual defense treaty and all official military ties with Taiwan), the administration disclosed that the United States would continue during 1979 to deliver military equipment already contracted for by Taiwan and that afterward the United States would continue to make available to Taiwan "selected defense weaponry" on a "restricted basis." Chinese leaders voiced objection to continued U.S. arms sales to Taiwan, but they did not block progress in U.S.-PRC normalization over the issue.

The Carter administration sidestepped Taiwan's repeated requests for permission to purchase a more advanced U.S. fighter. In mid-1980, seven members of the Senate Foreign Relations Committee sent a letter to the president expressing concern over the administration's continued delay on the fighter aircraft decision. On June 12, 1980, Senator Richard Stone, one of the signers of the letter, announced that the administration, in response, had decided to allow U.S. manufacturers to discuss the sales of more advanced fighter aircraft with Taiwan, but no agreement on the sales of aircraft was announced during the Carter administration.

Peking's public sensitivity on U.S.-Taiwan relations, including U.S. arms sales to Taiwan, rose markedly in mid-1980, coincident with the controversy in the U.S. presidential campaign over Ronald Reagan's criticism of the Carter administration's policy toward Taiwan and his call for an upgrading of U.S.-Taiwan relations. Peking media also implicated the United States in the December 1980 decision of the Dutch government to build two submarines for Taiwan, even though the United States subsequently denied any involvement in the Dutch decision. In an apparent demonstration of Chinese resolve to the United States and other nations considering possible sales of sensitive military equipment to Taiwan, Peking in early 1981 downgraded diplomatic relations with the Dutch from the ambassadorial to the chargé d'affaires level. Subsequently, the PRC repeatedly warned of an unspecified "strong response" if the United States continued to sell arms to Taiwan in spite of PRC objections. Western press reports said that Chinese dissatisfaction and uncertainty over U.S. policy regarding arms sales to

Taiwan was a major factor behind the PRC's refusal to send a high-level military delegation to the United States in late 1981, as had been announced by Secretary of State Haig during his visit to Peking in June of that year.

The recent U.S. debate over whether to sell advanced jet fighters to Taiwan focused, therefore, less on the strictly military implications of the possible sales than on their broader political implications for the seemingly zero-sum game of U.S. relations with the PRC and Taiwan. Most notably, the arms sales options most favored by Taiwan and by American advocates of stronger U.S.-Taiwan relations were almost invariably those most firmly opposed by the PRC and many American supporters of closer U.S.-PRC ties. U.S. congressional interest in the debate was strong and grounded in provisions of the Taiwan Relations Act and the Arms Export Control Act. The former stated that the Congress, along with the president, would determine what kinds of arms to sell to Taiwan, while the latter provided Congress with veto power over significant U.S. arms transfers abroad.

Taiwan's Military Considerations. Proponents of the U.S. sale of more sophisticated fighters to Taiwan argued strongly that Taiwan needed such planes to replace the ninety aged F-100 A/F aircraft in its current inventory with fighters capable of keeping pace with anticipated advances in PRC fighter aircraft development over the next decade. Those Taiwan supporters also noted that the Taipei government's five dozen F-5A/Bs were scheduled to reach the end of their utility in 1986. Without such sales, they asserted, the military situation in the Taiwan Straits would shift steadily in the PRC's favor, as the PRC continued to improve its fighter aircraft.

Proponents generally acknowledged that new modern fighter aircraft were not immediately needed to ensure Taiwan's survival, since military tensions in the Taiwan Straits were then at an all-time low. They stressed, however, that Peking had rapidly changed its policy toward Taiwan in the past and could do so again. Under conditions of renewed, hostile military pressure from the mainland, a strong and effective Taiwan air force of modern fighters would be an essential ingredient for Taiwan to continue deterring possible PRC attack or confronting PRC forces in the Taiwan Straits as far away from Taiwan as possible. Taiwan judged that it needed to purchase more advanced fighters, technically superior to PRC planes: There was a wide disparity in the size of the PRC and Taiwan air forces (the PRC, at least in theory, could muster a considerable portion of its 5,000 planes for use against Taiwan; Taiwan's air force had about 380 planes), and the PRC, unlike Taiwan, could increase the production of, and improve upon, the combat aircraft then in its inventory. Taiwan's best plane, the F-5E with

Sidewinder missiles, was rated equal or superior to the PRC version of the MiG-21—the best plane in production in the PRC.

Proponents of the Northrop Corporation's F-5G for sale to Taiwan added that a favorable U.S. decision was needed soon to avoid costly delays and to continue a steady supply of U.S. fighters for Taiwan. They noted that Northrop's current coproduction of F-5E fighters in Taiwan would end in mid-1983 and that more than one year and perhaps a full two years would be necessary from the time of a U.S. decision to go ahead with a coproduction arrangement with Taiwan for the F-5G before the first fighter for Taiwan's air force could be delivered.

Political-Economic Factors. Taiwan's leaders had been waiting since the 1970s for a favorable U.S. decision for a successor aircraft to the F-5E for their air force. They would have seen more delay or refusal by the United States as an important sign of further reduced U.S. support. The result reportedly could have been political instability and economic difficulty in Taiwan, with government leaders tightening security against perceived internal and external threats and international business confidence in Taiwan's future declining.

Effect on U.S.-PRC Relations. Opponents of the sale of more sophisticated U.S. fighter aircraft to Taiwan judged that Peking was likely to see the transfer of a new generation of U.S. aircraft to the island as a provocative demonstration of a U.S. intention to help keep Taiwan separate from mainland control for the foreseeable future. That could have prompted strong PRC reaction including:

- a downgrading of U.S.-PRC relations to the level that existed prior to the normalization of diplomatic relations;
- a halt in developing U.S.-PRC security cooperation;
- a cutback in U.S.-PRC exchange programs;
- a switch in the PRC's purchases of commonly available commodities (e.g., grain, cotton, soybeans) from the United States to other suppliers;
- a more hostile Chinese stance against the United States and Taiwan, perhaps including renewed PRC-Taiwan military tension to a level that prevailed before the normalization of U.S.-PRC relations; and
- a possible PRC move to seek a modus vivendi with the USSR.

Many opponents asserted that there was little need to risk such negative consequences since tensions in the Taiwan Straits were then at their lowest level in over three decades. Some added that Taiwan's security against the mainland rested not so much on improvement in Taiwan's forces as on the international constraints on PRC policy regarding Taiwan. They tended to dismiss concern about any possible negative impacts that U.S. delay or refusal of sales of jet fighters could have on Taiwan's political and economic stability. They based their arguments upon claims that Taiwan's stability depended mainly on its economic performance in relation to other world economies and that the United States could substantially reassure Taiwan with economic gestures.

The Reagan administration announced on January 11, 1982, that it had decided not to sell Taiwan jet fighters more advanced than the F-5E then in production in Taiwan. It seemed likely, however, that competing U.S.-PRC-Taiwan interests soon would come to a head once again over the issue of U.S. arms sale to Taiwan. In particular, as part of its decision in January 1982 not to sell more advanced fighter aircraft to Taiwan, the Reagan administration announced that it would continue to provide Taiwan with unspecified numbers of F-5E aircraft. Since the Northrop Corporation needed about one year's lead time to provide materials to extend its F-5E coproduction arrangement in Taiwan beyond mid-1983, important decisions on fighter aircraft sales to Taiwan had to be made soon. And yet PRC comment clearly implied that Peking would downgrade diplomatic relations with the United States, and perhaps take other negative measures, if such a major sale occurred. Taiwan, however, regarded a sale of that sort as essential to its security; U.S. refusal or delay would have been seen as a retreat from past U.S. commitments and as potentially destabilizing to the island's economic and political well-being.

Negotiations between the PRC and the United States managed to produce an at least temporary compromise that was able to bridge the gaps among the major competing interests. In an August 17, 1982 communiqué the Reagan administration said that U.S. arms sales to Taiwan would not exceed "either in qualitative or in quantitative terms" the level of those supplied during the past four years and that the United States intended gradually to reduce its sales of arms to Taiwan, leading to what the communiqué called a "final resolution." The United States also disavowed a policy of "two Chinas" or "one China, one Taiwan," and said that the U.S. government "understands and appreciates" the PRC policy of seeking a peaceful resolution of the Taiwan question as seen in recent PRC proposals for reunification talks with Taiwan. The U.S. side strongly implied that its agreement to curb arms supplies to Taiwan was contingent on a continuation of Peking's peaceful approach to the island.[11]

For its part, Peking strongly affirmed its "fundamental" peaceful policy toward Taiwan. In addition, the PRC leaders agreed to the communiqué even though it contained no reference to a fixed date for a U.S. arms cutoff, as they had demanded in the past. Moreover, Peking did not downgrade relations when the Reagan administration formally notified Congress on August 19 that the United States would extend its current coproduction arrangement in Taiwan for F-5E fighters for over two more years.

Both sides averred in the joint communiqué that they would take unspecified future measures to achieve a "final settlement" of the issue of U.S. arms sales to Taiwan "over a period of time."

The popular and congressional reaction was mixed, especially among conservatives. Critics tended to focus on the possible implications of the communiqué and related PRC demands for the future U.S. relationship with Taiwan. In particular, they asked whether the United States would have sufficient leeway under the current agreement to provide for what it viewed as Taiwan's legitimate security needs, as mandated by the Taiwan Relations Act. They also questioned whether the language of the communiqué, in which the United States disavowed any intent to pursue a "One China, One Taiwan" policy and expressed its appreciation of Peking's goal of reunifying Taiwan with the mainland, meant that the United States was committing itself to support Taiwan's eventual return to the mainland. (Some critics charged that such a stance would deny the vast majority of people on Taiwan—who opposed reunification with the PRC—the future option of continued U.S. support for Taiwan remaining separate from mainland control.)

Those who supported the agreement stressed that it avoided a rupture or downgrading of relations with the PRC without, in their view, compromising Taiwan's future or U.S. relations with Taiwan. They tended to see the ambiguities in the agreement in a positive, rather than negative, light.

An Alternative Policy Choice

Today, a suitable middle course for U.S. policy would involve the opportunity afforded by the ambiguities of the agreement to work out a strategy that adheres to the U.S. commitment gradually to curb arms sales to Taiwan and to provide for Taiwan's defense needs. So long as peace prevails in the Taiwan Straits, it seems fair for the United States gradually to cut back its sales of weapons to Taipei, arguing that existing circumstances do not require more weapons transfers. One way to provide for Taiwan's needs in the future would be quietly to transfer the know-how Taiwan requires to produce weapons on its own. At present, Taipei can provide many of its needs regarding ground forces, but it still will take several years of strenuous efforts, and some outside support, for the island to be capable of supporting itself in important areas of naval and air defense.

U.S.-PRC Military Ties

Americans will almost certainly continue to disagree strongly about the proper U.S. policy regarding military cooperation with the PRC. Support for such cooperation is likely to build so long as U.S. relations with the Soviet Union remain characterized more by hostility than by consultation, U.S. relations with China develop more closely, and Sino-Soviet relations remain cool. Peking's present stance on Taiwan, however, has placed an impediment to what many see as the next logical step forward in U.S.-PRC military ties, the sale of U.S. weapons to Peking. If and when this impediment is removed, U.S. policy makers are likely to be faced with the difficult task of satisfying conflicting American views on this sensitive issue.

A flat U.S. refusal to sell arms to the PRC would almost certainly prompt expressions of strong disappointment by PRC leaders, who would see it as a clear sign both of the United States's lack of trust in them and of U.S. determination to maintain an "arms embargo" against their country. When taken together with the Reagan administration's well-known differences with Peking over U.S.-Taiwan relations, the refusal could lead to a major reversal in Sino-American relations.

The main worry about the arms transfers and increased military cooperation is their symbolic importance, especially their implications for future U.S. policy toward the PRC and their meaning for U.S. relations with the USSR, Japan, and other Asian states. The incrementally developing U.S. security relationship with the PRC over the past decade has led from time to time to misperceptions of U.S. intentions on the part of U.S. interest groups, the Soviet Union, Asian countries, and even the PRC leaders. If U.S. officials maintain a vagueness about the PRC's place in U.S. security policy while they move ahead with more military transfers to the PRC, various interested parties could misinterpret U.S. objectives, and their reactions could well be contrary to U.S. interests. Thus, PRC leaders could incorrectly see such transfers as signaling a major strengthening of what they may view as the United States's commitment to protect the PRC's security against the USSR. Soviet leaders might perceive them as the consummation of a de facto U.S.-PRC military alliance that must be actively resisted by the USSR. Japan and other U.S. allies and friends in Asia could see them as signaling a fundamental shift in U.S. interest in Asia, away from them and toward the PRC as the main backer of U.S. security concerns in the region.

By contrast, a different approach that would allow the United States to make clearer to the various interested parties the limited objectives of its China policy could reduce the possible adverse consequences for

U.S. interests. Under this alternative, the United States would agree to increase to a carefully limited degree its military transfers to China, including some defensive weapons or related technology, and would use the opportunity to serve notice to Peking that the PRC leaders should expect no more such military help until Sino-American relations have matured over several years. This policy would remain in effect unless there were a gross change in the international balance of power or a substantial increase in Soviet military power in Asia designed to pressure China into a less pro-U.S. posture. The United States could continue to solidify its ties with the PRC in economic and political areas that are seen as having few negative consequences for U.S. interests.

Clarifying the limits of Sino-American military cooperation to the leaders of the Soviet Union would be particularly important. U.S. officials could note in conversations with the Soviets that U.S. supplies to China are in part governed by a desire to maintain, but not to narrow substantially, the current gap in the military capabilities of Sino-Soviet forces along China's northern border. Thus, Moscow would know that any major Soviet effort to expand its military power in Asia to intimidate the PRC would likely prompt increased U.S. support for Peking's military modernization.

Japan and other Asian states would also have to be reassured. A solid consensus in the United States in support of the limited military relationship with China would appear to be required. Such a consensus might prove difficult to build and yet remain within the confines of the limited military relationship noted above, since some members of Congress might be inclined to ask for a quid pro quo for U.S. military help to the PRC. Although this could involve preferential treatment granted by Peking to U.S. business representatives in trade with the PRC, some U.S. representatives might also demand that the United States be compensated with increased military access to China (e.g., basing rights or more intelligence-gathering facilities). Of course, such a move would be likely to increase further the risks of Soviet and other foreign reactions contrary to U.S. interests.

Another option would be to use limited military transfers as the first in a series of steps to some sort of mutual security arrangement with the PRC against the USSR. Those steps could include U.S. training of Chinese military personnel, the stationing of U.S. military experts in China, the presence of more U.S. intelligence facilities there, Sino-American maneuvers and exercises, and U.S. planning with Chinese forces. While such an approach would clearly have at least a short-term positive impact on U.S.-PRC relations, it would make almost impossible any lasting U.S. reassurance of the Soviet Union and other interested Asian nations about U.S. intentions toward China. Should

U.S. planners pursue this option, they probably ought to continue an ambiguous and secretive policy in regard to U.S.-PRC security ties. As noted above, such a policy would carry the risk of prompting extreme international reactions that could seriously complicate U.S. interests both at home and abroad.

In sum, U.S. refusal to sell any weapons or related technology to the PRC or to move ahead with Peking in other areas of military cooperation could seriously affect Sino-American relations and, by extension, a variety of important U.S. interests in world affairs. But the risks of moving ahead with such sales—whether or not they are designed to foster a closer Sino-American mutual security arrangement against the Soviet Union—will remain great so long as U.S. leaders remain vague about the objectives of their strategic relationship with China. The risks of a carefully limited U.S. military transfer to China could be reduced substantially if U.S. leaders shifted to a more clearly defined policy of moderate objectives toward Peking that could assure friends and foes alike of American intentions toward the PRC.

U.S.-PRC Economic Relations

More clarity and caution will also be needed in U.S. planning for economic relations with the PRC. Even though developing purely economic relations has few of the drawbacks that make Sino-American military cooperation so controversial and potentially dangerous for U.S. interests, there are pitfalls that should be avoided in the road ahead.

At present, a consensus seems to support encouraging increases in Sino-American trade and completing previously announced U.S. plans for economic relations with China. Many of the latter proposals were mentioned during Vice President Mondale's trip to the PRC in 1979 and have already been fulfilled—China now receives MFN tariff treatment and is eligible for Ex-Im Bank loans and OPIC guarantees. The United States, however, has still only begun to deliver on Mondale's pledge of up to $2 billion worth of Ex-Im Bank loans for U.S. trade with the PRC through 1984.

Recently, officials in the Reagan administration and Congress have proposed changes in U.S. laws to reduce and eliminate residual legal barriers, imposed during the cold war, on economic interchange with the PRC.[12] It is unlikely that these changes will have anything but a positive effect on U.S. interests, at least over the short term. For the most part, the legal barriers are minor irritants in Sino-American relations.

A notable exception is the Foreign Assistance Act, which prohibits the United States from giving aid to the PRC. Once that law is changed,

U.S. leaders will confront a new and much more controversial series of options on aid to China. If recent practice is any guide, Chinese leaders are likely to encourage the United States to become an active supporter of their economic and military modernization drive. Also, some U.S. leaders are likely to view increases in U.S. aid as a barometer of the "forward movement" they seek in U.S.-PRC relations.

The result could be a rapidly growing U.S. aid program in China that could have several important disadvantages for U.S. interests. For one thing, it would identify the United States very closely with the current "four modernizations" programs in the PRC. If those programs do not succeed—and U.S. specialists tend to agree that they will be only a partial success at best—Chinese leaders may portray the U.S. aid effort as a main cause of failure.[13] (PRC leaders followed a similar practice in the late 1950s when they blamed alleged inadequacies of the major Soviet aid effort for Chinese economic failure.)

In their enthusiasm to show support for and to build closer relations with China, U.S. leaders may commit the United States to backing economic development projects in the PRC that later might appear ill advised. This is especially likely now, since the Chinese have no clear program for modernization and development and are constantly changing their priorities. A case in point is Japan's major commitment in 1979 to assist the PRC's multibillion dollar steel mill in Baoshan, near Shanghai. At the time, the commitment was hailed by both sides as a paradigm of foreign efforts to help the PRC's modernization, but within two years the PRC so changed its economic priorities that it came to view the Japanese-aided plant as an enormously expensive white elephant sucking scarce economic resources away from the nation's modernization. As a result, in 1981 the Chinese tried to cancel contracts with Japanese suppliers of equipment for the plant, which led to strong Japanese protests and the rise of the most serious friction in Sino-Japanese relations in recent years.

U.S. leaders may also make aid commitments that will fail because of changed circumstances in the United States—e.g., the Ex-Im Bank's inability, because of growing budgetary constraints, to meet the $2 billion loan commitment made by Vice President Mondale in 1979. Meanwhile, current recipients of U.S. foreign assistance are likely to resent any new, large-scale U.S. aid to the PRC. Recognizing that foreign aid is unpopular in the United States and unlikely to be substantially increased, they see U.S. aid as a zero-sum game in which any new aid for China will come at their expense. As a result, large and rapid increases in U.S. aid for the PRC could seriously alienate those states from the United States. (In recent years, the members of the Association for Southeast Asian Nations—Thailand, Singapore, Malaysia, Indonesia, and the Philippines—have been particularly sensitive that their interests will suffer in the event of increased U.S. assistance to the PRC.)

Perhaps the greatest potential danger concerns possible U.S. military aid to China. As the United States ends legal restrictions on assistance to the PRC, it will be able to develop an arms sales relationship with Peking well beyond its current, largely symbolic importance. Recent large-scale U.S. offers of military aid to other countries in Asia important to U.S. competition with the Soviet Union (e.g., Pakistan) also appear to set a precedent for large military aid offers to the anti-Soviet Chinese. As was noted in the earlier discussion of U.S.-PRC military cooperation, such a large-scale relationship would risk having seriously negative consequences for important U.S. interests in relations with the Soviet Union, non-communist Asian countries, and the PRC.

Secrecy Versus Openness in U.S. China Policy

Ever since the beginning of the Sino-American reconciliation, U.S. policy makers have found it easier to develop relations with the PRC from behind a veil of secrecy than by consulting broadly and building a consensus among U.S. leaders. Such an approach prevents leaks that could offend Chinese sensitivities, avoids signaling U.S.-PRC intentions to the USSR, and allows the United States to deal with the Taiwan issue and other sensitive problems free from pressure and interference from partisan groups in the United States. It also allows the administration to hide internal differences and mistakes over China policy from public view.

The main disadvantages of this approach are that it has led to distorted American perceptions and expectations of the PRC, precluded the building of a solid consensus on China policy, and contradicted basic U.S. ideals of democracy and popular sovereignty. By restricting access to information about the PRC, U.S. policy makers—in an effort to win support for forward movement in relations with Peking—have been able to cover over negative aspects of China and to accentuate its positive accomplishments and compatibility with U.S. interests as a "friend" of the United States. President Carter hailed the Chinese as "our new and great friends"[14] while other U.S. administration spokesmen have noted in briefings, speeches, and off-the-record comments during the ongoing PRC power struggle how "stable" and "unified" PRC leaders were. They have frequently added during the painful Chinese economic readjustment since 1978 how "pragmatic" and "wise" those leaders have been on economic affairs.[15]

Such rhetoric overemphasizes the PRC's positive aspects and the commonness of Sino-American interests. It also does little to prepare the American people and their government representatives for the probable frictions, disputes, and disappointments that will arise in Sino-American relations in the future. As a result, the United States is likely to be surprised and perhaps sharply disillusioned when Chinese leaders fail to support U.S. interests or otherwise live up to U.S. expectations at some future time. (American historians of U.S.-PRC relations remember all too clearly how the United States went through similar "love-hate" extremes the last time that the United States became closely involved with a Chinese leadership—Chiang Kai-shek's Chinese Nationalists during the 1930s and 1940s. They recall the disastrous results of that episode for U.S. interests and want to avoid repetition in the current era.)

Meanwhile, because secrecy has made the implications of China policy poorly understood in the United States, support for U.S.-PRC reconciliation has been potentially unstable—a development vividly seen at the start of the Reagan administration. If China policy were more open and better understood among the American people and their government representatives, probably no U.S. president would be able even to consider endangering the entire substance of the U.S.-PRC relationship for the sake of a political gesture by reestablishing official relations with Taiwan.

Secrecy in China policy is also antithetical to the important ideal in U.S. government that the American people, through their representatives in both the executive and legislative branches, should be informed of the full implications of new policies, such as the developing relationship with the PRC, and should have some say in the formulation of those policies. Such a popular representative role seems all the more appropriate at a time when the United States is considering spending U.S. tax revenue to improve economic relations with China and after ten years of gradual U.S. efforts to build up a strategic relationship with the PRC—a commitment that may have to be backed in the future by the use of U.S. military personnel.

In sum, it seems clear that the time is long overdue for the establishment of a better balance between consensus-building and forward movement in U.S. relations with the PRC. It will, of course, be difficult and extremely time consuming for U.S. leaders to establish a consensus over China policy. It will probably lead to a further slowing of progress in U.S.-PRC relations, as Americans try to sort out their differences and their interests vis-à-vis China. Issues like Taiwan and U.S.-Soviet-PRC relations are likely to continue to divide them well into the future.

But without a better understanding of where they agree and disagree, U.S. leaders will likely be prone to follow past practice and push the relationship with the PRC further, only to see the potentially unstable structure of Sino-American reconciliation come crashing down around them if they meet serious difficulties or make mistakes in relations with China in the years ahead. For those interested in building a lasting Sino-American relationship, based on the long-term interests of both sides, it seems essential that U.S. leaders begin opening up China policy to greater public discussion and review so that the U.S. approach to the PRC will truly reflect U.S. national interests and intentions.

10

Notes

Chapter 1

1. Quoted by the New China News Agency (cited as NCNA), May 28, 1980, and replayed in U.S., Foreign Broadcast Information Service, Daily Report, *China* (cited as FBIS DR China), May 29, 1980.

2. Thus, for example:

• The PRC called for the establishment of a long-term strategic relationship with the United States as a vital link in the international united front it was developing against the USSR. Following the Soviet-backed Vietnamese invasion of Cambodia in 1978 and the Soviet invasion of Afghanistan in 1979, the United States increased efforts to foster international resistance to Soviet expansion and gave more favorable attention to the PRC's role in opposing the USSR. By the end of 1980, the United States and the PRC had established a successful record of close collaboration to help check the growth of Soviet and Soviet-backed power via Afghanistan in Southwest Asia and via Vietnam in Southeast Asia.

• The United States showed repeated surpluses in its trade with the PRC, and the PRC gained access to important U.S. agricultural products, technical expertise, and equipment needed for its economic modernization efforts.

• Cultural, educational, and tourist exchanges grew enormously, with tens of thousands of Americans traveling to the PRC each year and many thousands of Chinese coming to the United States for study or official tours.

3. Typical of the prevailing discord in the United States, some leaders in the Reagan administration have asserted that the United States should base its policy toward Taiwan on the Taiwan Relations Act. (The law, passed in April 1979, regulates U.S. relations with the island following the normalization of U.S.-PRC diplomatic relations.) Since the law both assumes that Taiwan will remain separate from the mainland for the foreseeable future and states that the United States will protect Taiwan from PRC pressure to change that status, Peking's leaders have said that it is totally unacceptable to them and incompatible with PRC interests. They have added that the law also contradicts U.S. commitments made in the Sino-American normalization communiqué of December 1978, in which the United States acknowledged the PRC position that Taiwan is part of China and recognized the PRC as the sole legal government

of China. In effect, the communiqué placed the United States on record as implicitly but unmistakably supporting the eventual union of Taiwan and the mainland. Other American leaders who are sensitive to Peking's views and mindful of past U.S. commitments have judged that U.S. policy toward Taiwan should be based on American statements made in the December 1978 communiqué—an approach more compatible with PRC interests.

Of course, Sino-American relations have also been affected by differences and difficulties in China as well as in the United States. For example, erratic progress in Peking's economic modernization, leadership differences over ideology and political and social reform, and other concerns have combined to foster serious problems in the 1980s. As a result, the already serious difficulties faced by Chinese Communist Party (CCP) Standing Committee member Deng Xiaoping and his associates in the PRC have been compounded as they strive to push China toward economic and political modernization.

Even though Deng and other reformers have been outspoken in favoring closer ties with the United States as an important part of their programs for the PRC's development, Chinese internal difficulties have threatened to upset the new Sino-American relationship. In particular, as the PRC was forced to cut back on imports of Western technology, the importance of economic ties with the United States was reduced. As leaders of the Reagan administration called for developing closer ties with Taiwan, the compromises Deng and his associates made in reaching the normalization agreement with the United States in December 1978 were called into question. Moreover, as the PRC's inability to provide both rapid economic development and effective military modernization became more evident, Chinese leaders began to debate the wisdom of Deng's policy of favoring the United States and opposing the Soviet Union. Some argued that a more evenhanded Chinese policy toward the superpowers would be more suitable, especially since the PRC needed to focus on economic development and to reduce military spending for the next several years. (For a useful wrap-up on the situation in the PRC, see U.S., Congress, Joint Economic Committee, *China Under the Four Modernizations* (Washington, D.C.: U.S. Government Printing Office, 1982).

4. Stanley Backrack, *The Committee of One Million: The China Lobby and U.S. Policy, 1953–1972.* (New York: Columbia University Press, 1976).

5. For background on the Sino-American reconciliation begun under Nixon, see A. Doak Barnett, *China and the Major Powers in East Asia* (Washington, D.C.: Brookings Institution, 1977); Michel Oksenberg and Robert B. Oxnam, *Dragon and Eagle* (New York: Basic Books, 1978); and Robert G. Sutter, *China Watch: Toward Sino-American Reconciliation* (Baltimore: Johns Hopkins University Press, 1978).

6. In the course of preparing this book, the author conducted more than one hundred interviews with U.S. officials and other American leaders concerned with China policy questions, including over thirty interviews with Carter administration officials. Some of the latter had been at high levels in the administration; one had held cabinet rank. Since the intent of the interviews was to elicit as frank an assessment as possible of differing perspectives on

issues in U.S. China policy, and many of these issues remain matters of institutional and personal sensitivity, individuals with whom the author spoke were assured that their comments would not be for attribution.

For general background information on the normalization decision, see Stanley Karnow, "East Asia in 1978: The Great Transformation," in William P. Bundy, ed., *Foreign Affairs: America and the World in 1978* (New York: Pergamon Press, 1979), pp. 589–612.

7. The views of Vance and Shulman were publicly laid out after their departures from office. See Cyrus Vance's article, "American Foreign Policy for the Pacific Nations," *International Security* 5, no. 3 (Winter 1980/81): 3–13, and Marshall Shulman's article in the *Los Angeles Times,* July 5, 1981.

8. This view was widely held among officials interviewed, although Dr. Brzezinski was not known to articulate it for the record while he was in office. For a clear, early indication of his assessment of the PRC's potential role in U.S. foreign policy, see his speeches during his May 1978 visit to China and his remarks at the Department of State briefing on China on January 15, 1979. The former are available in FBIS DR China, May 24–30, 1978. The latter are replayed in U.S., Department of State, Bureau of Public Affairs, *U.S. Policy Toward China, July 15, 1971–January 15, 1979,* Selected Documents no. 9, pp. 61–64.

Since leaving office, Dr. Brzezinski has been more frank in talking about his assessment of the PRC's role in U.S. foreign policy as well as of what he calls "the fierce struggle" within the U.S. government over expanding relations with China during the Carter administration. See his interview in the *Asian Wall Street Journal,* March 24, 1981.

9. See NCNA, March 23, 1979, in FBIS DR China, March 26, 1979.

10. The statement is replayed in *Congressional Record,* August 28, 1980, pp. E 4112–13.

11. See, in particular, comment on the sale in the *People's Daily,* January 20, 1981, and February 5, 1981.

12. For background on this issue, see U.S., Library of Congress, Congressional Research Service, *China-U.S.-Soviet Relations,* Issue Brief no. IB 79115 (Washington, D.C.: periodically updated).

13. See the testimony of Reagan administration witnesses at a hearing on U.S.-PRC economic relations held on July 16, 1981, by the U.S., Congress, House Foreign Affairs Committee, Subcommittee on Asian and Pacific Affairs.

Chapter 2

1. Some observers in the United States and in the PRC insist that the China lobby remains a strong influence on U.S. politics, particularly in the Congress, and blame the lobby for some of the dilemmas in contemporary U.S. China policy. They have alleged, for example, that the work of the lobby is reflected in large measure in Congress's protection of U.S. ties with Taiwan by adding controversial amendments to the Taiwan Relations Act in 1979 and in its sale of U.S. fighter aircraft to Taiwan. In fact, the record shows that the lobby's importance in formulating U.S. China policy has been on the wane since the

late 1960s. The record demonstrates as well that congressional attitudes have come to be based far more on an increasingly sophisticated view of the PRC, Taiwan, and U.S. interests in relations with them than on the influence of any lobby group.

2. Cited in William Watts et al., *Japan, Korea and China: American Perceptions and Policies* (Lexington, Mass.: D. C. Heath, 1979), p. 128.

3. The hearings are reviewed in Congressional Quarterly, *China: U.S. Policy Since 1945* (Washington, D.C., 1980), p. 33.

4. Ibid., p. 36.

5. For a good wrap-up of congressional reaction to Nixon's policy and the UN vote, see ibid., pp. 36–39.

6. For background on U.S.-PRC relations during the Nixon and Ford administrations, see A. Doak Barnett, *China and the Major Powers in East Asia* (Washington, D.C.: Brookings Institution, 1977); Michel Oksenberg and Robert B. Oxnam, *Dragon and Eagle* (New York: Basic Books, 1978); Robert G. Sutter, *China Watch: Toward Sino-American Reconciliation* (Baltimore: Johns Hopkins University Press, 1978); and U.S. Library of Congress, Congressional Research Service, *China-U.S. Relations,* Issue Brief no. 76053 (Washington, D.C., December 13, 1978), pp. 1–4.

7. See Barnett, *China and the Major Powers;* Oksenberg and Oxnam, *Dragon and Eagle;* Sutter, *China Watch;* and Watts et al., *Japan, Korea and China,* pp. 103–123.

8. U.S., Congress, Senate, *Journey to the New China* (Washington, D.C.: U.S. Government Printing Office, 1972), p. 6.

9. U.S., Congress, House, *Report of a Visit to the People's Republic of China* (Washington, D.C.: U.S. Government Printing Office, 1976), p. 4.

Meanwhile, delegates led by Congressman Melvin Price said in regard to their visit during 1976 that "the message that the Chinese wanted us to hear came through loud and clear: detente is a myth and efforts to appease the Soviet Union in the hope of postponing or avoiding war will simply repeat the errors of Chamberlain and Daladier in seeking to appease Hitler prior to World War II." (U.S., Congress, House, Committee on Armed Services, *Visit to the People's Republic of China.* [Washington, D.C.: U.S. Government Printing Office, 1976], p. 8.)

10. U.S., Congress, *Report of a Visit to the People's Republic of China,* p. 8.

11. U.S., Congress, *Ninth Congressional Delegation to the People's Republic of China* (Washington, D.C.: U.S. Government Printing Office, 1976), p. 2.

12. U.S., Congress, Senate, *The United States and China* (Washington, D.C.: U.S. Government Printing Office, 1976), pp. 2–3.

13. U.S., Congress, Senate, *China Enters the Post-Mao Era* (Washington, D.C.: U.S. Government Printing Office, 1976), p. 8.

14. U.S., Congress, *Ninth Congressional Delegation to the People's Republic of China,* p. 21.

15. Ibid., p. 28.

16. Congressional delegates led by Senator Charles Percy noted some of the basic impediments in U.S.-PRC trade in reporting on their visit to Peking in 1975. They said:

> For the future, China's government will not ask for loans and will accept only "genuine export credits," meaning medium-term deferred payments. There is no willingness to accept joint investments. . . . The emphasis is on self-reliance and self-sufficiency, principles permitting little opportunity for international collaboration on either a bilateral or multilateral basis. The Chinese in the main will rely on their own labor, not on significant imports of capital technology or equipment. [U.S., Congress, *The United States and China*, A Report by the Seventh Congressional Delegation to the People's Republic of China (Washington, D.C.: U.S. Government Printing Office, 1976), p. 18.]

17. U.S., Congress, *Journey to the New China*, p. 21. Some congressional visitors expressed dissatisfaction with the relatively strict format imposed upon travelers to the PRC; they also questioned Peking's willingness to reciprocate U.S. visits by sending delegations to the United States. They noted, for one thing, that while many thousands of Americans had traveled to the PRC, only a small fraction of that number of Chinese had visited the United States. Congressman Edward Derwinski commented that the delegation he accompanied to the PRC in 1975 "had a very carefully controlled schedule with visits to model factories, model communes, model workers apartments—which I personally feel utilized the 'Potemkin village' strategy. We were permitted limited but carefully arranged conversations with selected factory and commune workers, who, I believe, were well coached in advance of our visit. . . . At the official level, there was a similar lack of genuine conversation." (U.S., Congress, *Ninth Congressional Delegation to the People's Republic of China*, p. 27.) "Potemkin village" refers to idyllic villages built by a Russian official to give touring Russian rulers the impression that rural conditions were good.

18. Senator Henry Jackson summed up the Chinese world view when he reported on his visit to Peking in July 1974:

> At the center of Chinese concern is what they perceive to be the unreliable and expansionist nature of the Soviet Union. While the Chinese are optimistic about their capacity to handle their border situation and defend themselves on the basis of self-reliance—relying on their own strength—they see Soviet policy as directed in part at the encirclement and isolation of China.
>
> The Chinese have reiterated regularly that their long-run goal is the withdrawal of all foreign troops and elimination of all foreign bases, wherever they are situated abroad. But for the present the Chinese are far more concerned about what they perceive to be expansionist pressures of current Soviet policy in areas of strategic importance.
>
> China's current stated position is that the Russians are "feinting to the East in order to attack in the West." The Chinese are troubled by the weakness of Europe and the need for greater unity among the Western allies. They recognize that security in their own region is affected by what happens in Europe, and they are encouraging a strong North Atlantic Treaty Organization and discouraging any immediate withdrawal of United States troops from Europe. They fear that if the Soviets no longer had to reckon with a credible NATO in the West they could

further intensify their political and military pressure in the East. . . . While in principle the Chinese favor the elimination of all foreign bases, they recognize that Japan is under threat from Soviet missiles and troops, and they do not now criticize the U.S.-Japan security treaty or the presence of American bases in Japan. [U.S., Congress, Senate, *China and American Policy* (Washington, D.C.: U.S. Government Printing Office, 1974), pp. 1–2.]

19. U.S., Congress, *Ninth Congressional Delegation to the People's Republic of China,* p. 20.

20. As Senator Mansfield said following a visit to the PRC in November 1976:

> For more than two decades the United States closed its official mind to China and the channels of effective communication between the two nations were blocked. The consequences of this period of know-nothingness still linger. Miscalculations about China may well have been the main factor in the involvement of the United States in two major wars in Asia in a single generation. Pressures are at work which would cause another major miscalculation over Taiwan. [U.S., Congress, *China Enters the Post-Mao Era,* p. 40.]

21. U.S., Congress, House, *China: One Step Further Toward Normalization* (Washington, D.C.: U.S. Government Printing Office, 1975), p. 4. In a similar vein, Senator Sam Nunn noted following his trip to the PRC in 1975 that:

> The PRC, in their words, are committed to supporting revolution in the world but are opposed to all form of hegemony and to exporting revolution. They explain this vague and subtle distinction by their expressed belief that revolution can only be generated and controlled by a country's own people. They vigorously deny all efforts to dominate others except, of course, Taiwan, which they consider to be part of the PRC.
>
> Only future events will determine whether supporting but not exporting revolution is a distinction without a difference. Actions, not words, will also make clear, in the future, whether the PRC will gradually begin to play a useful and constructive role in Asia and the world. [U.S., Congress, *Ninth Congressional Delegation to the People's Republic of China,* p. 32.]

Congressional visitors devoted special attention to assessing the future of the Sino-Soviet rift. While most expressed confidence that a Sino-Soviet reconciliation—and possible attendant difficulties for the United States—remained remote so long as Zhou Enlai and Mao Zedong were alive, some raised questions about the possible courses Peking might follow in the post-Mao period. Congressmen Lester Wolff and J. Herbert Burke noted such questions in response to signs of leadership instability in Peking during a visit there in April 1976. The death of Zhou Enlai and the purge of Vice Premier Deng Xiaoping in early 1976 were followed by a mass demonstration at Tien An Men square on April 5, 1976, which was seen by many observers as an unusual breakdown of authority in the Chinese capital. Congressmen Wolff and Burke judged that these events indicated a strong difference of opinion between so-called radical and moderate leaders in Peking, and they wondered "what are the implications for the world scene should the post-Mao era be marked by visible upheavals?" They added the question, "Should a relatively stable leadership emerge, does continuity in foreign policy necessarily follow?" (U.S., Congress, House, *United States–China: Future Foreign Policy Directions* [Washington, D.C.: U.S. Government Printing Office, 1976], p. 15.)

22. U.S., Congress, *Ninth Congressional Delegation to the People's Republic of China*, p. 27.

23. U.S., Congress, *The United States and China*, p. 1.

24. U.S., Congress, House, *Impressions of the New China* (Washington, D.C.: U.S. Government Printing Office, 1972), p. 1. Noting that PRC officials' management of foreign visitors might pose a possible impediment to understanding Chinese internal affairs, Senator Hugh Scott said in regard to his trip to the PRC in 1976 that:

> As many other American visitors to China, including Members of the Congress, over the past four years have discovered, the Chinese are generous and exacting hosts. They learn of your interests and wants and do the best they can to satisfy them. They expose you to a staggering variety of impressions by means of a complete schedule of visits to institutions and with leading persons. They ask you to listen respectfully to their explanations of what it is that you are seeing. The visitor to China is a beholder of the scene, and a passive listener to the words of hospitable, earnest and dedicated persons responsible for the place, the program, the event or the institution concerned. Visitors do not cross question. . . .
>
> Chinese management of an itinerary of this sort allows even the most well prepared and perceptive traveler very limited opportunity for research or systematic interrogation of those who obviously are in possession of information of interest or value. A traveler must be either very bold or very foolish to make claim to accuracy in his impressions or to assert that impressions formed in one location fairly represent anything more than that. [U.S., Congress, *The United States and China*, pp. 5, 10.]

Of course, some congressional delegates did not share Senator Scott's views. Senator Mike Mansfield, for instance, judged that he had ample opportunity during his three visits to the PRC to move about and obtain information through on-the-spot observation and talks with PRC representatives. (U.S., Congress, *Journey to the New China*, pp. 1–2.)

In contrast, Congressman Derwinski was more pointed than Senator Scott when he asserted that the Peking leaders appeared to have deliberately orchestrated his visit in order to portray a very positive image and prevent him from seeing the actual conditions inside China. (U.S., Congress, *Ninth Congressional Delegation to the People's Republic of China*, p. 27.)

25. The Shanghai Communiqué established the basis for exchanges between the United States and the PRC. It said that: "The two sides agreed that it is desirable to broaden the understanding between the two peoples. To this end, they discussed specific areas in such fields as science, technology, culture, sports, and journalism, in which people-to-people contacts and exchanges would be mutually beneficial. Each side undertakes to facilitate further development of such contacts and exchanges."

26. Typical of this view was the comment of Senator Warren Magnuson in regard to his group's visit to the PRC in 1973:

The object for which we were invited, however, and for which we went, was not to sit in judgment of another society, but rather to enlarge our understanding of that society and of how our two countries might further develop a relationship based on the principle of equality and mutual benefit. Whatever our group's individual political philosophies, and they vary greatly within a common value system, none of us came away with any doubt as to the wisdom, indeed the necessity, for increased understanding and continuing improvement in U.S.-PRC relations. The very seriousness of purpose of the Chinese, with a population of 800 million and a rapidly developing military force, brought home to us the importance of seeking to build a bridge of confidence now, when for the first time in 25 years conditions in both our countries are favorable for rapprochement. [U.S., Congress, *China Report* (Washington, D.C.: U.S. Government Printing Office, 1973), p. 11.]

27. U.S., Congress, *China Enters the Post-Mao Era,* p. 40.

28. U.S., Congress, *Ninth Congressional Delegation to the People's Republic of China,* p. 4.

29. The members of Congressman Anderson's delegation said: "Both countries should continue to build on the foundation that has been laid to enlarge the areas of common interest. The task is not an easy one. The Chinese view the relationship with hard-headed realism; we must do the same, avoiding the illusions and romanticism which sometimes characterized the American attitude towards China in the past." [Ibid., p. 4.]

30. U.S., Congress, *Journey to the New China,* p. 2.

31. Ibid., p. 4.

32. U.S., Congress, Senate, *China: A Quarter Century After the Founding of the People's Republic* (Washington, D.C.: U.S. Government Printing Office, 1975), p. 3. The senator also offered a positive assessment of medical care and the educational system in the PRC. He noted in his report:

After the establishment of the People's Republic of China in 1949, the new government was faced with a population plagued by malnutrition, communicable and parasitic diseases, and inadequate health facilities and personnel. Everywhere there were scurvy-ridden, lice-infested, potbellied children with inflamed eyes, and countless beggars. An open prostitution problem existed as did rampant venereal disease and tuberculosis. . . . Now there has evolved a system which provides universal basic health care. It is a system which has eliminated venereal disease, controlled tuberculosis, partially controlled malaria and schistosomiasis, and made world-recognized achievements in burn therapy, re-implantation of amputated extremities and digits, and in the treatment of fractures. The system has given rebirth and new significance to traditional Chinese medicine in the usage of acupuncture. [Ibid, p. 4.]

He went on to note:

Education is free and compulsory for seven to nine years, varying in length from area to area. . . . Education in China is directed to practical application, not to learning for the sake of learning. Young children are taught to read and write and are generally prepared for limited specialized training. Work and other ethical values are also instilled in them in accordance with Maoist concepts. At the secondary level, education is usually combined with practical experience keyed to turning out persons capable of going directly to jobs in the communes and factories. Additional on-the-job training takes place later. Those destined to be skilled technicians, for instance, go through an apprenticeship of several years. [Ibid., p. 10.]

33. For example, Congressman Anderson's delegation pointed out that "massive inputs of human labor" were required to construct irrigation systems, which had significantly alleviated China's age-old problems of flood and drought. They noted that the leveling of incomes in the PRC had been "forced" on the people by the government and added that "millions of urban youth who could not be absorbed into the urban work force have been sent down to the countryside to work in communes."

The delegates also pointed out that the PRC system appeared not always to live up to its own stated objectives and principles. Thus, they said that a PRC "objective is an egalitarian society—but in one factory we visited the wage differential was about five to one." Noting a contrast of achievements and shortfalls in the PRC educational system, they said that "China undoubtedly has the largest primary school system in the world—but many universities have not resumed normal activities since the disruption of the Cultural Revolution in the mid 1960s." (U.S., Congress, *Ninth Congressional Delegation to the People's Republic of China,* pp. 3–6.)

The delegates did not comment extensively on medical care in the PRC, but other congressional visitors noted that Peking's record in raising the standard of basic health care had been achieved by turning out a large number of paramedics while giving less attention to broadly qualified and well-trained doctors. (U.S., Congress, *Journey to the New China,* pp. 19–20.)

34. U.S., Congress, *Visit to the People's Republic of China,* pp. 24–25.

35. U.S., Congress, *Ninth Congressional Delegation to the People's Republic of China,* p. 28.

36. U.S., Congress, *China: A Quarter Century After the Founding of the People's Republic,* p. 34. The senator viewed the current system as both consistent with Chinese tradition and accepted well by the Chinese people as a means to advance unity and national development. He pointed out that:

Politics permeates China's daily life, from the high government officials in Peking to peasants in the remote communes. The traditional Chinese concepts of family loyalty and group activity have been extended to make the Chinese people into a pyramid of families. At the apex is the leadership of an integrated Chinese nation. Pride in common accomplishment and faith in a common future are evident everywhere. China today is more united than ever before in its history. [U.S., Congress, *China: A Quarter Century After the Founding of the People's Republic,* p. 1.]

The senator also stated that women enjoyed equality with men in the PRC and that "a casual sense of freedom" and "easy egalitarianism" marked relations between citizens of the PRC and their leaders. He also pointed to the organization of the rural commune in positive terms, noting: "The communes are in the nature of agro-towns and are a fundamental economic unit of the new China. They are also a new concept in social organization which acts to broaden and extend the virtues of interdependence of the old Chinese family system into a community of cooperation and group-action by many families." (U.S., Congress, *Journey to the New China,* p. 3.)

37. U.S., Congress, *Ninth Congressional Delegation to the People's Republic of China,* p. 9. Congressmen Hale Boggs and Gerald Ford recited a list of "troubling impressions" following their visit to the PRC in 1972. They said that:

> Chairman Mao [Zedong], despite rare public appearances, is ubiquitous: his presence is felt everywhere. Enormous color portraits of the Chairman are found atop major public buildings. His portrait adorns the walls of virtually all public rooms, factories, classrooms and homes we visited. Quotations from Mao's writings— usually exhorting the population to greater production or increased vigilance—are spread over gigantic banners hung from public buildings, or lettered in white on huge red billboards. Radios and public loudspeakers give forth an undeviating fare of martial music, political instruction, and songs whose themes ordinarily extol the nobility of peasant labor, the heroism of factory workers, the decency and courage of the people's liberation army, and the omnipresence of hostile outside forces.
>
> No non-Chinese newspapers, books, films or magazines are anywhere in evidence. Instead, all Chinese books, newspapers and magazines are state produced. Literature appears to consist of dogmatic collections of news, stories or poems whose unalterable themes are those of overcoming obstacles, exercising vigilance, and performing acts of heroism in the struggle to meet factory or farm production goals.
>
> The individual is important only as a tiny part of the whole; there seems to be no place for individual freedom to dissent, to disagree, to seek, discover or pursue alternatives. The political discourse is a scramble toward the center to avoid the perilous extremes of ultra-leftism or ultra-rightism.
>
> The highly organized system of child-care, from pre-school to after-school— and the use of that system to inculcate in the children a veneration of the state and obedience to its leaders—is awesome in its possible implications for the future. Writing, art, music, dance, drama and even supervised play—all teach a complete devotion to the heroes, the tasks, the purposes and policies of the system. [U.S., Congress, *Impressions of the New China,* pp. 2–3.]

38. U.S., Congress, *United States–China,* pp. 14–15.

39. U.S., Congress, *The United States and China,* p. 8.

40. U.S., Congress, *China: A Quarter Century After the Founding of the People's Republic,* p. 1.

41. Agriculture was said to be the foundation of the PRC economy and the primary economic concern of PRC planners. Next in the list of priorities was light industry, followed by heavy industry. As Senator Mansfield pointed out:

> Agriculture comes first, followed by light industry, and last, heavy industry. Light industry and agriculture are closely linked because two thirds of the raw materials for light industry come from agriculture. Growth in agriculture and light industrial sections provides the basis for financing as well as the market for heavy industry, which in turn produces the machinery, transport, and so on that sustain progress in agriculture and light industry. [U.S., Congress, *China Enters the Post-Mao Era,* p. 23.]

Regarding military strategy, Congressmen Wolff and Burke appeared to sum up the PRC view as seen in other congressional reports when they noted that:

> China will pursue an independent and self-reliant course in the conduct of her military affairs as well as in her foreign policy. Her posture toward the Soviet Union is a defensive one, we were told; her war preparedness consists primarily of sheer weight of millions of land forces and a massive network of underground tunnels and shelters. . . .
>
> It was maintained that the Chinese defense would be such that its meat would be too tough to bite. It was indicated that the combination of conventional troops, the people's militia and networks of underground tunnels are the main line of defense against the danger from the north. [U.S., Congress, *United States–China: Future Foreign Policy Directions,* pp. 4–5.]

42. For a discussion of PRC leadership debate over treatment of the United States and the Taiwan issue during this period, see Robert G. Sutter, *Chinese Foreign Policy After the Cultural Revolution* (Boulder, Colo.: Westview Press, 1978), pp. 33–38, 70–84, 94–112.

43. This section is based heavily on the series of special reports and weekly publications of the U.S. Foreign Broadcast Information Service (FBIS) Analysis Group. The weekly publication is known as *Trends in Communist Media.*

44. These NCNA and *People's Daily* Reports are replayed in FBIS, Daily Report *China* (cited as FBIS DR China), July 29 and July 30, 1974.

45. See the PRC press coverage of this issue replayed in FBIS DR China, November 10, 1975.

46. Speech replayed in FBIS DR China,, October 20, 1975,

47. Speech replayed in FBIS DR China,, December 2, 1975.

48. PRC media coverage of Nixon's visit replayed in FBIS DR China, February 22–25, 1976.

49. See, in particular, FBIS *Special Memorandum,* "Changes in PRC Leadership, Current Propaganda Suggest Continued Moderate Peking Policy Toward U.S.," December 27, 1976.

50. This section is based heavily on FBIS *Special Report on Communist Media,* "Peking Media Treatment of the Taiwan Issue, 1972–1976," October 29, 1976.

Chapter 3

1. See Secretary of State Cyrus Vance's remarks on this issue in the *New York Times,* February 10, 1977.

2. See Secretary Vance's remarks to reporters after he met with the head of the PRC Liaison Office in the *New York Times,* January 12, 1977.

3. *New York Times,* August 28, 1977.

4. *Washington Post,* September 7, 1977.

5. U.S., Congress, House, Committee on International Relations, Subcommittee on Asian and Pacific Affairs, *Normalization of Relations with the People's Republic of China: Practical Implications* (Washington, D.C.: U.S. Government Printing Office, 1977).

6. William Watts et al., *Japan, Korea and China: American Perceptions and Policies* (Lexington, Mass.: D. C. Heath, 1979), pp. 125–38.

7. See, for example, earlier congressional hearings on this issue—notably, U.S., Congress, House, Committee on International Relations, *United States–Soviet Union–China: The Great Power Triangle* (Washington, D.C.: U.S. Government Printing Office, 1976); and *United States–China Relations: The Process of Normalization of Relations* (Washington, D.C.: U.S. Government Printing Office, 1976). See also the review of U.S. leaders' attitudes on this issue contained in U.S., Library of Congress, Congressional Research Service, *U.S.-PRC Normalization: Arguments and Alternatives,* Report no. 77-182 F (Washington, D.C., August 3, 1977).

8. U.S., Congress, *Normalization of Relations with the People's Republic of China,* p. vi.

9. Testimony of Robert Barnett, ibid., pp. 165–68.

10. Testimony of Ross Terrill, ibid., pp. 137–40.

11. Ibid., pp. 80–136.

12. Ibid., p. xi.

13. Testimony of Hungdah Chiu, ibid., pp. 215–31; and testimony of Eugene Theroux, ibid., pp. 96–103.

14. Testimony of A. Doak Barnett, ibid., pp. 1–13.

15. Senator Goldwater based his suit against President Carter's termination of the U.S.-Taiwan defense treaty on these grounds.

16. Testimony of Jerome Cohen, U.S., Congress, *Normalization of Relations with the People's Republic of China,* pp. 80–83.

17. Testimony of Victor Li, ibid., pp. 83–96.

18. A poll by the Foreign Policy Association in 1977 appeared to substantiate this point. The association tabulated approximately five thousand ballots concerning the China issue in its annual nationwide foreign policy discussion program. Among this group, whose members had a far greater than average interest in foreign affairs and the international arena, 33 percent were willing to accept Peking's preconditions—severance of U.S. diplomatic and military ties with Taiwan—as the cost of normalization of our relations, while 53 percent were opposed. Support jumped sharply—to 74 percent in favor and only 14 percent opposed—if Peking were prepared to give "firm assurances" that it would use only peaceful means to resolve the status of Taiwan. (Cited in Watts, *Japan, Korea and China,* pp. 128–29.)

19. Testimony of Hugh Scott, U.S., Congress, *Normalization of Relations with the People's Republic of China,* pp. 322–40.

20. In regard to Peking's claim to Taiwan, the Japanese formula represented one of the most moderate arrangements Peking had used in normalizing relations with Western-aligned countries. In negotiations before diplomatic relations were established, Peking had generally insisted that the country recognizing the PRC also formally endorse the PRC claim to Taiwan. A sign of moderation on the Taiwan issue was introduced in 1970 when Canada established relations with the PRC without formally supporting the PRC claim to Taiwan; the Canadians merely "took note" of the claim. Japan used an even more roundabout path

in acknowledging Peking's claim to the island, stating in the September 1972 communiqué establishing relations with the PRC that Tokyo "fully understands and respects" the PRC claim and adhered to Article 8 of the 1945 Potsdam Declaration. The following month, West Germany said nothing of Peking's claim to Taiwan in its agreement establishing diplomatic relations with the PRC, but this rare exception appeared related to the fact that the Bonn government had never had official ties with the ROC and had not recognized Taiwan as anything other than a part of China.

Of course, if the United States had formally endorsed Peking's claim to Taiwan, it could have seriously undercut the legal basis for continuing any distinct U.S. relationship with Taiwan. This problem could have become particularly serious if the Taipei government had ever decided to abandon any claim as the government of China and to declare Taiwan an independent state.

21. For a useful study of the "Japanese formula" in practice, see David Nelson Rowe, *Informal "Diplomatic Relations": The Case of Japan and the Republic of China, 1972–1974* (Hamden, Conn.: Shoestring Press, 1975).

22. Testimony of Robert Scalapino, U.S., Congress, *Normalization of Relations with the People's Republic of China,* pp. 18–24; and testimony of Nathaniel Thayer, ibid., pp. 24–42.

23. *Boston Globe,* July 17, 1977.

24. Testimony of Robert Barnett, U.S., Congress, *Normalization of Relations with the People's Republic of China,* pp. 160–68; and testimony of Ross Terrill, ibid., pp. 137–46.

25. Testimony of Donald Zagoria, ibid., pp. 150–60.

26. Testimony of Ray Cline, ibid., pp. 195–206.

27. Testimony of William Roth, ibid., pp. 341–51.

28. Testimony of Allen S. Whiting, ibid., pp. 13–18.

29. Testimony of Robert Barnett, ibid., pp. 161–62.

30. Testimony of Donald Zagoria, ibid., pp. 150–60.

31. See discussion in U.S., Congress, House, Committee on International Relations, *United States–Soviet Union–China: The Great Power Triangle* (Washington, D.C.: U.S. Government Printing Office, 1977).

32. Testimony of Robert Scalapino, ibid., pp. 24–42.

33. Testimony of Ray Cline, ibid., p. 198.

34. See discussion in U.S., Library of Congress, *U.S.-PRC Normalization,* p. 25.

35. Testimony of Nathaniel Thayer, U.S., Congress, *Normalization of Relations with the People's Republic of China,* pp. 22–23.

36. See discussion in U.S., Library of Congress, *U.S.-PRC Normalization,* pp. 26–27.

37. See testimony of Nathaniel Thayer and Robert Scalapino, U.S., Congress, *Normalization of Relations with the People's Republic of China,* pp. 18–42.

38. See testimony of Donald Zagoria and Robert Barnett, ibid., pp. 150–70.

39. See remarks of A. Doak Barnett on normalization and Korea, ibid., p. 10.

40. Ibid.

41. See discussion in U.S., Library of Congress, *U.S.-PRC Normalization,* pp. 30–31.

42. Testimony of Parris Chang and Hungdah Chiu, U.S., Congress, *Normalization of Relations with the People's Republic of China,* pp. 210–12, 215–31.

43. For a review of U.S. views on human rights conditions in the PRC and Taiwan at this time, see U.S., Library of Congress, Congressional Research Service, *Human Rights in China,* Report no. 78-50 F (Washington, D.C., February 28, 1978).

44. See discussion in U.S., Library of Congress, *U.S.-PRC Normalization,* p. 36.

45. Testimony of Robert Barnett, U.S., Congress, *Normalization of Relations with the People's Republic of China,* pp. 160–65.

46. See discussion of this issue in U.S., Library of Congress, *U.S.-PRC Normalization,* pp. 34–35.

47. Ibid.

48. Testimony of Marinus Van Gessel, U.S., Congress, *Normalization of Relations with the People's Republic of China,* pp. 254–66.

49. Testimony of Dwight Perkins, ibid., pp. 282–90.

50. Testimony of Donald Zagoria, ibid., pp. 150–60.

51. Discussed in U.S., Library of Congress, *U.S.-PRC Normalization,* pp. 42–43.

52. Testimony of A. Doak Barnett, U.S., Congress, *Normalization of Relations with the People's Republic of China,* pp. 7–13.

53. Testimony of Ross Terrill, ibid., p. 145.

54. Testimony of Robert Scalapino, ibid., p. xviii.

55. Remarks of Ray Cline, ibid., p. 195.

56. Testimony of Lester Wolff, ibid., pp. 43–44.

57. Testimony of Ralph N. Clough, ibid., pp. 146–50.

58. U.S. ambiguity on the status of Taiwan was judged to be of particular importance to the United States if Taipei eventually ended its claim of being the government of China and declared Taiwan an independent state. By remaining equivocal on Taiwan's status, the United States would not preclude the legal possibility of establishing full relations with an independent Taiwan state while maintaining normal diplomatic relations with Peking.

59. U.S., Congress, Senate, *China and American Policy* (Washington, D.C.: U.S. Government Printing Office, 1974), p. 5.

60. See the discussion in U.S., Library of Congress, *U.S.-PRC Normalization,* p. 46.

61. Testimony of Les AuCoin, U.S., Congress, *Normalization of Relations with the People's Republic of China,* pp. 248–54.

62. Testimony of Selig Harrison, ibid., pp. 266–82.

63. Testimony of Hugh Scott, ibid., p. 324.

64. Testimony of Victor Li, ibid., pp. 86–87.

65. This section is based on testimony given by Jerome Cohen, Victor Li, Eugene Theroux, and former Secretary of the U.S. Senate Francis Valeo, U.S., Congress, *Normalization of Relations with the People's Republic of China,* pp.

80–136. It also draws heavily on studies of the subject, including William Clarke and Martha Avery, "The Sino-American Commercial Relationship," and Theroux, "Legal and Practical Problems in the China Trade." Both articles are contained in U.S., Congress, Joint Economic Committee, *China: A Reassessment of the Economy* (Washington, D.C.: U.S. Government Printing Office, 1975). Another study of particular use is Victor Li, *Derecognizing Taiwan: The Legal Problems* (Washington, D.C.: Carnegie Endowment for International Peace, 1977). See also U.S., Library of Congress, *U.S.-PRC Normalization,* pp. 48–59.

Chapter 4

1. For background, see:

U.S., Congress, House, Committee on Armed Services, *Report of the Delegation to the Far East* (Washington, D.C.: U.S. Government Printing Office, 1979).

————— , *Report of the Delegation to the People's Republic of China* (Washington, D.C.: U.S. Government Printing Office, 1979).

U.S., Congress, House, Committee on Foreign Affairs, *Implementation of the Taiwan Relations Act,* Hearings, October 23 and November 8, 1979 (Washington, D.C.: U.S. Government Printing Office, 1980).

————— , *Taiwan Legislation,* Hearings, February 7 and 8, 1979 (Washington, D.C.: U.S. Government Printing Office, 1979).

————— , *Taiwan Relations Act,* Conference Report, March 24, 1979 (Washington, D.C.: U.S. Government Printing Office, 1979).

————— , *United States–Taiwan Relations Act,* Report, March 3, 1979 (Washington, D.C.: U.S. Government Printing Office, 1979).

————— , Subcommittee on Asian and Pacific Affairs, *China and Asia—An Analysis of China's Recent Policy Toward Neighboring States* (Washington, D.C.: U.S. Government Printing Office, 1979).

————— , *Playing the China Card: Implications for United States–Soviet–Chinese Relations* (Washington, D.C.: U.S. Government Printing Office, 1979).

————— , *Implementation of the Taiwan Relations Act: Issues and Concerns,* Hearings, February 14 and 15, 1979 (Washington, D.C.: U.S. Government Printing Office, 1979).

————— , *The United States and the People's Republic of China: Issues for the 1980s,* Hearings, April 1, July 22, August 26, and September 23, 1980 (Washington, D.C.: U.S. Government Printing Office, 1980).

————— , *Security and Stability in Asia: 1979* (Washington, D.C.: U.S. Government Printing Office, 1979).

U.S., Congress, Senate, Committee on Foreign Relations, *Implementation of the Taiwan Relations Act: The First Year* (Washington, D.C.: U.S. Government Printing Office, 1980) (cited with subtitle).

————— , *Sino-American Relations: A New Turn* (Washington, D.C.: U.S. Government Printing Office, 1979).

————— , *Some Recent Developments Related to Human Rights in the People's Republic of China* (Washington, D.C.: U.S. Government Printing Office, 1979).

————, *Taiwan,* Hearings, February 5, 6, 7, 8, 21, and 22, 1979 (Washington, D.C.: U.S. Government Printing Office, 1979).

————, *Taiwan Enabling Act,* March 1979. (Washington, D.C.: U.S. Government Printing Office, 1979).

————, *The United States, China, and Japan,* September 1979 (Washington, D.C.: U.S. Government Printing Office, 1979).

————, *United States Foreign Policy Objectives and Overseas Military Installations,* April 1979 (Washington, D.C.: U.S. Government Printing Office, 1979).

————, *U.S. Troop Withdrawal from the Republic of Korea: An Update, 1979* (Washington, D.C.: U.S. Government Printing Office, 1979).

————, Subcommittee on East Asian and Pacific Affairs, *U.S. Policy in East Asia,* Hearing, July 12, 1979 (Washington, D.C.: U.S. Government Printing Office, 1979).

2. See Ralph N. Clough, Robert B. Oxnam, and William Watts, *The United States and China: American Perspectives and Future Alternatives* (Washington, D.C.: Potomac Associates, 1977).

3. See Chapter 1, note 6.

4. For an excellent analysis of the roots and developments of this issue in U.S. foreign policy, see Banning Garrett, *The China Card and Its Origins: U.S. Bureaucratic Politics and the Strategic Triangle* (Berkeley, Calif.: University of California Press, forthcoming).

5. See, for example, the letter from Congressmen Zablocki and Wolff to President Carter contained in U.S., Congress, *Implementation of the Taiwan Relations Act: Issues and Concerns.*

6. For a wrap-up of congressional and administration views on this issue, see U.S., Congress, House, Committee on Foreign Affairs, *Executive-Legislative Consultations on China Policy, 1978–1979* (Washington, D.C.: U.S. Government Printing Office, 1980).

7. This was done notably with the so-called Dole-Stone amendment to the International Security Assistance Act of 1978, which is discussed below.

8. See, for instance, U.S., Congress, *Implementation of the Taiwan Relations Act: The First Year;* and U.S., Congress, *Implementation of the Taiwan Relations Act.*

9. See, for example, *The United States and the People's Republic of China.*

10. For background on the administration's public position, see U.S., Department of State, Bureau of Public Affairs, *U.S. Policy Toward China: July 15, 1971–January 15, 1979,* Selected Documents no. 9 (Washington, D.C., 1979).

11. The text of the proposed bill is seen in U.S., Congress, *Taiwan Enabling Act,* pp. 61–63.

12. See, for instance, ibid., pp. 7–8.

13. Ibid., p. 7.

14. U.S., Congress, *Taiwan,* pp. 51–52.

15. U.S., Congress, *Taiwan Legislation,* p. 113.

16. See *New York Times,* February 13, 1979.

17. See U.S., Congress, *Taiwan Enabling Act,* p. 4.

18. Ibid., pp. 20–22.

19. U.S., Congress, *Taiwan Relations Act.*

20. U.S., Congress, *Taiwan Enabling Act,* p. 9.

21. Ibid., p. 84.

22. *New York Times,* October 18, 1979. The Senate on June 6, 1979, passed by a vote of 59 to 35 an amendment to a resolution (S.Res. 15) that said the "approval of the U.S. Senate is required to terminate any mutual defense treaty between the United States and another nation." While it did not specifically mention Taiwan, the resolution was seen as a rebuke of President Carter for his decision to end the U.S. defense treaty with Taiwan. The Senate action was also related to Judge Gasch's decision earlier on June 6, 1979, to dismiss the suit against the president's action on the Taiwan defense treaty brought by Senator Goldwater and other members of Congress. The judge reportedly indicated that he could take no action on the suit unless the Senate or both houses of Congress went on record in opposition to the president's decision. The judge's subsequent favorable ruling on the suit came in October.

23. For a review of these steps, see U.S., Library of Congress, Congressional Research Service, *China-U.S. Relations,* Issue Brief no. IB 76053. (Washington, D.C., periodically updated).

24. For background, see U.S., Congress, *Implementation of the Taiwan Relations Act: The First Year.*

25. U.S., Congress, *Implementation of the Taiwan Relations Act,* p. 37.

26. U.S., Congress, *Implementation of the Taiwan Relations Act: The First Year,* p. 2. For background on U.S.-Taiwan military relations, see U.S., Library of Congress, Congressional Research Service, *Taiwan's Future: Implications for the United States,* Issue Brief no. IB 79101 (Washington, D.C., periodically updated).

27. *New York Times,* June 13, 1980.

28. For background, see:

U.S., Congress, House, Committee on Foreign Affairs, *Prospects for U.S.-China Economic Cooperation* (Washington, D.C.: U.S. Government Printing Office, 1980).

————, Subcommittees on Asian and Pacific Affairs and on International Economic Policy and Trade, *OPIC Services for Investors in China* (Washington, D.C.: U.S. Government Printing Office, 1981).

U.S., Congress, House, Committee on Ways and Means, *Approving the Extension of Nondiscriminatory Treatment to Products of the PRC* (Washington, D.C.: U.S. Government Printing Office, 1980).

————, Subcommittee on Trade, *U.S.-China Trade Agreement* (Washington, D.C.: U.S. Government Printing Office, 1980).

U.S., Congress, Senate, Committee on Banking, Housing, and Urban Affairs, Subcommittee on International Finance, *Amending the Export-Import Bank Act and the Trade Act* (Washington, D.C.: U.S. Government Printing Office, 1979).

U.S., Congress, Senate, Committee on Finance, *Extension of Nondiscriminatory Treatment to Products of the PRC* (Washington, D.C.: U.S. Government Printing Office, 1980).

————— , Subcommittee on International Trade, *Agreement on Trade Relations Between the United States and the People's Republic of China* (Washington, D.C.: U.S. Government Printing Office, 1980).

U.S., Congress, Senate, Committee on Foreign Relations, *Hearing on S. 1916, a Bill to Authorize Operations of O.P.I.C. in China* (Washington, D.C.: U.S. Government Printing Office, 1980).

29. For a review of the views of congressional, administration, and other U.S. leaders on this issue, see U.S., Congress, *Playing the China Card.*

30. *Washington Post,* October 2, 1979.

31. These steps are reviewed in U.S., Library of Congress, *China-U.S. Relations.*

32. For detailed background on this issue, see U.S., Congress, *Playing the China Card.* See also U.S., Library of Congress, Congressional Research Service, *China-U.S.-Soviet Relations,* Issue Brief no. IB 79115 (Washington, D.C., periodically updated).

33. See reportage of Dr. Brzezinski's visit to the PRC in May 1978 in U.S., Foreign Broadcast Information Service, Daily Report, *China,* May 22 and 23, 1978.

34. *Christian Science Monitor,* June 15, 1978.

35. Statement of Secretary of State Cyrus Vance, November 3, 1978.

36. Reviewed in U.S., Library of Congress, *China-U.S.-Soviet Relations.*

37. U.S., Congress, *The United States and the People's Republic of China,* p. 1.

Chapter 5

1. See Chapter 1, note 6. This chapter is based largely on interviews conducted in 1979 and 1980 with more than twenty-five officials, divided approximately equally between the legislative and executive branches and representing a high percentage of those who were centrally involved at the working level in congressional-executive relations over China policy at the time. Given that the intent of the interviews was to elicit contrasting perspectives, and that many of the episodes remain matters of institutional and personal sensitivity, those interviewed were assured that their comments would not be for attribution.

For more information on this and other recent episodes in executive-congressional relations over Chinese and other foreign policy issues, see the series of reports published by U.S., Congress, House, Committee on Foreign Affairs, under the general heading *Congress and Foreign Policy Series.* See, in particular, the first in this series, *Executive-Legislative Consultations over China Policy, 1978–1979* (Washington, D.C.: U.S. Government Printing Office, 1980).

2. Some congressional aides saw Secretary Vance's cautious approach to the Taiwan issue as reflective of congressional influence on the administration's China policy.

3. Of the fifteen congressional staff members interviewed in 1979, only one indicated that he had been informed in advance of the Carter administration's decision. This was so even though each of these staff members had important roles to play in the conduct of U.S. China policy.

4. U.S., Congress, House, Committee on International Relations, Subcommittee on Asian and Pacific Affairs, *Normalization of Relations with the People's Republic of China: Practical Implications* (Washington, D.C.: U.S. Government Printing Office, 1977), p. v.

5. An important participant in the passage of the amendment, Robert Downen, has written extensively on this subject and on China policy in general. See his books, *The Taiwan Pawn in the China Game* (Washington, D.C.: Georgetown University Center for Strategic and International Studies, 1979) and *Of Grave Concern: U.S.-Taiwan Relations on the Threshold of the 1980s* (Washington, D.C.: Georgetown University Center for Strategic and International Studies, 1981).

6. For background on these views, see:

U.S., Congress, House, Committee on Armed Services, *Report of the Delegation to the Far East* (Washington, D.C.: U.S. Government Printing Office, 1979).

————, Investigations Subcommittee, *Report on the Impact of Intelligence Reassessment on Withdrawal of U.S. Troops from Korea* (Washington, D.C.: U.S. Government Printing Office, 1979).

U.S., Congress, Senate, Committee on Foreign Relations, *U.S. Troop Withdrawal from the Republic of Korea: An update, 1979* (Washington, D.C.: U.S. Government Printing Office, 1979).

U.S., Library of Congress, Congressional Research Service, *Republic of Korea: U.S. Commitments and the Question of Human Rights,* Issue Brief no. IB 74115 (Washington, D.C., periodically updated).

————, *Vietnam: Problems of Normalizing U.S.-Vietnamese Relations,* Issue Brief no. IB 77018. (Washington, D.C., periodically updated).

7. On the controversy surrounding arms transfers to Turkey, see U.S., Congress, House, Committee on Foreign Affairs, *Congressional-Executive Relations and the Turkish Arms Embargo,* Congress and Foreign Policy Series no. 3 (Washington, D.C.: U.S. Government Printing Office, 1981).

8. Ralph N. Clough, Robert B. Oxnam, and William Watts, *The United States and China: American Perspectives and Future Alternatives* (Washington, D.C., Potomac Associates, 1977).

9. Policy toward Korea and Vietnam were most notable in this regard. See note 6 for this chapter.

10. These diverse administration views are reviewed in U.S., Congress, House, Committee on Foreign Affairs, *Executive-Legislative Consultations on China Policy, 1978-1979* (Washington, D.C.: U.S. Government Printing Office, 1980), pp. 22-24.

11. On December 19, 1978, in an interview with Walter Cronkite of CBS News, President Carter said in reference to consultations in the United States over the decision to normalize with the PRC, "I might say in complete candor that in the last two or three weeks, when the negotiations were building up to

a climax in an unanticipated degree of rapidity of movement, we did not consult with anyone outside a very tiny group within the executive branch of government about the prospective success."

12. Thus, for example, initial briefings of the press failed to convey the condition that the United States would halt all new arms transfers to Taiwan during 1979. See *Washington Post,* December 16 and 17, 1978.

13. See, in particular, Deputy Secretary of State Warren Christopher's remarks on treaties with Taiwan to the Senate Foreign Relations Committee in U.S., Congress, Senate, Committee on Foreign Relations, *Taiwan* (Washington, D.C.: U.S. Government Printing Office, 1979), p. 15.

14. The disclosure came during Vice President Mondale's trip to China. See *Baltimore Sun,* September 1, 1979.

15. Accusations of the administration's pro-Peking bias are seen in U.S., Congress, Senate, Committee on Foreign Relations, *Implementation of the Taiwan Relations Act: The First Year* (Washington, D.C.: U.S. Government Printing Office, 1980), p. 4.

16. Administration spokesmen pointed to section 4(c) of the Taiwan Relations Act, which said:

> For all purposes, including actions in any court in the United States, the Congress approves the continuation in force of all treaties and other international agreements, including multilateral conventions, entered into by the United States and the governing authorities on Taiwan recognized by the United States as the Republic of China prior to January 1, 1979, and in force between them on December 31, 1978, *unless and until terminated in accordance with law.* [emphasis added]

17. See Deputy Secretary of State Christopher's remarks in U.S., Congress, *Taiwan,* p. 15.

18. This episode is reviewed in U.S., Congress, *Implementation of the Taiwan Relations Act,* pp. 11–12.

19. For a reflection of congressional complaints, see ibid. pp. 9–10.

20. For background on congressional resistance, see:

U.S., Congress, House, Committee on Ways and Means, *Approving the Extention of Nondiscriminatory Treatment to Products of the PRC* (Washington, D.C.: U.S. Government Printing Office, 1980).

————, Subcommittee on Trade, *U.S.-China Trade Agreement,* Hearings, November 1, 2, and 29, 1979 (Washington, D.C.: U.S. Government Printing Office, 1980).

U.S., Congress, Senate, Committee on Banking, Housing and Urban Affairs, Subcommittee on International Finance, *Amending the Export-Import Bank Act and the Trade Act,* Hearing (Washington, D.C.: U.S. Government Printing Office, 1979).

U.S., Congress, Senate, Committee on Finance, Subcommittee on International Trade, *Agreement on Trade Relations Between the United States and the People's Republic of China* (Washington, D.C.: U.S. Government Printing Office, 1980).

—————, *Extension of Nondiscriminatory Treatment to Products of the PRC* (Washington, D.C.: U.S. Government Printing Office, 1980).

21. These views are reflected in U.S., Congress, House, Committee on Foreign Affairs, Subcommittee on Asian and Pacific Affairs, *The United States and the People's Republic of China: Issues for the 1980s* (Washington, D.C.: U.S. Government Printing Office, 1980).

22. See *New York Times,* September 7, 1977.

23. For background on difficulties in executive-legislative consultations on foreign policy, see U.S., Congress, House, Committee on Foreign Affairs, *Executive-Legislative Consultations on Foreign Policy* (Washington, D.C.: U.S. Government Printing Office, 1981).

24. See, for example, U.S., Congress, *Implementation of the Taiwan Relations Act,* p. 3, which states, ". . . the executive branch appears at times to be implementing that version of the act which it drafted, not the Taiwan Relations Act passed by Congress."

25. This view was reflected in ibid., p. 1.

Chapter 6

1. Section 36(b) of the AECA allowed Congress to disapprove by concurrent resolution the transfer of any "major defense equipment" worth at least seven million dollars or any other defense articles or services worth twenty-five million dollars or more. Sections 38(b)(3) and 36(c) of the AECA regarding commercial transactions allowed Congress to disapprove by concurrent resolution transfers of "major defense equipment" valued at one hundred million dollars or more. Also regarding commercial transactions, under a new provision in P.L. 96-533, section 38(a)(3) was created and gave the president discretionary authority to require that any defense article or service be subject to government-to-government sales restrictions such as those noted in section 36(b) above.

At the same time, the Foreign Assistance Act, section 620(f), appeared to limit the furnishing of U.S. grant military assistance to any communist country unless the president issued a narrowly defined waiver. The section specified that the president had to determine and report to Congress that such assistance was vital to U.S. security, the recipient country was not controlled by the international communist conspiracy, and such assistance would further promote the independence of the recipient country from international communism. The phrase "communist country" expressly included the PRC.

Section 505(b) of the Foreign Assistance Act limited the ability of the president to grant defense articles at a cost over three million dollars in any fiscal year unless he issued a specific waiver. According to this section, the president had to determine that the recipient country conformed to the principles of the U.N. Charter, that the articles transfered would be used to defend the country or the free world, that the recipient country was making reasonable efforts to build up its own defense, and that the increased ability of the recipient country to defend itself was important to the security of the United States.

Regarding the possible sending of military advisors to the PRC, section 515 of the Foreign Assistance Act stated that no military assistance advisory group, military mission, or other organization of U.S. military personnel performing similar military advisory functions under either that act or the Arms Export Control Act could operate in a foreign country like the PRC without specific authorization by Congress.

2. The following articles and books represent a sampling of some of the most relevant publications dealing with the issue of U.S.-PRC military and security cooperation:

A. Doak Barnett, "Military-Security Relations Between China and the United States," *Foreign Affairs* 55, no. 3 (1977).

Roger G. Brown, "Chinese Politics and American Policy: A New Look at the Triangle," *Foreign Policy* 24 (Summer 1976).

Banning Garrett, "The China Card: To Play or Not to Play," *Contemporary China,* Spring 1979.

Edward Luttwak, "Against the China Card," *Commentary* 70, no. 4 (1978): 37–43.

Robert L. Pfaltzgraff, Jr., "China, Soviet Strategy, and American Policy," *International Security* 5, no. 2 (1980).

Michael Pillsbury, "Future Sino-American Security Ties: The View from Tokyo, Moscow and Peking," *International Security* 25, no. 4 (1977).

————, "U.S.-China Military Ties," *Foreign Policy* 21 (Fall 1975).

Richard H. Solomon, ed., *Asian Security in the 1980s: Problems and Policies for a Time of Transition* (Santa Monica, Calif.: The Rand Corporation, November 1979).

Ross Terrill, "China and the World: Self-reliance or Interdependence," *Foreign Affairs* 55, no. 2 (1977).

————, "The Strategy of the Chinese Card," *Asian Wall Street Journal,* July 20, 1978.

U.S., Congress, House, Committee on Foreign Affairs, Subcommittee on Asian and Pacific Affairs, *Playing the China Card: Implications for United States–Soviet–Chinese Relations* (Washington, D.C.: U.S. Government Printing Office, 1979).

————, *The United States and the People's Republic of China: Issues for the 1980s* (Washington, D.C.: U.S. Government Printing Office, 1980).

U.S., Congress, House, Committee on International Relations, *United States–Soviet Union–China: The Great Power Triangle,* Summary of hearings conducted by the Subcommittee on Future Foreign Policy Research and Development of the Committee on International Relations, October–December 1975 and March–June 1976 (Washington, D.C.: U.S. Government Printing Office, 1977).

————, Subcommittee on Future Foreign Policy Research and Development, *United States–Soviet Union–China: The Great Power Triangle.* Hearings (Washington, D.C.: U.S. Government Printing Office, 1976).

U.S., Library of Congress, Congressional Research Service, *Increased U.S. Military Transfers to China: Arguments and Alternatives.* [Washington, D.C.] Report no. 81-121 F. (Washington, D.C., May 20, 1981).

Allen S. Whiting, "China and the Superpowers: Toward the Year 2000," *Daedalus,* Fall 1980.

This chapter is based on published sources such as these, as well as on interviews conducted in late 1980 and early 1981 with over thirty U.S. foreign policy and defense specialists, both in and out of government, who have been closely involved with this issue. Each of those interviews was conducted on a nonattribution basis to elicit as frank an assessment as possible and to avoid personal or institutional embarrassment over sensitive issues in U.S. foreign policy.

3. See, in particular, Michael Pillsbury, "U.S.-China Military Ties."

4. For a thorough review of these steps, see Banning Garrett's forthcoming book, *The "China Card" and Its Origins: U.S. Bureaucratic Politics and the Strategic Triangle* (Berkeley, Calif.: University of California Press).

5. For more information on the Brown visit and subsequent developments in U.S.-PRC military ties, see U.S., Library of Congress, Congressional Research Service, *China-U.S.-Soviet Relations,* Issue Brief no. IB 79115 (Washington, D.C., periodically updated).

6. Thus, the United States was legally restricted from giving free military equipment to the PRC, while the PRC was too poor to be able to afford to buy much from the United States.

7. For a good wrap-up on the PRC's military capabilities, see U.S., Congress, Senate, Committee on Foreign Relations, *Sino-American Relations: A New Turn* (Washington, D.C.: U.S. Government Printing Office, 1979), pp. 39–46. See also U.S., Library of Congress, *Increased U.S. Military Transfers to China,* pp. 43–56.

8. In this regard, several military specialists pointed to the seeming inconsistency in Peking's defense procurement process, noting in particular the PRC's on-again, off-again interest in the British "Harrier" aircraft. The PRC also was reported to be very interested in French anti-tank missiles, but no agreements on this item were reached. The reasons given for this seeming Chinese inconsistency varied: Some pointed to the PRC's recently heightened awareness of its inability to pay for foreign equipment. Others noted the reluctance of some Western countries to offend the USSR by being one of the first Western powers to sell weapons to the PRC. Still others emphasized that Western countries were unwilling to supply Peking with sophisticated military equipment that they judged would be of little practical use for China given the current, relatively low technical competence in the PRC.

9. See, for example, PRC Vice Foreign Minister Zhang Wenjin's interview in the *Washington Post,* November 23, 1980.

10. For varied assessments of China's military power against likely adversaries see:

John M. Collins, *U.S.-Soviet Military Balance, 1960–1980* (New York: McGraw-Hill, 1980).

Angus M. Fraser, "Military Modernization in China," *Problems of Communism* 27 (September–December 1979).

International Institute for Strategic Studies, *Military Balance, 1980–1981* (London, 1980).

————, *Strategic Survey 1979* (London, 1980).

Leo Yueh-yun Liu, "The Modernization of the Chinese Military," *Current History* 79, no. 458 (1980).

Thomas A. Marks, "Two Chinese Roads to Military Modernization—and a U.S. Dilemma," *Strategic Review* 8, no. 3 (1980).

Drew Middleton, *The Duel of the Giants: China and Russia in Asia* (New York: Charles Scribner's Sons, 1978).

Lelands Ness, "Chinese Army," *Armies and Weapons,* June 1978.

Clarence A. Robinson, "China's Technology Impresses Visitors," *Aviation Week and Space Technology,* October 6, 1980.

Francis J. Romance, "Modernization of China's Armed Forces," *Asian Survey* 20, no. 3 (1980).

William Schneider, "China's Military Power." In William Schneider, ed., *About Face: The China Decision and Its Consequences* (New Rochelle, N.Y.: Arlington House, 1979).

U.S., Department of Defense, Defense Intelligence Agency, *Handbook of the Chinese Armed Forces* (Washington, D.C., July 1976).

Robert L. Worden, *Chinese Militia in Evolution,* Defense Intelligence Agency Report no. DDB-1100-285-80 (Washington, D.C., May 1980).

Peter L. Young, "China's Military Capabilities," *Asian Defense Journal,* February 1979.

11. See discussion of this issue by Thomas Robinson in U.S., Congress, Joint Economic Committee, *China Under the Four Modernizations* (Washington, D.C.: U.S. Government Printing Office, 1982).

12. For background on Soviet policy toward the PRC, see William Hyland, "The Sino-Soviet Conflict: A Search for New Security Strategies," in Richard H. Solomon, ed., *Asian Security in the 1980s,* pp. 39–53.

13. Indeed, several analysts claimed that the U.S. leaders had not even defined what role the United States would like to see the PRC play in future global and regional development and therefore found it difficult to determine how U.S. military transfers would help or hinder the PRC in that role.

14. For background on differing U.S. assessments of the USSR, see U.S., Library of Congress, Congressional Research Service, *Soviet Strategic Objectives and SALT II: American Perceptions,* Report no. 78-119 F (Washington, D.C., May 25, 1978).

15. Technically speaking, "window of vulnerability" refers to the period when U.S. land-based ICBMs will be vulnerable to Soviet attack—a period that is supposed to end with the deployment of the planned MX missile. However, the phrase is sometimes used more broadly to refer to what is seen as a general superpower imbalance against the United States.

16. For an assessment of Japan's defense effort, see U.S., Library of Congress, Congressional Research Service, *Japanese Attitudes Toward Defense and Security Issues,* Report no. 81-158 F (Washington, D.C., July 7, 1981).

17. In this regard, see Banning Garrett, *Soviet Perception of China and Sino-American Security Ties,* Study prepared for SALT/Arms Control Support Group, Office of the Assistant Secretary of Defense (Atomic Energy) (Washington, D.C., June 1981).

18. Soviet military planners are thought to assess the PRC's limited military capabilities much more realistically than the shrill Soviet media commentaries that warn of the China "threat." Nevertheless, the Soviet's logistical problems and other weakness in Asia, as well as their assessment of the probable cost of any protracted conflict with the PRC, are thought to promote general Soviet concern about the Asian front.

19. This point of view was voiced by a number of U.S. military analysts who were interviewed, although they acknowledged that public attention to their approach was sparse. For a classic example of this point of view, see Michael Pillsbury, "U.S.-Chinese Military Ties," *Foreign Policy* 21 (Fall 1975).

These military planners tended to stress that even though PRC military capabilities were not expected to increase rapidly as a result of increased U.S. military transfers to the PRC, closer Sino-American security ties were beneficial to the United States. They would help ensure that the PRC remained on the U.S. side in the event of a major East-West confrontation and would increase Soviet worry about the PRC taking action—in conjunction with moves by the United States—against the USSR.

20. Testimony of Malcolm Toon in U.S., Congress, *The United States and the People's Republic of China,* pp. 75–78.

21. Testimony of Raymond Garthoff, ibid., pp. 78–92.

22. Testimony of Richard Pipes, ibid., pp. 136–39.

23. For a variation on this view, see Brown, "Chinese Politics and American Policy."

24. See the article by Ray Cline in the *Washington Star,* October 14, 1980.

25. U.S., Congress, *The United States and the People's Republic of China,* pp. 34–60.

26. Testimony of Harry Harding submitted to the U.S., Congress, House Committee on Foreign Affairs, Subcommittee on Asian and Pacific Affairs, September 25, 1980.

27. These developments reportedly would increase the likelihood that the PRC would play a stabilizing rather than disruptive role in the economically important East Asian region. This view was voiced by some U.S. businesspersons with a special interest in East Asian affairs.

28. These observers were predictably vague in defining the outlines of this proposed mutual security arrangement, although they repeatedly compared it directly with the North Atlantic alliance.

29. For instance, it was claimed that U.S. military transfers to the PRC might so increase the PRC's perceived leverage over the United States in Asia that Peking might take more forceful actions—such as a naval blockade—against the island. U.S. arms were not thought to increase substantially the PRC ability to conduct such an operation, at least for several years. But the transfers could signal Peking, Taiwan, and Taiwan's leading trading partners of a shift in U.S. priorities in the region, suggesting that the United States would not react strongly if the PRC resorted to force against the island. In the event of a PRC blockade—which was thought by many to be within the range of the PRC's current military capabilities—the United States would have to

decide whether to confront its strategically important friend in Asia or to allow Taiwan to be pressured into an accommodation with the mainland.

30. Some U.S. officials would welcome an increase in Soviet deployments against the PRC because they would reduce Soviet ability to confront the West elsewhere.

31. Although a few officials saw Moscow as possibly reacting immediately with force to U.S. sales to the PRC, others stressed that Soviet military planners had not yet been rash in their military actions against the PRC. Several added that the United States should be wary that even though Soviet planners might appear cautious, U.S. military cooperation could quickly build to a point where it would cross an ill-defined "threshold" of Soviet tolerance and lead to a harsh military response against the PRC and, possibly, the United States.

32. Some China specialists argued that the PRC was unlikely to change its anti-Soviet posture and would continue to tie down Soviet forces, whether or not the United States increased military transfers to the PRC. They therefore saw little need for the United States to risk the possible disadvantages to closer United States-PRC military ties.

33. See discussion of this issue in Garrett, *Soviet Perception of China and Sino-American Security Ties.*

34. Some observers noted that since the PRC's military leaders received less benefit than other PRC leaders from their country's modernization program and its opening to the West, they would have less to lose, and possibly more to gain, if that program and the PRC's pragmatic, relatively pro-Western leadership under Deng Xiaoping were changed. U.S. concern over the loyalty of the PRC military to the current Deng leadership in Peking was increased in late 1980 by press reports that Deng's opponents were trying to appeal to the military to undercut Deng's programs and to enhance their own leading positions.

35. It was said that the United States could not expect relations with the PRC to remain cordial if Washington continued, as expected, to sell hundreds of millions of dollars of military equipment to Taiwan while maintaining a de facto arms embargo against the PRC. In particular, some said that the United States could avoid a downturn in U.S.-PRC relations and still go ahead with the proposed sale of the FX fighter aircraft to Taiwan by simultaneously allowing the transfer to the mainland government of sophisticated U.S. aircraft engine technology needed for the PRC fighter aircraft program.

36. One China specialist went further in this regard, asserting that the PRC gave better treatment and more advantageous trade to those individual American companies that had been most helpful in promoting U.S. military transfers to the PRC.

37. A few observers claimed that Japan's leaders were privately arguing against U.S. arms sales to the PRC in part for selfish reasons. The Japanese allegedly judged that if the United States moved ahead with such sales, the PRC would favor U.S. businesses over Japanese competitors for potentially lucrative trade deals.

38. One Asia specialist said that some countries in the Association for Southeast Asian Nations (ASEAN), in response to U.S.-PRC military ties, would

begin to reassess their views of the Soviet presence in Southeast Asia and might come to see the USSR and its ally, Vietnam, as a useful buffer to growing Chinese power in the region. Several other observers doubted that the transfer of arms to the PRC would automatically result in such a shift of ASEAN attitudes.

39. Some officials claimed that the PRC leaders lacked a fixed and viable defense strategy and that U.S. military supplies could prove to be less than fully useful if Chinese defense plans changed in the future. PRC leaders might be inclined to blame the United States for transferring "inappropriate" equipment at great cost to their country's limited economic resources.

Chapter 7

1. Roger Sullivan, "The Value of the Chinese Connection," *The International Trade Law Journal* 5, no. 1 (Fall-Winter 1979):35–38. (Sullivan was deputy assistant secretary of state in charge of China policy when he wrote the article.)

2. The best recent assessment of U.S.-PRC economic relations is contained in A. Doak Barnett's comprehensive analysis of the PRC economy, *China's Economy in Global Perspective* (Washington, D.C., Brookings Institution, 1981).

3. U.S., Congress, House, Committee on International Relations, Subcommittee on Investigations, *United States–China Relations: The Process of Normalization of Relations,* Hearings (Washington, D.C.: U.S. Government Printing Office, 1976), pp. 22–23.

4. Stanley B. Lubman, "Trade and Sino-American Relations," in Michel Oksenberg and Robert B. Oxnam, eds., *Dragon and Eagle* (New York: Basic Books, 1978), pp. 187–213.

5. U.S., Congress, House, Committee on International Relations, Subcommittee on Asian and Pacific Affairs, *Normalization of Relations with the People's Republic of China: Practical Implications,* Hearings (Washington, D.C.: U.S. Government Printing Office, 1977), p. 285.

6. See assessment made by Martha Avery and William Clarke in U.S., Congress, Joint Economic Committee, *Chinese Economy Post-Mao* (Washington, D.C.: U.S. Government Printing Office, 1978), pp. 747–48.

7. See William Clarke, "Commercial Implications of Normalization," *The International Trade Law Journal* 5, no. 1 (Fall–Winter 1979): 95.

8. See, for example, *Chicago Tribune,* January 22, 1979; and *Washington Post,* January 14, 1979.

9. Clarke, "Commercial Implications of Normalization," p. 93.

10. Louis Kraar, "China's Narrow Door to the West," *Fortune,* March 26, 1979.

11. Norman Pearlstine and Flora S. H. Ling, "The China Trade: A Note of Caution," *Forbes,* February 5, 1979.

12. *New York Times,* January 16, 1979.

13. The settlement of this and other U.S.-PRC economic issues during the Carter administration are discussed in U.S., Library of Congress, Congressional Research Service, *China-U.S. Relations,* Issue Brief no. IB 76053. (Washington, D.C., periodically updated).

14. For background on the PRC's recent economic policy, see U.S., Congress, Joint Economic Committee, *China Under the Four Modernizations* (Washington, D.C.: U.S. Government Printing Office, 1982). For a very useful short review of PRC economic policies, see "Prospects for China Trade Through 1985," *Business America,* August 11, 1980, pp. 3–8; and U.S., Library of Congress, Congressional Research Service, *China's Future,* Issue Brief no. IB 81151. (Washington, D.C., periodically updated).

15. Zhao's report is replayed in U.S., Foreign Broadcast Information Service, Daily Report, *China,* December 16, 1981.

16. A Doak Barnett, *China's Economy in Global Perspective,* p. 569.

17. Ibid., p. 570. See also U.S., Congress, House, Committee on Foreign Affairs, Subcommittee on Asian and Pacific Affairs, *The New Era in East Asia,* Hearings (Washington, D.C.: U.S. Government Printing Office, 1981), pp. 195–260.

Chapter 8

1. See Reagan's statement in the *Congressional Record,* August 28, 1980, pp. E 4112–E 4113.

2. The Reagan administration also worked hard to reassure traditional U.S. allies and friends in East Asia, and their supporters in the United States, that it intends to maintain U.S. military strength and economic interest in the region. The administration has consolidated relations with South Korea and Japan during the visits of the South Korean and Japanese government leaders to the United States in early 1981 and with the Philippines during Vice President Bush's visit there in May 1981.

3. For example, Representative Solarz was the first member of Congress to travel to North Korea. See his report in U.S., Congress, House, Committee on Foreign Affairs, *The Korean Conundrum* (Washington, D.C.: U.S. Government Printing Office, 1981).

4. This view is well set forth in Robert Downen, *Of Grave Concern: U.S.-Taiwan Relations on the Threshold of the 1980s* (Washington, D.C., Georgetown University Center for Strategic and International Studies, 1981).

5. Ray Cline of Georgetown University is closely associated with this view.

6. This view was raised repeatedly at a conference on dual-system nations, held at the Georgetown University Center for Strategic and International Studies on June 23, 1981.

7. See, for instance, the June 10, 1981, PRC Foreign Ministry Information Department spokesman's statement on U.S.-Taiwan arms sales.

8. Senator Robert Byrd suggested that the United States undertake such a mediating role in an article written in the *Washington Post,* September 30, 1980.

9. The agreement was reported on March 23, 1981.

10. For background analysis on the FX decision, see A. Doak Barnett, *The FX Decision* (Washington, D.C.: Brookings Institution, 1981); Hua Xiu, "China Won't Accept U.S. 'Balanced Arms Sale,'" *Beijing Review,* no. 25 (June 22, 1981):11–12; and Chi-wu Wang, "Military Preparedness and Security Needs:

Perceptions from the Republic of China on Taiwan," *Asian Survey* 21 (June 1981):651–63. See also U.S., Library of Congress, Congressional Research Service, *Fighter Aircraft Sales to Taiwan: U.S. Policy,* Issue Brief no. IB 81157 (Washington, D.C., periodically updated). On the technical capabilities of various U.S. planes proposed for sale to Taiwan, see U.S., Library of Congress, Congressional Research Service, *Issues Concerning Pakistan's Possible Acquisition of the U.S. F-16 Fighter Bomber Aircraft,* Report no. 81-225F (Washington, D.C., October 5, 1981), pp. 15–42.

11. The communiqué and PRC statements are reprinted in U.S., Foreign Broadcast Information Service, Daily Report, *China* (cited as FBIS DR China), August 17, 1982.

12. See, notably, testimony by Assistant Secretary of State John Holdridge before the U.S. House Foreign Affairs Committee, Subcommittee on Asian and Pacific Affairs, on July 16, 1981.

13. See U.S., Congress, Joint Economic Committee, *China Under the Four Modernizations* (Washington, D.C.: U.S. Government Printing Office, 1982).

14. Cited by New China News Agency, May 28, 1980, and reprinted in FBIS DR China, May 29, 1980.

15. See in this regard U.S., Department of State, *China and the United States: Into the 1980s,* Current Policy Paper no. 187 (Washington, D.C., June 4, 1980).

Index